TRADE IN THE GLOBAL ECONOMY

TRADE IN THE GLOBAL ECONOMY

SAMUEL EDWARDS (EDITOR)

Nova Science Publishers, Inc.
Huntington, NY

Senior Editors: Susan Boriotti and Donna Dennis
Senior Editorial Coordinator: Tatiana Shohov
Office Manager: Annette Hellinger
Graphics: Wanda Serrano
Book Production: Cathy DeGregory, Matthew Kozlowski, Jonathan Rose and Jennifer Vogt
Circulation: Ave Maria Gonzalez, Ron Hedges and Andre Tillman

Library of Congress Cataloging-in-Publication Data
Available Upon Request

227 Main Street, Suite 100
Huntington, New York 11743
Tele. 631-424-6682 Fax 631-425-5933
E Mail Novascil@aol.com

Printed in the United States of America

CONTENTS:

TRADE POLICY IN AN ECONOMIC PERSPECTIVE

Craig K. Elwell

SUMMARY

Trade liberalization, by removing barriers to free trade among nations, raises the economic welfare of trading nations. This economic insight while readily accepted by the professional economist, finds a more skeptical audience in the wider population. Despite the apparent economic benefit, numerous barriers to free exchange among nations still exist. Some are measures of political coercion or economic warfare. Some are party to public health protections. Usually, however, trade barriers, including trade subsidies, reflect the political strength of special interests threatened by free international trade, but they also may be a reflection of a general apprehension that trade among nations is different than exchange among individuals, and requires some degree of protection to secure national advantage.

The popularity of the notion of "competitiveness" in policy debates is likely a manifestation of this apprehension. It is usually a misunderstood notion, however, that obscures the fact that one nation's good economic fortune is most often not at other nations' expense. Through trade some amount of benefit accrues to all nations.

The gains from trade grow out of a number of economic forces given wider scope by trade liberalization. These are comparative advantage (i.e., increased specialization), economies of scale, greater competitive pressures, and greater inducement for investment and innovation.

While free trade generates net economic gains for the nation, the adjustment to a more efficient allocation of resources imposes significant costs on particular workers and sectors of the economy. In this regard, there may be some latitude for government policies to provide temporary support and facilitate retraining and relocation.

The economic case for free trade is compelling, but there are theoretical exceptions which demonstrate that some degree of protection or special support could raise economic welfare above the free trade level. These exceptions usually fail at the practical level where successful implementation is problematic and the size of benefit often small. If not always the best policy in theory, free trade is most often the best policy in practice.

While trade liberalization will make the nation richer, it will not change the size of the trade deficit, nor will it change the total level of employment. These phenomenon are rooted in domestic macroeconomic conditions largely unrelated to the process of trade liberalization.

*****

There is no notion more central to economics than that of the "gains from trade." This is true whether one talks of trade among individuals, regions, or nations. In each case, free exchange improves the economic welfare of the participants. It follows that the removal of barriers to free exchange will raise economic well being. Yet, while the economic fruits of free exchange are readily accepted for economic transactions within a nation's borders, this is far less true when one comes to the matter of trade among nations. We find that man made barriers to trade are most prevalent for transactions between nations. Whether or not to remove such barriers is the central issue of trade policy.

If nations stand to be richer with free trade, why have barriers been erected? Some barriers deny the gains for trade for non-economic goals, for example to reduce proliferation of certain weapons, to impose costs on objectionable human rights practices, or prevent import of products injurious to plant, animal and human health. Economic welfare occasionally erupts. Most often however trade barriers protect domestic industries. While free trade may raise the well-being for the nation it does to necessarily raise the welfare of particular industries, groups, or individuals. Free trade enriches by guiding scarce resources toward more efficient uses, but this will also mean that resources will also be guided out of less efficient uses. Firms and individuals in the latter circumstance will often find their economic well being reduced, even as the wider economy's welfare is increased. To the extent that those who stand to lose from trade are politically more focused and more capable of influencing public policy, trade barriers have been erected to protect their interests. Second, even among those who may have nothing directly to gain from trade restrictions, there is perhaps an inclination to see exchange between nations as fundamentally different than exchange within a nation, and often requires some degree of protection to secure national advantage. The great popularity of the notion of "competitiveness" may be a manifestation of this mindset. In this case, trade is seen as a "zero sum" game where one nation's gain must be another nation's loss.

Trade is Mutually Beneficial

While a country's exports do compete with exports from other countries on the world market, each country is an export market and a supplier of desirable imports for other countries. Our exports are exchanged for the exports of other nations. Exporting more is useful only because it allows a nation to import more, thereby raising the level of exports of our trading partners. Economic well-being rises as the level of trade rises.

This complete interaction among countries is better characterized as a "positive sum game" with "mutual gain," than as competition. One nation's gain is not at the other nation's expense. A more prosperous rest-of-the-world does not make the United States worse off. The nation's standard of living is not threatened by other countries' good fortune. More likely their good fortune will provide enhanced opportunities for U.S. exports as well as an augmented selection of quality goods at lower cost for domestic consumers. Both raise living standards in the United States.

In the "zero-sum" framework exports become a measure of national advantage and imports a measure of national disadvantage. From this framework, it is easy to conclude that "mercantilist" policies to promote exports and discourage imports will enhance a nation's economic well-being. From the economist's perspective of trade as a "positive sum game," quite the opposite conclusion emerges. Exports are the means (the cost) of acquiring desirable imports that raise economic well being. To promote the former and discourage the latter must lower our *economic* welfare.[1] Adam Smith compellingly argued against the follies of "mercantilism" in 1776. Subsequent generations of economists have strongly reiterated that message. A nation's economic well being is enhanced by expanding, not restricting, trade among nations.

Due to changes in relative productivity and consumer tastes, a nation may find that over time its share of the gains from trade can rise or fall. If the latter it may seem that trade is reducing the nation's economic welfare. The 'gains from trade" have become smaller in this circumstance, but there are "gains" nevertheless, and the nation's economic welfare is still higher than if trade were restricted.

As a general proposition, in the post-war period, economic experience confirmed what economic theory predicted: the expansion of trade, promoted by the removal of barriers, has generated economic gains to all trading nations. The sizable reduction of trade barriers by the industrial economies in the 1950s and 1960s contributed importantly to that period's fast-paced economic growth. (See chart 1.) In the 1970s and 1980s, several developing economies, most notably in East Asia, adopted more outward-looking trade policies as part of a successful program for rapid economic growth. During this same period in the industrial economies, however rising external deficits and deteriorated wage and employment performance generated protectionist pressures and a growing interest among policy makers in alternatives to free trade. More recently, we have seen renewed momentum toward free trade with major trade liberalization initiatives in the European Union, NAFTA, and the Uruguay Round, and most projections suggest each will secure sizable economic gains for the participating nations. Despite these policy actions trade liberalization, nevertheless, remains a contentious political issue.[2]

---

[1] For a fuller discussion of the concepts of "competitiveness" see U.S. Library of Congress. Congressional Research Service. *Competitiveness: Issue or Illusion.* CRS Report No. 94-424 E, by Craig Elwell. Washington, D.C., 1993.

[2] For example See: U.S. Library of Congress. Congressional Research Service. *A Reappraisal of the Economic Effects of the 1994 GATT Agreement.* Report No. 94-288 E, by Craig Elwell and Alfred Reifman. Washington, 1994; Lustig, Nora, Barry Bosworth, and Robert Lawrence. *Assessing the Impact of North American Free Trade.* Washington, Brookings Institution, 1992; and, Baldwin, Richard. The Growth Effect of 1992. *Economic Policy*, October 1989. p. 247-281.

CHART 1. Growth of World Exports and Production of Goods
Annual Percent Change

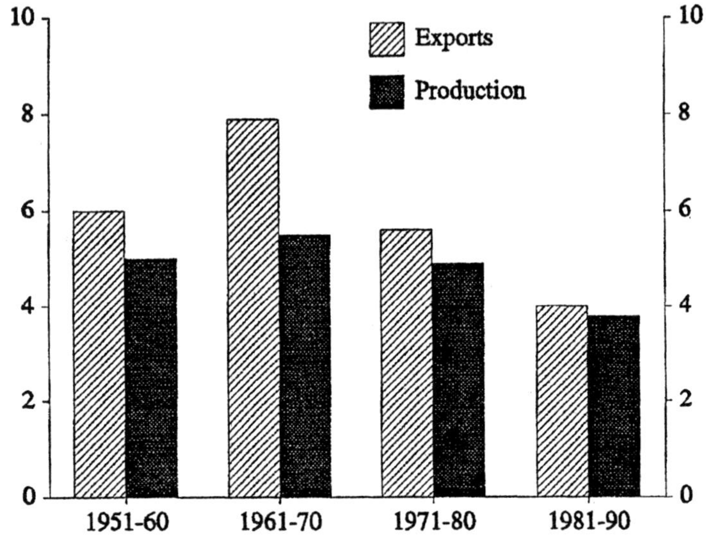

Source: General Agreement on Tariffs and Trade. *International Trade*, several issues.

SOURCES OF THE GAINS FROM TRADE

A number of economic forces give rise to the mutual gains from international trade.

First, international trade, like domestic trade, allows a country to specialize in the production of goods and services which it does relatively well. This is known as the doctrine of *comparative advantage.* Since a country (or an individual) cannot do everything with equal proficiency, trade allows specialization and greater efficiency. By concentrating on what one does relatively well and trading for goods that is relatively less efficient at producing, a nation can consume more of all goods than is possible without trade. (These gains are possible even if a nation has an absolute disadvantage in the production of all traded goods and services.) This doctrine, first articulated by David Ricardo in 1817, explains why an attorney who is also the best secretary in the world still would hire someone to do his typing and why, in the 1800s, Britain exported cloth in exchange for wine from France.

Trade is also enriching because it allows countries to take advantage of *economies of scale.* The longer production run a firm has, the lower its costs may be. Many products require huge initial investments in research and development as well as large investments in highly specialized physical plant and equipment; the ability to reach a larger world market through trade can greatly reduce the average production cost and the final price consumers must pay for that product. This is important even for a country with a large internal market, such as the United States.

In addition to comparative advantage and scale economies, the increased globalization of markets that comes from reducing barriers and expanding trade increases the economic *flexibility* of the United States. The economy's ability to respond quickly and efficiently to rapidly changing world market conditions is enhanced by improved access to foreign markets, technologies, and capital resources. Expanding trade increase *competitive pressures* in the market place, pushing firms to cut waste, keep prices down, and raise quality – clear benefits to the nations' consumers.

These forces give rise to what economists call the "static gains from trade" – that is, the one-time increment to the nation's economic welfare that arise from the more efficient allocation of resources afforded by free trade. In addition, trade liberalization may generate "dynamic" gains that are harder to measure, but are perhaps many times larger than the static gains. Dynamic gains emerge as a sustained, but not necessarily permanent, acceleration of the economy's rate of growth, generating income gains that multiply in each subsequent year.

Many theorize that dynamic effects grow out of an improved environment for investment and innovation that trade liberalization fosters. Improved efficiency and lowered risk of government intervention on trade matters raise the rate of return to investment, inducing a rise in the capital stock and, in turn, an acceleration in the nation's medium-term rate of economic growth. Similarly, trade liberalization expands the market for innovation, raising the expected rate of return to successful innovation and spreading research and development costs more widely. Expanding the scope of competition to a wider world market can force firms to accelerate the pace of innovation, or risk business failure. Moreover, open trade enhances the exchanges of technical knowledge among nations as goods and human and physical capital move more freely. A higher pace of innovation will likely have a strong positive effect on the nation's long-term growth rate.[3]

THE PROBLEM OF ADJUSTMENT COSTS

While trade liberalization will likely lead to *net* gains for the nation, the adjustment to the more efficient allocation of resources may impose significant costs on particular workers and sectors of the economy. These costs involve the retraining and relocating of workers in declining industries and the shifting of capital. The costs are often overstated in popular discussion, but they may be significant nevertheless. To a large degree, the forces of the market will facilitate such adjustment, but there may also be considerable scope for public policy to provide temporary support and to facilitate retraining and relocation. The economic case for government support is no more or less compelling than if the disruption stemmed from a purely domestic source but, trade related disruption carries more emotive force. Such government actions may be necessary to make securing the larger economic benefits of free trade politically feasible.

While adjustment is costly, the efficiency cost of protecting jobs is usually far higher. A recent study estimates that, for the United States, the average cost to the consumer per job saved by protection is about $170,000, many times the average wage in the protected industries.[4]

---

[3] See also International Monetary Fund. Trade as an Engine of Growth. *World Economic Outlook.* Washington, 1993. p. 70-80.

[4] Hufbauer, Gary Clyde, and Kimberly Ann Elliott. *Measuring the Costs of Protection in the United States.* Washington, D. C., Institute for International Economics, 1994. p. 3-14.

IS FREE TRADE ALWAYS THE BEST POLICY?

There are theoretical exceptions to the economic case for free trade. Numerous theoretical models have been devised over the decades that demonstrate that a deviation from free trade policy world, via a special program of subsidization and protection, enhance national economic well-being beyond the free trade outcome.[5] The most recent such exception is the case for government promotion of "strategic industries." Like previous "exceptions" to the free trade doctrine, this approach is less than compelling o a practical level. First, there is the problem of accurately *identifying* such industries. Second, there is the problem of devising a "promotion" program that does not create costly distortions in resource allocation. Third, there is the problem of avoiding a nullifying retaliation by one's trading partners. Most important, the evidence usually shows that the potential gains from such policies are not large and often not sufficient to offset the direct cost of such a program. In the end, such policy deviations from free trade carry the risk of doing more harm than good. We are then left with the insight that if not always best in theory, free trade is most often the best policy in practice.[6]

WHAT TRADE POLICY WON'T DO

While trade liberalization will make the nation richer, it will not change the size of the trade deficit, nor will it change the total level of employment.

The Trade Deficit: The trade deficit occurs not because of systemic inability of the United States to sell goods on the world market, but because of macroeconomic conditions at home stimulating more imports than exports to satisfy domestic demand. In effect, the Untied States spends beyond current production, and a net inflow of goods and services from abroad (a trade deficit) fills the gap. This excess of demand occurs because the United States continues to save less than is needed to finance domestic investment. That domestic imbalance leads to the trade imbalance.

The investment undertaken by an economy will be equal to the saving – income not used for public and private consumption – that is available to finance it. However, neither the level of saving available nor the level of investment undertaken need be limited by sources and used in the domestic economy. In an open world economy, a nation which finds that domestic saving falls short of domestic investment, can attract through an increase in domestic real interest rates, an inward flow of foreign saving (financial capital) to help finance domestic investment. Such a nation becomes a net importer of foreign saving, using that borrowed purchasing power to acquire foreign goods - a trade deficit – to meet domestic demand for consumption and investment. The

---

5 Two often cited examples of using protection to raise economic welfare above its free-trade level are "the optimum tariff" and "infant industry protection." For a discussion of these see Kenen, Peter. *The International Economy.* 2nd edition. Englewood Cliffs, NJ, Prentice-Hall, 1989. p. 182-209..

6 See also U.S. Library of Congress. Congressional Research Service. *U.S. Trade Policy: Free Trade-FairTrade and their Discontents.* CRS Report No. 92-377 E, by Craig Elwell and Alfred Reifman. Washington, D.C., 1992.

United States has been in this category for well over a decade. (See table 1.) This condition will not be changed by the removal of trade barriers.

Jobs: Popular discussion of trade policy do not proceed too far before the issue of jobs arises: Are jobs being created, or are jobs being lost? This likely reflects the commons sense perception that if foreign goods enter the American economy they must displace domestic production and employment. In this view, trade barriers can be seen as protecting jobs, whereas trade liberalization eliminates jobs.

The total level of employment in the economy, however, is a macroeconomic phenomenon rooted in the domestic forces governing the aggregate supply of labor - the number of people who want to work. The U.S. economy is capable of fully employing that labor force with or without trade. An increase in exports may raise employment in the exporting industries, but for a given supply of labor it must also force a contraction of employment in other parts of the economy. Similarly, much is often made of the statistic that it requires 20,000 workers to produce a billion dollars of exports. Expanding exports will increase the number of workers producing exports but it does not increase total employment. If U.S. exports shrink, employment in the export industries may shrink, but, after adjustment, resources used in the production of exports would find domestic sues, leaving total employment unchanged.

Trade and trade liberalization will likely alter the composition of employment among industries, but it does not affect the long term level of employment. Trade tends to raise the efficiency of any given level of employment, raising national income and economic welfare, but in the aggregate it does not create of lose jobs.

While trade liberalization does not affect overall employment it *could* have an adverse effect on the distribution and level of wages. Some observers are concerned that recent poor performance of real wages, especially for low-skilled workers, is the consequence of expanding trade with developing countries. As regards the distribution of wages, it is plausible economic conjecture that trade, by effectively expanding the supply of low-skilled workers, would reduce the wage of unskilled workers in the United States. While plausible, the preponderance of the evidence, so far, indicates that trade's contribution to growing wage inequality in the United States has been small. In part, this may reflect that U.S. trade with low-skill, low-wage economies remains a very small fraction of total trade. In addition, as suggested above, trade liberalization also generates important scale and dynamic effects that likely work to boost worker wages. The United States does have a real wage problem. The evidence available so far does not show trade to be a major source of that problem, however.[7]

---

[7] See also: U.S. Library of Congress. Congressional Research Service. *Does Trade Reduce the Wages of U.S. Workers?* CRS Report No. 94-288 E, by Craig Elwell. Washington, D.C., 1994.

Table 1. U.S. Saving-Investment Balance (percent of GDP)

	1987	1988	1989	1990	1991	1992	1993
Saving	16.0	16.6	16.4	15.3	15.4	14.3	14.6
Investment	18.9	18.4	18.2	16.9	15.3	15.4	16.1
Net Lending (= Current Account Balance)	-2.9	-1.8	-1.7	-1.6	0.1	-1.1	-1.5

Source IMF. *World Economic Outlook.* October 1994

THE MERCANTILIST BASIS OF MOST TRADE NEGOTIATIONS

It is interesting to note that the actual practice of trade liberalization negotiations are structured around the "mercantilist" premise that a nation's barriers are a benefit to be lowered only if a commensurate reduction of other nations barriers is forthcoming. Exports are good, imports are bad, so you can export more to the U.S. only if we can export more to you."

Economics tells us that the economic cost of trade barriers usually falls most heavily on the nation that imposes the barriers. Thus the tactic of most trade negotiations is to agree to not shoot oneself in the foot only if your trading partner aggress not to shoot himself in the foot. To the economist the nation's economic welfare would be raised by unilaterally dropping protectionist trade barriers, yet political reality suggests that such action is most unlikely to occur. It appears that the negotiation tactic of linking the reduction of trade barriers at home to the lowering of trade barriers abroad serves the economic goal of lower trade barriers world wide. In effect, "mercantilist" rhetoric may serve free trade goals.

TRADE AND ECONOMIC WELL-BEING

Craig Elwell

SUMMARY

The recent presidential primary revealed that many Americans do not see international trade contributing to their economic well-being. Much anecdotal evidence is mustered to reveal the hardship imposed by the expanding globalization of the U.S. economy. We can expect as this election year unfolds for there to be increased political pressure from some quarters for the Congress "to do something" about this perceived problem. Yet things are not always as they seem and trade may not be the problem many would suggest it is. The economic hardship is no doubt real, but an effective policy response to this problem would be aided by a clearer view of trade's effect on the U.S. economy.

International trade is a means to economic enrichment. It is, however, a process that creates winners and losers. Trade enriches by allowing a nation to specialize production according to "comparative advantage." In addition, trade raises economic well-being by giving scope to economies of scale, by increasing competitive pressure on firms, and by giving added inducement to the process of technological change and innovation. Workers and capital in relatively less efficient endeavors may find their economic prospects diminished, however.

Exports are a vehicle for acquiring imports. To export and not import would erode economic well-being not raise it. The interplay of market forces will establish an optimal level of trade for each trading nation and for the world economy. Trade barriers, because they distort this market process, will move trade away from its economic prospects diminished, however.

The Nation's global trade deficit is not necessary an indicator of poor trade performance, but rather, a measure of the degree to which the nation has chosen to use the world trading system to boost current spending above current output. As such, the deficit is a measure of our borrowing from the rest of the world. It does not cause a reduction in the total level of output and, therefore, does not cause a reduction the total level of employment. There is, however, a burden associated with the trade deficit, as rising foreign indebtedness, will also require rising debt service payments.

While elevating the level of real income, trade can also have strong effects on the distribution of income. So far, however, careful analysis does not suggest that trade has had a significant adverse effect on the distribution of income in the United States.

*****

The recent presidential primary campaign brought to the forefront the obviously simmering issue of international trade and U.S. economic well-being. It was clear that many Americans have at least the suspicion that trade has encroached on that well-being. This suspicion is often sustained by assorted anecdotal evidence of factories closing and jobs being lost at the same time as the tide of imports, particularly from low-wage countries, rises. These things have occurred, but they represent only a partial and, by themselves, an inaccurate picture of the total effect of international trade on the U.S. economy.

Economic theory and evidence indicate that trade is enriching, with a positive effect like that of technological change, whereby economic efficiency is enhanced and the level of output and consumption raised. But, also like technological change, trade will induce a reallocation of the economy's resources (capital and labor) toward relatively more efficient activities and away from less efficient activities. Such reallocation, while beneficial to the whole economy, can be costly to individual industries and workers in the relatively less efficient activities, who bear significant adjustment costs and find the new market value of their economic undertaking diminished.

This report will examine several aspects of trade and economic well-being, with the intent of clarifying what is accurate and what is not by examining economic theory and available evidence. First, the basic economic case for free trade is examined as well as possible exceptions to that case. Then the discussion will turn to consider several "hot issues" that always arise in debates about trade: lost jobs, falling wages, and rising income inequality. While anecdotes abound, what does careful economic analysis say about each of these issues?

Trade and the Level of Real Income

Trade raises economic well-being in several ways. The most important way is by allowing a nation to specialize in the production of what it is relatively efficient at producing and trade for things it is relatively less efficient at producing. The result of such specialization will be the ability to consume more of all goods with trade than without trade. This is the very same economic principle that guides our individual economic behavior writ large. Rather than build our own automobile, or provide our own medical services, or grow our own food, we find it far more efficient to specialize in an occupation we are good at and trade for these and most other goods and services that we want or need. Specialization and trade clearly allows each of us to consume more than we could if we tried to be self-sufficient. The same is true for a nation, albeit to a less extensive degree (i.e., U.S. imports among to only about 12% of Gross Domestic Product [GDP]).

What is also important to note about the gains from specialization and trade is that they will occur even if the trading parties have an absolute advantage or disadvantage in the efficiency with which they produce all goods. All that is required is a difference in relative efficiency, that is, a difference between nations in the rate at which the output of one good must be reduced to allow an increase in the output of a second good. If these rates are different, then gains from trade exist and specializing production in areas where relative efficiency is highest while trading for goods where relative efficiency is lowest will raise overall economic well-being in both countries. This principle is clearly true in our individual behavior, explaining why a lawyer who is a superior typist would still find it more efficient to hire a secretary to do her own typing. The time she would spend typing would contribute to a greater income if devoted to the law. Similarly, the secretary, with an absolute efficiency disadvantage in both activities, is benefited by this pattern of specialization. In the text books this arrangement of production is called specialization by "comparative advantage." First articulated by David Ricardo in 1817, it remains today a central and powerful insight into the economic basis for mutually beneficial international trade.

Relative productive efficiency will vary among nations because of differences in the relative abundance or scarcity of the various factors of production. For example, compared to most other countries the United States has a relative abundance of high-skilled labor and a relative scarcity of low-skilled labor extensively will, with trade, increase domestic real income. In contrast, a country such as China which has a relative abundance of low-skilled labor and a relative scarcity of high-skilled labor finds that specialization in the production of goods that use low-skilled labor finds that specialization in the production of goods that use low-skilled labor intensively will, with trade, raise that country's real income. In this circumstance there would be gains from trade between the Untied States and China. The pattern of trade that would emerge from these different factor endowments and relative productive efficiencies would be for the Untied States to be a net exporter of goods that use high-skilled labor extensively and a net importer of goods that use low-skilled labor extensively. China on the other hand would be a net exporter of goods that use low-skilled labor extensively and a net importer of goods that use high-skilled labor extensively. Establishing comparative advantage on the basis of differences in factor proportions is based on the Hecksher-Ohlin theorem, a central structure of the modern theory of international trade. (In addition to factor endowments, differences in productive technology could also create differences in relative efficiency and form a basis for trade. On the demand side, differences in tastes in consumption among countries could also form a basis for trade.)[1]

Trade is also enriching because it allows countries to take advantage of economic scale. By providing greater scope for specialization and by spreading often substantial fixed costs over a larger production level, the ability to reach a world market through trade can greatly reduce unit production costs and the final price the consumer must pay.

---

[1] For a fuller discussion of comparative advantage, factor proportions, and the basis for trade see Lindert, Peter and Thomas Pugel. *International Economics.* 3rd edition. Chicago, IL, Irwin, 1996, p. 19-95.

It is probably clear that this benefit will flow from domestically produced goods that are consumed at home and also exported, but the benefit will also be derived from trade's favorable effect on the cost of goods produced by foreign industries which we consume as imports.

In addition to comparative advantage and scale economies, the expansion of trade increases competitive pressures in the marketplace, pushing companies to cut waste, keep prices down, and raise quality—clear benefits to the nation's consumers.

These several forces give rise to what economists call the "static gains from trade"—that is, the onetime increment to the nation's economic well-being that arises from a more efficient allocation and scale of use of the nation's and the world's scarce resources. Beyond such gains, many economists theorize that international trade may also generate "dynamic gains." These gains are harder to measure, but in their cumulative effect are perhaps many times larger than static gains. Dynamic gains would be evidenced by a sustained acceleration of the economy's long-term rate of growth. As such dynamic gains would represent an increase in the rate of improvement of the efficiency with which any given endowment of resources is used—an increase in the long-term rate of growth of output per unit of input. (Such an increase would be measured as an improvement in the rate of total factor productivity, that is, the increase n output not explained by the increase of inputs.)

Dynamic gains occur, it is argued, because trade expands the market for innovation, raises the economic return for successful innovation, and spreads the research and development costs of innovation more widely. A faster pace of technological change and productive innovation increases the pace of efficiency improvement and the economy's long-term growth rate. And, of course, only a small increase in the pace of long-term efficiency improvement yields large improvements in the standard of living over the stretch of several decades.[2]

Taken together, these several forces make most economists strong advocates of the power of international trade to enrich. This power was made evident in a recent empirical study by Sachs and Warner.[3] They examined the growth performance of 111 countries divided into two groups: those "open" to trade and those "closed" to trade. The "open" economies showed much faster growth than the "closed" economies. Having said this, it is also important to keep a sense of proportion. While beneficial, trade is still a relatively small source of enrichment for a large continental economy like the United States. Despite tremendous growth in the post-war era, imports to the Untied States still amount to only about 12% of GDP in recent years. (This is up from about 5% in the 1960s, however.)

---

[2] See also Baldwin, R.E. Measurable Dynamic Gains From Trade. *Journal of Political Economy*, v. 100, no. 11, February 1992. p. 162-174; Elwell, Craig, and Alfred Reifman. *The Uruguay Round: A Macroeconomic Assessment.* Washington, Congressional Research Service, 1993. Report No. 93-533 E.

[3] Sachs, Jeffery and Andrew Warner. *Economic Reform and the Process of Global Integration.* Washington, Brookings Papers on Economic Activity, 1995.

The Economic Role of Exports and Imports

Much popular discussion of trade proceeds as if exports are "good" and should be increased and as if imports are "bad" and should be decreased. Yet the economic framework outlined above indicates that such a program would make the nation poorer. It is the expansion of trade (exports and imports) not just export sales that raises economic well-being.

Consider for a moment what an "export" by itself represents: the nation's scarce resources have been used to produce a product that will not be consumed by any of its citizens. If the transaction ended there the home economy would surely be worse off than if those resources had been used to produce a good for domestic consumption. But, the transaction does not end there because to the nation exports are a vehicle for acquiring imports. In effect, the cost to the economy of exporting is more than offset by the benefit of being able to import. As discussed above, such trading will expand the nation's consumption possibilities.

At any point in time we would expect there to be some optimal level of trade for each trading nation and the world economy that is consistent with the most efficient allocation of the world's scarce resources and reflective of the current state of relative production costs and consumption preferences across trading nations. The interplay of global market forces will move trade toward this optional level.

The Terms of Trade: It is possible, however, given the optimal level of trade, for a trading nation to increase its share of the total gains from trade. In the text books this is called an improvement in the nation's "terms of trade," and essentially means that for a given level of trade the nation's share of the gains from trade is rising. This can occur if a trading nation steadily reduces the volume of exports needed to acquire any given volume of imports. The terms of trade is commonly defined as the ratio of export prices to import prices. Other factors unchanged, a rise of the terms of trade increases the import purchasing power of any given volume of exports. The same volume of imports can be purchased for a reduced volume of exports. This means that the amount of resources needed to produce any given volume of exports is reduced, freeing resources to produce added output for other uses. In this circumstance the nation raises its share of the overall gains from trade and its real income.[4]

Of course, if one nation's "terms of trade" is rising then another nation's terms of trade is falling, as would its share of the gains from trade (more on this later). Nevertheless, even if one's share is getting smaller, there is still a gain, albeit smaller to the nation from trade.

It is also useful to distinguish between short-run and long-run movements of the terms of trade. Changes in national spending and saving can lead to short-run changes in the terms of trade and real income, but such movements, often unrelated to enduring

---

[4] See Lindert, Pugel, *International Economics*, 3rd ed., p. 48. Other, more complex measures of the terms of trade have been devised. They attempt to also take into consideration the effect of changes in productivity in the export sector; recognizing that real income need not fall with a decline of export prices if productivity has increased efficiently to commensurately reduce the resource cost of export production. There are no consistent measures of such "factorial" terms of trade nor is there any strong opinion that the simple measure used here misrepresents the effect of terms of trade changes on real income.

changes in underlying thrift, innovation, or productivity, tend to reverse themselves. A long-term rise in a nation's terms of trade is likely if it steadily brings forth new, innovative, high quality products widely desired in the global market place. There are, however, no direct and easily exploitable policy levers that can assure such an outcome.

Trade Barriers

It follows reasonably from the above discussion that trade barriers are a distortion that prevent the world economy from reaching an optimal level of trade and in so doing must reduce real income.

Tariffs and tariff-like barriers that aim at reducing the level of imports will lead to an over-allocation of resources to the protected import-competing sectors and an under-allocation of resources to the tradeable goods sectors of the economy. Thus, the level of exports must also fall. The overall level of trade must be reduced as must the level of real income. Such barriers often exist because they benefit politically influential groups. Their gain, however, is at the larger expense of the wider community. It is theoretically possible to specify conditions where a tariff could be used to increase the nation's real income. But, this occurs at the greater expense of its trading partners. The likely prospect of foreign retaliation makes it unlikely that such an advantage could be secured in practice. With retaliation, all parties lose as a still larger shrinkage of trade reduces real income all around. A recent estimate of the costs of existing U.S. trade barriers indicated that U.S. consumers pay an extra $70 billion per year and that the average annual cost per protected job was about $170,000.[5]

The political economy of trade policy puts the nation in the curious position where it must use the threat of imposing costly trade barriers on itself to deter a trading partner from raising a trade barrier or to encourage the removal of one that already exists. In fact, the substantial progress made in reducing trade barriers in the post-war era largely under the auspices of the General Agreement on Tariffs and Trade (GATT), proceeds on the un-economic presumption that a trade barrier is a benefit to the home economy to be negotiated away for reduction of its trading partners' barriers. In effect, I promise to stop shooting myself in the foot, if you do the same. This un-economic premise has led to quite excellent economic results, however.

Export subsidies and other forms of export promotion also distort the allocation of the nations resources, in this case causing an over allocation of resources to the tradeable goods sector. Real income is reduced because the added resources diverted by the subsidy to the tradable goods sector would have generated a greater return in some non-export activity. Again a theoretical case can be made for what are called "strategic" export subsidies. In this circumstance it is argued that an industry has the potential to realize extras normal returns but that potential will not be fulfilled if left to the will of the private market place. Therefore public nurturing through subsidies are called for. Such an argument is valid from the standpoint of economic theory. Yet, because success in this endeavor is conditional on the unlikely existence of a complex array of special

[5] See: Hufbauer, Gary and Kimberly Elliott. *Measuring the Costs of Protection in the United States.* Washington, Institute for International Economics, 1994. p. 5-7.

conditions and because there is little evidence that the potential gains are significant it is not a compelling option in practice.[6]

Some might counter that Japan is a good example of a nation that successfully used a program of government support for selected industries and export promotion to boost that country's economic well-being. Not so, says a recent study by Beason and Weinstein.[7] They found that Japan's industry and export programs did not pick "winners," rather they found a high correlation of level of support and slow growth industries. This suggests that Japan's economic success has been in spite of costly policies aimed at "strategic exporting."[8]

As a general observation, examination of major examples of industrial targeting across countries does not reveal that governments have had much success in their industrial targeting.[9]

The removal of trade barriers and the promotion of open markets benefits all trading nations. This understanding has sustained U.S. trade policy in the post-war era and made this country an active supporter of successive rounds of multilateral lowering of trade barriers under the GATT; as well as, the recent NAFTA agreement. Gaining such economic enrichment likely will form the economic basis for possible future policy initiative such as the Free Trade Area of the Americas (FTAA) and Asia-Pacific Economic Cooperation (APEC).

The Global Trade Deficit

A global trade deficit is taken by many to be a sign of a nation's international economic failure, and a measure of the degree to which foreign goods have diminished total domestic production and reduced economic well-being. This is not true in theory or in fact.

A trade deficit is really a measure of the degree to which a trading nation has chosen to use the international trading system as a vehicle to push domestic spending beyond current production. In effect the deficit country has borrowed from the rest of the world so as to supplement current spending. In this framework a trade deficit is not a force that reduces total domestic output, but a force that allows a deficit country like the United States to spend beyond what the domestic economy can currently produce.

Similarly a trade surplus is a measure of the degree to which a nation is using the international trading system to keep current domestic spending below current output. The surplus represents a nation's willingness to be a lender of real output to the rest of

---

6 For a more in-depth discussion of trade barriers see: Krugman, Paul and Maurice Obsegeld. *International Economics: Theory and Policy.*, Third Edition. Harper Collins, New York, 1994. 195-254. See also: Bhagwati, Jagdish. *Protectionism.* Cambridge, Mass., MIT Press, 1988.

7 Beason, Richard and David Weinstein. *Growth Economics of Scale and Targeting in Japan (1950-1990).* Discussion Paper 1644. Harvard Institute of Economic Research, June 1994.

8 A discussion more favorable to Japan's targeting efforts can be found in: Tyson, Laura D'Andrea. *Who's Bashing Whom? Trade Conflict in High-Technology Industries.* Washington, Institute for International Economics, 1992.

9 For a good survey of such programs, see: Krugman and Obstfeld, p. 277-297.

the world. Of course, the ability to run a deficit requires the existence of another nation willing to run a surplus and vice versa. There is no necessary economic reason to see one position as being more or less desirable than the other.

To understand how this is possible and why both a global deficit and a surplus can be desirable, one has to understand that, corresponding to each trading nation's transactions in goods and services, there is an equivalent corresponding, but opposite in direction, exchange of financial capital. Trade is not barter. Transactions for goods also involve the exchange of some form of financial asset. This might be currency acceptable as foreign exchange, but could also involve some other type of financial instrument such as stocks, bonds, or real capital.

If a nation is running a trade deficit, then, by definition, export earnings fall short of what is needed to pay its import bill. The shortfall is made up by its trading partners' willingness to accept some form of financial asset in lieu of payment. (In effect, they have taken an IOU.) The foreign holder of these assets will be able to make some future claim on the home economy's output, but in the current period the deficit nation has a net inflow of financial capital and a net inflow of real resources allowing it to augment domestic spending.

The key point, however, is that in addition to a net inflow of goods the deficit nation has also received a like sized net inflow of financial capital. The capital inflow increases the supply of capital available to the home economy and in turn pushes down domestic interest rates. Thus, while the excess of imports over exports, by itself, may have a dampening effect on sectors of the domestic economy that compete with imports, the net inflow of financial capital will have an equal sized stimulative impact on sectors such as housing, consumer durables, and investments in plant and equipment that are sensitive to the level of interest rates. Thus a global trade deficit will likely alter the composition of total output; however, it does not reduce the overall level of output.

The Level of Employment: If the trade deficit does not cause a reduction in total output then neither can it lead to any *net* loss of jobs. While it may mean that the composition of employment changes, there is no reason to expect the total level of employment to fall. The economy can fully employ its labor-force with or without a trade deficit. In the United States, since the end of the last recession in 1991, the trade deficit has steadily risen as the unemployment rate has steadily fallen.

Some argue that a shift in the composition of employment by a trade deficit has an adverse effect on U.S. real income. It is argued that because wages paid in the tradeable goods sectors, adversely affected by the trade deficit, are higher than in the favorably affected sectors there is a net loss of wage income due to the changed mix. This could occur, but the critical question is what is the magnitude involved? It is often argued that the wage differential is 30% (a great overstatement, but let's use it for the sake of argument) and the sectoral employment loss is about 1% of the labor force. If so, that would calculate the induced annual wage loss to the economy to be about 0.3%--a rather modest deterioration.

The Burden on Future Generations: Recurring trade deficits do mean that the economy has been incurring debt to foreigners as it has financed its excess of spending. The burden of that debt becomes manifest when it must be paid back plus interest at some point in the future. At that time the economy's level of consumption will be pushed lower than would be true if no foreign borrowing had occurred. How sizeable this burden will be depends of course on the size of the obligation, but also on what was done with the borrowed funds. If the foreign borrowing was used primarily to finance an increase of investment rather than consumption, then the burden could be wholly or substantially reduced. Because investing the borrowed financial and real resources means that they were used to give an added boost to the economy's productive capacity, and to that degree, avoids the need to reduce future consumption.[10] For the United States, however, the large trade deficits of the last twelve years have been used largely to finance public and private consumption.

The U.S. Commerce Department keeps a tally of our net foreign indebtedness that it reports as the Net International Investment Position (NITP). Through 1994, that indebtedness stood at $650 billion, a substantial amount, but not of overwhelming size for a $7 trillion plus economy. The burden of this net indebtedness will be measured by the annual debt service costs. That magnitude is best judged by changes in the U.S. investment income flow, a portion of the U.S. current account balance. That series has seen a steady fall since the 1980s. In 1981, the Untied States had a net inflow of investment income of about $32 billion, by 1990, that inflow had dwindled to about $20 billion, and in 1995, it had become a net outflow of about $11 billion. Thus, there has been a net in fall international investment earnings of over $40 billion. This is a significant loss of purchasing power, but again not overwhelming in a $7 trillion plus economy.

To stem this growing debt service burden the United States must reduce its persistent large global trade deficit. Trade policy measures are expected to have little or no effect on the overall trade deficit. To narrow that imbalances the nation must reign in the excess of its domestic spending over domestic production. The most promising way of achieving that is to reduce the large federal budget deficit. Reduced federal expenditure directly reduces national spending, while higher taxes, indirectly reduces private sector spending.

Bilateral Trade Balances: While to the economy exports are the means to acquiring imports, with any individual trading partner it is not necessary for what is sold as exports to be equal in value to what is purchased as imports. Since trade is not barter, but is undertaken with an associated exchange of financial assets, it is a reasonable economic occurrence to have bilateral trade imbalances even if there is balance in total trade and even if all trade barriers were removed. With some trading partners a nation will export much and import little, with others import much and export little. The pattern of trade across trading partners will be strongly rooted in different resource endowments, different comparative advantage in production, and different tastes in final consumption. Bilateral surpluses with some trading partners can be used to pay for bilateral deficits with others. There is not necessary economic harm in such a pattern of trade and it can persist indefinitely. For example, even if Japan's global trade surplus vanished that country would have sizable bilateral imbalances with its trading partners: sizable deficits with low-income countries from whom it must acquire the raw materials it does not itself possess and sizable trade surpluses with high income countries such as the United States who are the principal markets for Japan's expensive manufactured goods. Surpluses in manufactures trade would be needed to offset deficits in raw materials trade. Thus, even

---

10 See also, U.S. Library of Congress. Congressional Research Service. *The U.S. Trade Deficit: Implications for U.S. Living Standards.* Report No. 91-907 E, by Craig Elwell. Washington, 1991.

with balanced global trade, Japan would likely still have a $20-$30 billion bilateral surplus with the United States.

Can the Nation Be Hurt By Trade?

It is possible for the expansion of international trade to erode the nation's level of economic well-being? Many people see the cases where competition with low priced imports forces domestic producers to slow the rise or even reduce worker wages to remain competitive. Clearly these workers are worse off as a result of trade. But, total income to the economy does not necessarily decline. We must also consider that the lower price of the imported goods raises the real income of those who consume them. The gain to these people is most often not as visible as the cost of those whose wage has been reduced, buy it will be equal in economic value.

Of course, trade is not just in goods that we also produce and consume at home. As a general proposition, trade can certainly reduce domestic real income if over time it drives down the price of the goods we export or raises the price of the goods we import. The ratio of these two groups of prices we have said above is called the nation's "terms of trade." This is a telling measure of whether the nation's share of the mutual gains from trade are rising or falling. A rising terms of trade says that the "export cost" of gaining any given volume of imports is falling, meaning that the real cost of importing is falling, that the economy's share of the gains from trade is rising, and that real income in the economy is also increased. It follows that a falling "terms of trade" will reduce the rate of increase of real income. Such a reduction does not mean that it is not in the nation's interest to continue to trade just, that the gain is being reduced.

Since the "terms of trade" is regularly measured by the U.S. Commerce Department, it is easy to judge how expanding world trade has affected U.S. real income over the last few decades. For a period stretching from the end of World War II through the late 1960s, the U.S. terms of trade rose, not an unexpected early post-war period. This trend changed in the 1970s with a steady decline of the U.S. terms of trade. This, no doubt, largely occurred because the war-damaged industrial powers had regained their industrial capacity and American goods faced heightened competition on the world market. The associated decline in U.S. real income was not great, however. The reduction amounted to about a 2% fall of real income from what it otherwise would have been. Since 1980 the U.S. terms of trade has been essentially trendless, showing no sustained tendency to rise or fall. One could not conclude from this performance that trade has been particularly deleterious to U.S. real income and economic well-being.[11]

Trade and the Distribution of Income

The coincident occurrence over the last twenty years of poor wage performance and expanding trade with low wage countries leads some to see causality running from trade

[11] See also: Krugman, Paul. Does Third World Growth Hurt First World Prosperity? *Harvard Business Review*, July-August, 1994. p. 113-120.

to American wage and pressure often grows to create policies that would curtail such trade. It is certainly true that while most careful economic analysis concludes that trade is a boon to the level of overall economic well-being, it also recognizes that it has the potential to exert very strong effects on the distribution of income, perhaps deteriorating the income position of labor relative to capital or of certain types of labor (i.e., unskilled versus skilled) relative to each other.

The standard prediction of mainstream trade theory is that, given certain conditions and assumptions, trade should improve the position of the abundant factor of production and cause the position of the economy's scarce factor to deteriorate. This occurs because trade allows the nation's abundant factor to compete in the rest of the world where it is relatively scarce, thereby bidding up its return; but trade also makes the nation's scarce factor compete in a world economy where it is relatively more abundant, thereby bidding down its return. For the United States, this might mean that capital would gain and labor lose or that high-skilled labor would gain and low-skilled labor lose.

A related prediction of trade theory is there to e a strong tendency for trade to equalize the returns to all factors. Therefore, if trade forces U.S. workers to compete with low wage foreign workers, U.S. wages would be pushed down towards the foreign level. Or, if the relevant example is relatively scarce low-skilled U.S. workers facing competition with relatively abundant low-skilled foreign workers, then the wages of low-skilled U.S. workers would fall relative to their high skilled counterparts.

In all of this, a key point to keep in mind is that American labor does not compete directly with foreign labor but indirectly through the prices of traded goods. Domestic labor's wages are pushed down as the price of the product those workers produce is pushed down by foreign competition.[12]

Trade and the Average Level of Wages

It is true since the late 1970s the rate of growth of average wages in the United States has slowed markedly. But, it is quite unlikely that international trade had much to do with this poor performance.

Earlier we observed that the movement of the U.S. terms of trade since the late 1970s shows no evidence of trade causing a significant reduction of total real income. Therefore, trade can drive down wages only as it reduces labor's share of total income. Yet that share has been remarkably stable at about 73% for the last 20 years.

Another strand of the trade-hurting-wages argument observes that over the period of weak wage growth real worker compensation has not kept up with productivity growth.[13] Just such a divergence would occur if trade were leading to a process of factor price

[12] For further discussion of the distributional predictions of mainstream trade theory see Lindert and Thomas, p. 57-75.

[13] These arguments rely on measure of "average" productivity, while economic theory argues that wages will correlate with "marginal" productivity, which is not commonly estimated. While it is possible that average and marginal productivity move together , it is also possible that they do not. It could occur that average productivity rises while marginal productivity does not. Thus, if this occurred, wages would not be expected to rise even as average productivity does. We have no evidence to suggest that this has occurred, however.

equalization that divers domestic real income toward foreign workers. Yet, in comparing real wages to productivity one must be careful in choosing the deflator used to generate the real wage series (real wages or real compensation are determined by dividing nominal wages or compensation by a relevant measure of the level of prices). Economic theory is clear in saying that the appropriate comparison in determining whether labor is receiving the value of its incremental contribution to output is that of real product wages to productivity, that is, wages should be deflated by an index of the prices of goods produced by U.S. workers, not by an index of prices of goods consumed by workers. If trade and factor price equalization were working to slow wage growth, real product wages would have grown slower than productivity. In fact, real product wages closely track productivity since the late 1970s. This does not change the economic plight of workers, but it does indicate that trade was not the source of poor wage growth.

The U.S. problem of slow growth in real wages would then seem to be rooted in the combined effect of slower productivity growth and the tendency for the average price of the goods U.S. workers consume to rise significantly faster than the average price of the goods they produce. The principal culprits in this last regard are the falling price of capital goods (particularly computers) which are a large share of what workers produce, but a small share of what they consume; and the sharply rising price of housing services which are a large share of what workers consume, but a small share of what they produce. It has nothing to do with international trade, however.[14]

Trade and the Inequality of Wages

The second dimension of the U.S. real age problem is rising inequality of worker earnings. It is a credible empirical observation for the United States that relative to most trading partners the abundant factor of production is high skilled labor whereas the relatively scarce factor is low-skilled labor. It is also true that recent years have seen an increase of trade with nations with just the opposite factor proportions. As stated earlier, a standard prediction of international trade theory in such a circumstance is that high skilled U.S. workers gain and low-skill U.S. workers lose as trade according to comparative advantage expands the output of the high-skill abundant exporting industries and contracts the output of the low-skill abundant import-competing industries.[15]

While certainly plausible, a careful look at the evidence does not support this scenario. As discussed above, what must initiate the factor price equalization process is a change in the relative price of the traded goods. In this case we would expect to observe a decline in the relative price of U.S. goods produced using low-skilled labor intensively. A detailed empirical study by Lawrence and Slaughter could not find that such a change in relative prices had occurred.[16] In fact, they found that over the relevant

---

[14] See also: Krugman, Paul and Robert Lawrence. *Trade, Jobs and Wages.* NBER Working Paper. No. 4478. Cambridge, MA 1993.

[15] For an analysis along these lines see: Murphy, Kevin, and Finis Welch. The Structure of Wages. *Quarterly Journal of Economics,* 107.1, February 1992. p. 285-326.

[16] Lawrence, Robert A., and Matthew J. Slaughter. *International Trade and American Wages in the 1980s; Giant Sucking, Sound on Small Hiccup* Brookings Papers on Economic Activity.

time period the price of goods produced primarily with low-skilled labor rose slightly relative to that of goods produced primarily with high-skilled labor. Thus in the context of the factor price equalization process trade in recent years should have decreased wage inequality in the United States.

In addition the Lawrence and Slaughter study considered a collateral prediction of the factor price equalization process. If international competition was pushing down the wage of low-skilled American workers we would also expect to see the now relatively cheaper low-skilled workers used more intensively in the production process. What Lawrence and Slaughter, found, however, was that just the opposite had occurred. Throughout U.S. manufacturing there has been a significant increase in the ratio of skilled to unskilled workers. Again this suggests that trade has not been the force behind widening wage inequality.

This conclusion does not mean that a factor price equalization process has not been at work. But if occurring, it is being overwhelmed and offset by other forces. First of all, the effect of factor price equalization on wages may be small. Through U.S. trade with economies with abundant low-skill and low-wage workers has grown greatly it still remains a very minor share of total U.S. trade, amounting to no more that 3% of total U.S. GDP. Second we know that trade will unleash other forces such as scale economies and improved efficiency that could be sufficiently strong to counteract the downward push of factor price equalization on the wages of U.S. low-skill workers.

Most economists look for the cause of widening wage inequality in a more general process of "biased" technological change that has induced a shift towards more intensive use of skilled labor and away from intensive use of low-skilled labor. While expanding international trade carries the potential to increase wage inequality and while this effect could exert itself more strongly in the future, so far expanding international trade does not provide an adequate explanation of the inequality problem.[17]

CONCLUSION

Mainstream economic analysis generally sees international trade to be an enriching process. While it is possible to identify theoretical circumstances where trade might be harmful, they are without practical significance. This process of enrichment does, however, bring with it both winners and losers. There are more pluses than minuses, but the tough policy issue is how to secure the gains from the trade and at the same time assure equitable treatment for those who are hurt by the process.

Poor wage growth and rising inequality are troublesome characteristics of the United States recent economic history, and some would conjecture that expanding international trade is a cause of this problem. The best research available to date indicates otherwise. Poor average wage growth is rooted in poor productivity growth, particularly in the

No. 2. Washington 1993. p. 161-225. See also: Symposia: Income Inequality and Trade. *Journal of Economic Perspectives,* Summer 1995, v. 9, no.3. p. 15-80.

[17] This conclusion is supported by other research for example: Berman, Eli, John Bound, and Zvi Grilliches. *Changes in the Demand for Skilled Labor Within the U.S. Manufacturing Industries.* Working Paper 4255. Cambridge, MA, National Bureau of Economic Research, January 1993.

service producing sectors of the U.S. economy. A deteriorating distribution of worker earnings is most likely caused by a strong bias in the process of technological advance that favors high-skilled workers relative to low-skilled workers. International trade can unleash forces that hurt domestic workers but, so far, such effects have not been found to be significant enough to account for the adverse overall wage trends of recent years. Rather than curtail trade, efforts aimed at helping distressed workers are likely more efficiently focused on getting these workers the skills they need to prosper in the emerging global economy.

Since trade still only accounts for a minor share of economic activity in the United States its capacity to do good or bad is also minor. The effects on domestic real income of most international economic events are significant but small in size when compared to the largely domestic economic concerns such as recession, inflation, or productivity growth.

TRADE AND INTERNATIONAL COMPETITION POLICY

Dick K. Nanto

SUMMARY

International competition policy is aimed at prohibiting private activities that restrict or distort competition –particularly as they affect trade. It is both a process of harmonizing national competition policies and a goal of negotiating a multinational agreement on antitrust policy. Although every industrialized nation has national antitrust and competition laws, there is no consensus on the need for, shape of, or reach of an international competition policy. The World Trade Organization is exploring the possibility of including competition policy in its negotiating agenda. Congressional action on competition policy centers mainly on its oversight of trade, economic, and antitrust relations with foreign countries. This report will be updated as events warrant.

Competition policy refers to the administration of antitrust and other laws aimed at ensuring competition in markets. It has gained importance in international economic relations because successive reductions in tariff and non-tariff barriers have shifted the focus from government-controlled import barriers to restrictive practices by private companies. As trade is liberalized, governments no longer can impose impediments to products from abroad. Private companies, however, can erect barriers with similar effect. International competition policy tries to prohibit agreements and practices which restrict and distort competition among trading states. It also is aimed at preventing the misuse by a firm of its dominant position in a market in a way that adversely affects international trade. It is intended to protect consumers from private firms who unilaterally, or collectively, set prices that are higher than otherwise would prevail.

The pressure for governments to act on competition policy emanates mainly from multinational corporations that operate indifferent world markets and often face anticompetitive practices there that may be considered illegal in the United States. It also emanates from domestic industries competing with imports from companies that may be engaged in unfair trading practices (e.g. dumping) that may be financed by excess profits generated through exercising monopoly power at home or through international cartels.

Congressional action on competition policy centers mainly on its oversight of trade, economic, and antitrust relationships with foreign countries. The first area of oversight deals with U.S. efforts to open markets for American exports and business abroad. The second is the activities of multilateral organizations, such as the World Trade Organization (WTO) and the Organization for Economic Cooperation and Development (OECD). The third is in cooperative (comity) activities with other national antitrust authorities. In the 106th Congress, H.R. 1120 (S. Levin, et al.) would require an investigation by the International Trade Commission to collect information on and assess the adverse effects of anticompetitive practices in international steel trade. Hearings dealing with international competition policy also are being scheduled.

BACKGROUND

Competition policy has heretofore been mostly a domestic issue. It centers on identifying, regulating, and dealing with restrictive economic structures and practices, collusive business behavior, barriers to entry into industry, and other activities that may deter companies or other economic actors from engaging in free and open market competition. The targets of competition policy include restrictive business practices such as public and private monopolies, cartels (including export cartels), vertical or horizontal restraints, certain mergers and acquisitions, predatory pricing, price fixing, price discrimination, and abuse of market power. Some trade restrictions also can inhibit competition. These practices usually cause economic inefficiencies, abnormally high prices, or may retard the advance of technology.

Monopoly power or restrictive business practices are usually a question of degree. Anti-competitive behavior can range from that of a huge corporation that may destroy all competitors through predatory pricing to producer with a unique product. The issue is not the existence of monopoly power, per se, but its effect on the marketplace.

Firms with monopoly or monopolistic power can diminish economic efficiency, but they also can enhance it. While governments recognize that monopolies cause inefficiencies, they often provide monopoly power to companies. They grant patents, copyrights, and licenses to operate. They establish standards that favor existing companies. They allow public utilities to service specific geographical areas, provide protection from import competition, and allow mergers and acquisitions that reduce competition. Governments recognize that some industries require large, oligopolistic companies to take advantage of economies of sale in production. A domestic company, moreover, may make the case that it requires some monopoly power to compete with foreign companies that dominate their home markets.

Some governments look aside as companies monopolize distribution channels and often are ambivalent about enforcing competition policy. Still, most agree that certain types of anti-competitive behavior should not be tolerated. Every industrialized nation has some form of domestic competition policy. There is no consensus, however, on the need for, shape of, or reach of an international competition policy.

International competition policy could proceed on three basic paths. The first is to harmonize national antitrust laws and rely primarily on cooperation among national antitrust authorities to enforce those laws. The second would be to devise a set of binding competition rules that would be enforceable through an international dispute settlement process. A third approach would be to have countries agree on a framework for rules or core principles (basic concepts upon which there could be broad agreement).[1]

Adopting an international competition policy agreement faces three major hurdles. The first is that the theory underlying the policy and a consensus on the appropriate measures necessary to achieve it are still being developed. There are no authoritative ways to measure restrictive business practices nor do definitive policy prescriptions exist.

The second hurdle is political. The appeal of competition policy depends partly on the level of economic development of a country. Developing nations seem more interested in pursuing industrial policies that will foster strong companies than in anti-trust policy aimed at keeping their companies within bounds. Developing nations also have gained greatly by raising their export prices through cartels or other arrangements in order to shift the terms of trade in their favor (particularly in raising the price of petroleum).

The third major hurdle is enforcement and dispute settlement. The initial responsibility for enforcement rests with the authorities in the countries themselves. Nations may or may not be willing to cede supranational authority to an international organization for enforcement. Extraterritorial enforcement of antitrust laws also carries problems, and comity does not always achieve desired results.[2]

At the international level, competition policy is being addressed by the OECD through its Committee on Competition Law and Policy and its Joint Group on Trade and Competition. These OECD groups have been doing considerable intellectual work on trade and competition policy. The OECD has worked to define best practices or common approaches of the enforcement of competition law. It has been seeking to promote the convergence of competition policy across countries. At the WTO, competition policy is under consideration as a new issue for its negotiating agenda.[3] In its Singapore Ministerial in December 1996, the WTO established a working group to study trade and competition policy. This group, however, has focused first on analytical and educational issues rather than on the possibility of negotiations. It is to issue its report in 1999. The United Nations Conference on Trade and Development (UNCTAD) works mainly with countries that are adopting or modernizing their antitrust laws.

As for support for including competition policy in WTO negotiations, in general, the U.S. Justice Department and Federal Trade Commission have been cool to the idea, while the U.S. Trade Representative has given it limited support.[4] In the private sector,

---

[1] Shelton, Joanna R. Competition Policy: What Chance for International Rules? Paper delivered at Wilton Park Conference 545 : The Global Trade Agenda, November 25, 1998. Wilton Park, UK. On Internet at [http://www.oced.org//news_and_events/release/sheltwiltonpark.htm].

[2] Alford, Roger P. The Extraterritorial Application of Antitrust Laws: The United States and European Community Approaches. *Virginia Journal of International Law*, v. 33, Fall 1992. p. 1.

[3] See: CRS Report 98-841 E, *The World Trade Organization: Future Negotiations*, by Arlene Wilson.

[4] See, for example: FTC Chairman Discussed Competition Policy. Trends in International Antitrust Enforcement. *Antitrust & Trade Regulation Report,* Nov. 12, 1998. Barshefsky, Brittan Take Stab at Fleshing Out New Trade Initiative. *Inside U.S. Trade,* September 25, 1998. p. 3-4.

U.S. multinational corporations tend to support wider WTO rules for competition policy. The European Union, which has its own supranational competition authority, in principle, has favored placing competition policy on the WTO negotiating agenda. The Competition Bureau in Canada has stated that it is time to contemplate an agreement on competition policy in the next round of the WTO.[5] Multinational corporations tend to support more work on competition policies by international organizations, but they are concerned about the exchange of confidential information dealing with their market positions.

In the United States, November 1997, the Department of Justice formed the International Competition Policy Advisory Committee (ICPAC) to address global antitrust problems.[6] In forming the committee, the Department noted that recently there have been dramatic increases in both international commerce and international anticompetitive activity. The number of transnational corporate mergers has been rising steadily, and the Department has numerous investigations involving international antitrust issues, such as transnational cartels, multi-jurisdictional merger reviews, and international anticompetitive business practices.

In 1992, the U.S. Justice Department stated that it would challenge anticompetitive conduct abroad if (1) the conduct has a direct, substantial, and reasonably foreseeable effect on exports of goods or services from the United States; (2) the conduct involves anticompetitive activities that violate U.S. antitrust laws, and (3) U.S. courts have jurisdiction over foreign persons or corporations engaged in such conduct.[7] In 1994, Congress passed the International Antirust Enforcement Assistance Ace (15 U.S.C.A. §§ 6201-6212) which emphasizes cooperation and mutual assistance between the Justice Department in the United States and foreign antitrust enforcement entities. These efforts rely heavily on positive comity or cooperation among antitrust authorities.

Competition policy has been at the heart of several recent trade disputes. On March 31, 1998, the WTO released a decision in a U.S.-initiated dispute involving access by Kodak to the photographic film and paper market in Japan. The WTO panel decided against the U.S. which highlighted the lack of an explicit competition policy agreement in the WTO that would have provided a better legal foundation for such cases.[8] Competition policy also came into play in a 1995 dispute over automobiles and parts with Japan. One aspect of this dispute dealt with access by U.S. automakers to dealerships and by automobile parts makers to repair garages in Japan.[9]

According to the U.S. Trade Representative, U.S. industries face anticompetitive practices in many other countries. For example, Asian industrial groups (*keiretsu* in

---

[5] Von Finckenstein, Konrad. Testimony before the U.S. International Competition Policy Advisory Committee. November 2, 1998. Hearing transcript, p. 18.

[6] The committee is co-chaired by former Assistant General for Antitrust James F. Rill and Former chairwoman of the U.S. International Trade Commission Paula Stern.

[7] Justice Department's April 3 Statement of Enforcement Policy: Department of Justice Policy Regarding Anticompetitive Conduct that Restricts U.S. Exports. *Antitrust and Trade Regulation Report,* April 9, 1992. p. 483.

[8] See CRS Report 98-442 E, *The Kodak-Fuji Film Case at the WTO and the Openness of Japan's Film Market,* by Dick K. Nanto.

[9] See: CRS Report 95-725 E, *The Japan-U.S. Automobile and Parts Trade Dispute,* by Dick K. Nanto, William Cooper, and Gwenell L. Bass.

Japan and *chaebol* in South Korea) are often accused of anticompetitive behavior. China has created industrial conglomerates to improve the profitability of state-owned enterprises, some of which are authorized to fix prices, allocate contracts and restrict competition among domestic suppliers. In South Korea, the government-affiliated Korean Broadcasting Advertising Corporation holds a monopoly over the allocation of television and radio advertising time. In India, both state-owned and private Indian firms can engage in mot types of anticompetitive practices with little or no fear of reaction from government overseers or action from a heavily backlogged court system. In 1996, Switzerland strengthened its anti-cartel law, but it still permits cartels under certain circumstances.[10] Also, even though virtually all industrialized and many developing nations have antitrust laws, enforcement varies widely from country to country.

Some of the newly industrializing nations have pressed for abolishing antidumping laws and replacing them with competition policy agreements. Dumping would be treated as an abuse of power. Although Australia and New Zealand have taken this approach in their free-trade agreement, U.S. policymakers have not supported this approach.

EXISTING COMPETITION POLICY AGREEMENTS

As with most other international economic policies, the competition policy agreements that do exist began with arrangements for cooperation or as part of the rules for international trading agreements or economic blocs. The General Agreement on Tariffs and Trade, which has been incorporated into the WTO, contains some provisions which address certain competition-related governmental actions dealing with monopolies, exclusive service arrangements, the effects of domestic regulation, and the need for transparency in all these matters. In the WTO Telecommunications Agreement, there is an obligation to allow service providers of other Members access to public telecommunications networks (which often are public monopolies) on "reasonable and non-discriminatory" terms and conditions.[11]

With respect to particular nations the European Union has the most well-developed policy. The commitment to economic integration there is strong enough that members have agreed to a common competition policy and ceded some of their sovereign rights to enforce it to The Commission of the European Communities and the European Court of Justice. In practice, those cases whose effects can be confined largely to the jurisdiction of a single EU member are acted upon solely by that state.[12]

The North American Free Trade Agreement (NAFTA) included a chapter on competition policy that requires each party to adopt or maintain measures to proscribe

---

[10] U.S. Trade Representative. *1999 National Trade Estimate Report* on Foreign Trade Barriers. Washington, U.S. Government Printing Office, 1999. 354 p. On Internet at [http://www.ustr.gov/reports/nte/1999].

[11] Organizations for Economic Cooperation and Development. *Competition Elements in International Trade Agreements: A Post-Uruguay Round Overview of WTO Agreements.* Report number COM/DAFFE/CLP(98)FINAL. Paris, OECD, January 1999. p. 14.

[12] Graham, Edward M. "Competition Policy and the New Trade Agenda." *New Dimensions of Market Access in a Globalizing World Economy*, by the Organization for Economic Co-operation and Development. Paris, OECD, 1995. pp. 111.

anti-competitive business conduct and to cooperate on issues of enforcement. It has, however, no mechanism for dispute settlement.

In the Australia-New Zealand Closer Economic Relations Trade Agreement (CER), the two countries agreed to extend their domestic antitrust laws to cover the combined two economies. They gave the competition authorities in each country new investigatory powers to obtain evidence in the other nation.[13] Australia and New Zealand also have taken a novel approach to competition policy and trade. In their CER agreement, they replaced antidumping laws between their two countries with provisions from their competition laws. The monopolization or abuse of dominant positions also applies to dumping cases.[14]

The Asia Pacific Economic Cooperation (APEC) council is examining competition policy as a complement to its goal of free trade. The aim is to facilitate trade and reduce trade friction – particularly between the United States and Japan.[15]

The OECD has long been addressing competition issues for this group of 25 industrial nations. It has formed a Joint Group on Trade and Competition, and its members have agreed to cooperate on anticompetitive practices affecting international trade and to continue to work informally for greater convergence in standards for competition law, more use of common analytical methods, and more international enforcement capacity and information sharing.

A competition policy agreement, therefore, is on the agenda for consideration and possible action by the WTO, OECD, and APEC. In a sense, international competition policy is both a goal and a process. As a process, nations are seeking to harmonize their antitrust laws and enforcement. As a goal, international organizations are studying the relationship between competition policy and trade. The WTO, however, is yet to decide whether to initiate activity leading to formal negotiations on international competition policy.

---

[13] Thomson, Graeme A. "Trade and Competition Policy Linkages: Some Ideas on a Framework for the Future." *New Dimensions of Market Access in a Globalizing World Economy*, by the Organization for Economic CO-operation and Development. Paris, OECD, 1995. pp. 142.

[14] Fels, Allan. Remarks before the U.S. International Competition Policy Advisory Committee. November 2, 1998. Hearing transcript page 10. On Internet at [http://www.usdoj.gov/atr/icpac/2232.htm].

[15] APEC Eminent Persons Group. *Implementing the APEC Vision.* Singapore, APEC Secretariat, 1995. p. 19-21.

U.S. International Trade: Data and Forecasts

Dick K. Nanto and Vivian C. Jones

Summary

In 1999 the Untied States incurred a trade deficit in goods of $328.8 billion on a Census basis and $345.6 billion on a balance-of-payments basis (BoP). A surplus in services trade of $80.6 billion gave a deficit of $265.0 on goods and services (BoP) for the year. For August 2000, the trade deficit in goods decreased to $36.4 billion from $38.5 billion in July.

Overall U.S. trade deficits reflect a shortage of savings in the domestic economy and a reliance on capital imports to finance that shortfall. They are a concern for Congress for several reasons. Financial, budgetary and other policies may affect the size of the trade deficit, while trade and capital flows affect the exchange value of the U.S. dollar. A large overall trade deficit may also indicate that certain U.S. industries are having difficulty competing with imports at home and in markets abroad. This may generate trade friction and pressures for the government do more to open foreign markets, shield U.S. producers from foreign competition, or assist U.S. industries to become more competitive.

Since 1976, the United States has incurred continual merchandise trade deficits. They increased dramatically from $36.5 billion in 1982 to a peak in 1987 at $159.6 billion. The deficit dropped to $74.1 billion in 1991 but rose to $345.6 billion in 1999 (BoP).

Much of the improvement in the U.S. trade deficit between 1987 and 1991 resulted from a depreciation of the dollar and the recession in 1990-91. The multilateral trade-weighted real value of the U.S. dollar reached a high in 1985, then dropped sharply from 1986 through 1988.

The worsening of the deficit in 1993-95 can be attributed primarily to the faster recovery from recession in the United States than in Europe or Japan. In 1997-99, the Asian financial crisis caused a sizable fall in U.S. exports to Asia and a marked increase in U.S. imports from Asia.

In 1999, total U.S. goods trade reached $1.7 trillion with exports of $695.8 billion and imports of $1.0 trillion (Census basis). In 1999, U.S. exports increased by 2.6% while imports increased by 12.8%.

The broadest measure of U.S. international economic transactions is the balance on current account. In addition to merchandise trade, it includes trade in services and unilateral transfers. The current account deficit increased in 1999 to a record $331.5 billion from $217.1 billion in 1998. After reaching a peak of $160.7 billion in 1987, the current account deficit had fallen steadily through 1991 when it reached a surplus of $6.6 billion. Economic projections indicate that the current account deficit may reach between $430-450 billion in 2000.

In trade in advanced technology products, the U.S. surplus decreased from $29.7 billion in 1998 to $19.1 billion in 1999.

In trade passenger automobiles, the United States has been running a deficit, particularly with Canada, Japan, Mexico, and Germany.

MOST RECENT DEVELOPMENTS

For August, the U.S. international trade deficit in goods and services decreased to $29.4 billion, down from $31.7 billion July (BoP basis). Exports of goods and services increased to $93.0 billion in August, up from $89.8 billion in July. August imports increased to $122.5 billion, up from $121.5 billion in July. Exports of goods alone increased to $68.0 billion, up from $65.1 billion in July, while imports of goods increased to $104.4 billion, up from $103.6 billion in June.

The deficit on goods trade with Mexico was $1.9 billion for the month of August 2000, down form $2.2 billion in August 1999(Census basis). The goods deficit with Japan was $6,8 billion in August 2000, up from $6.7 billion in August 1999, and the trade deficit in goods with China rose to $8.6 billion, up from 6.8 billion in August 1999. The deficit with the European Union rose to $4.7 billion for August 2000, up from $4.1 billion in August 1999. The deficit with the Asian Newly Industrialized Countries (Hong Kong, South Korea, Singapore, and Taiwan) was $2.6 billion for August 2000, up from $1.7 billion in August 1999.

BACKGROUND AND ANALYSIS

BACKGROUND

The rising U.S. trade deficit is one of the few negatives in the booming American economy. The U.S. deficits on goods trade and current account have roughly doubled over the past two years. Historically, between 1980 and 1987, both trade and current account deficits expanded but then decreased substantially between 1988 and 1991. Since then, both have risen again and have been running at record-breaking levels. The issue brief provides historical and current data as well as some forecasts on U.S. trade and current accounts.

U.S. trade balances are macroeconomic variables that may or may not indicate underlying problems with the competitiveness of particular industries or what some refer to as the competitiveness of a nation. The reasons is that overall trade flows are determined, within the framework of institutional barriers to trade and the activities of individual industries primarily by macroeconomic factors such as rates of growth, savings and investment behavior, exchange rates, and government budget deficits/surpluses. In 1998, for example, despite the competitive large nation (based on domestic strength, infrastructure, and management) while Japan was in twelfth place even though its trade surplus was increasing.

Increases in trade deficits may diminish economic growth, since net exports (exports minus imports) are a component of gross domestic product. In the late 1980s and early 1990s, export growth was an important element in overall U.S. economic growth. In 1999, merchandise exports accounted for about 8.5% of GDP, compared with 5.9% in 190. Recently, however, rising trade deficits have reduced total domestic demand in the economy, although they have been offset by rising consumer, business, and government demand.

The U.S. government compiles trade data in three different ways that result in different sets of figures for each data series. The data are first reported on a Census or Customs basis. These numbers are then adjusted and reported in terms of the balance of payments (BoP), and then national income and product accounts (NIPA). In 1999, for example, the U.S. merchandise trade deficit on Census basis was $328.8 billion, on a balance-of payments basis was $345.6 billion, and on a NIPA basis was $254.0 billion. Most bilateral and sectoral data are reported only on a Census basis.

Export and import data also may be adjusted for inflation to gauge movement in trade volumes as distinct from trade values. Conceptually, this procedure is analogous to adjusting on a c.i.f. (cost –insurance-freight) basis which includes the vale of insurance, international shipping, and other charges incurred in bringing merchandise to U.S. ports of entry. The Customs or f.a.s. (free-alongside-ship), data to not include these supplementary costs. The data on merchandise trade presented below do not include insurance and freight charges that are counted in U.S. services trade.

U.S. Merchandise Trade Balance

The merchandise (goods) trade balance is the most widely known and frequently used indicator of U.S. international economic activity (see Figure 1). In 1999, total U.S. merchandise trade on a Census basis amounted to $1.7 trillion, with exports of $695.8 billion and imports of $1.0 trillion. The U.S. merchandise trade deficit increased 43.6% in 1999 to $328.8 billion (Census basis), following a 27.3% increase in 1998. Prior to 1992, the deficit had decreased for 4 consecutive years, from a previous peak of $153.0 billion in 1987 to $67.0 billion in 1991. The recent increase in the trade deficit is due largely to sluggish demand for U.S. exports caused primarily by slow economic recovery in other countries and increasing demand for imports caused mainly by faster economic growth in the United States. As a share of gross domestic product (GDP), the deficit on goods trade rose from 1.9% in 1990 to 3.0% in 1999.

Figure 1. Merchandise Imports, Exports, and Exchange Rate

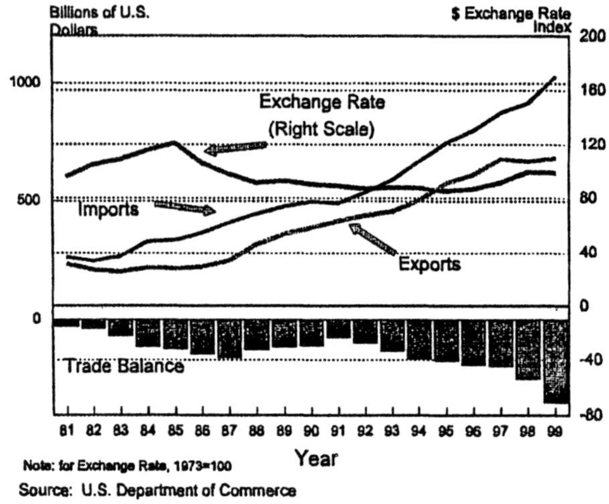

U.S. merchandise exports decreased in 1998 for the first time since 1986 (see Figure 2). In 1999, U.S. exports increased by 2.1% to $695.8 billion (Census basis). By comparison, exports decreased by 1.4% in 1998, but increased by 11.1% in 1997, and 6.3% in 1996. The rate of growth of imports, on the other hand, also has been high. Imports rose by 12.3% to $1.0 trillion in 1999, 4.7% in 1998, 9.1% in 1997 and 7.2% in 1996. Imports exceeded exports by 50.5% in 1999-a great improvement over the 1987 figure of 60.7%. The fact that imports exceeded exports by 51% in 1999, however, implies that U.S. exports must grow 51% faster than imports just for the trade deficit to stay the same.

Figure 2. U.S. Exchange Rage and Growth in Exports and Imports, 1981-1999

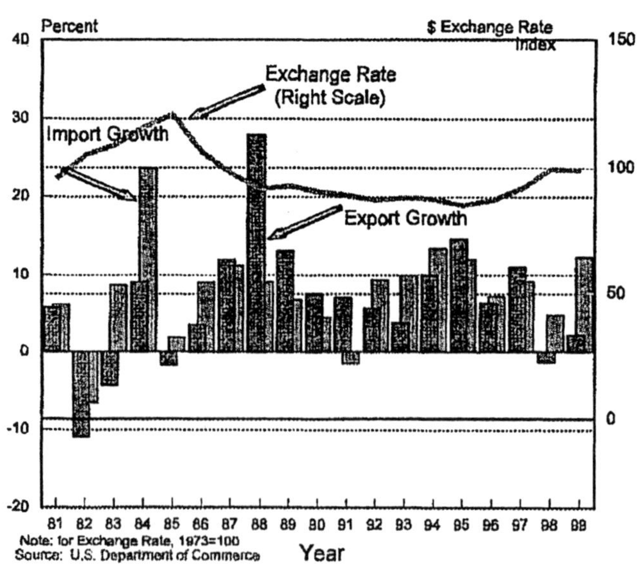

Merchandise Trade Balance in Volume Terms

Like other economic variables, exports and imports, reported in terms of their values, can change merely because prices change. Trade data, therefore, can be adjusted for inflation by dividing by a price index (currently based on prices and weights in 1996). Such corrected data are referred to as "volume" and not "real," because some trade commodities actually are reported in volume terms (e.g., tons of wheat). The volume data provide a more accurate picture of how the underlying flows of merchandise are changing.

Figure 3. U.S. Merchandise Exports, Imports, and Balances by Volume (1996 base) 1982-1999

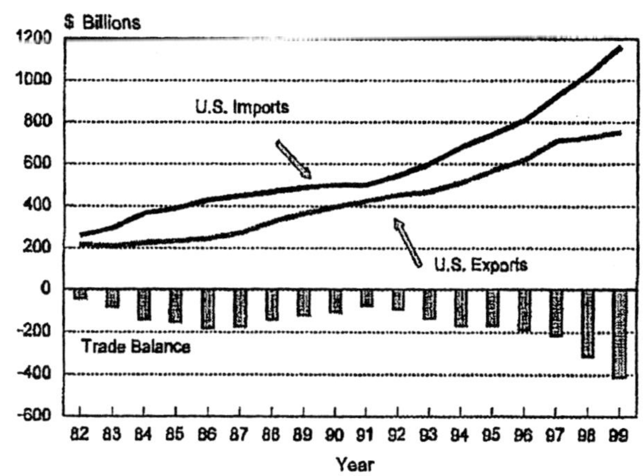

As shown in Table 2 and Figure 3, the constant-dollar value, or physical volume, of merchandise exports increased by 3.8% in 1999, 2.1% in 1998, and 14.5% in 1997. The physical volume of imports increased by 12.7% in 1999, as compared with 11.7% in 1998, and 14.2% in 1997. Because the growth in merchandise imports is higher than the growth of exports and because imports exceed exports by 54.9% on a physical volume basis, the U.S. trade deficit in terms of volume is also increasing. Since 1993, the deficit in volume terms has been larger than the deficit in value terms partly because of the decline in oil import prices. This trend may be reversed in the year 2000 because of an increase of the price of oil.

Current Account Balance

The current account provides a broader measure of U.S. trade because it includes services, investment income, and unilateral transfers in addition to merchandise. The balance on services includes travel, transportation, fees and royalties, insurance payments, and other government and private services. The balance on investment income includes income received on U.S. assets abroad minus income paid on foreign assets in the U.S. Unilateral transfers are international transfers of funds for which there is no quid pro quo. These include private gifts, remittances, pension payments, and government grants (foreign aid).

Figure 4. U.S. Current Account and Merchandise Trade Balances, 1980-1999

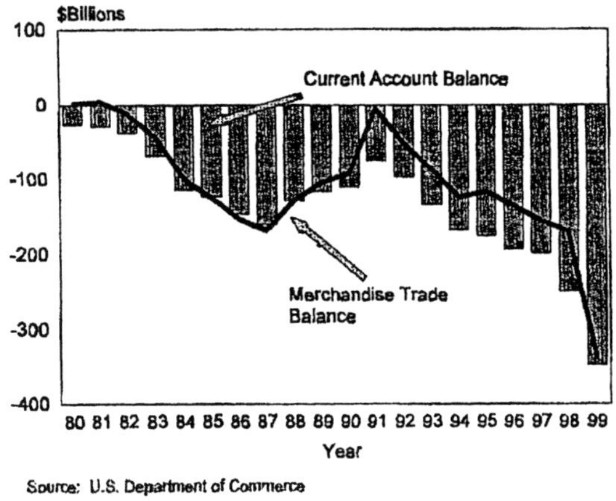

Table 3 summarizes the components of the U.S. current account. The U.S. deficit on current account fell from a record-high $160.7 billion in 1987, to $77.0 billion in 1990, and rose to a $6.6 billion surplus in 1991. However, in 1992, the current account deficit increased significantly to $47.7 billion and again to $82.7 billion in 1993, $118.6 billion in 1994, $123.3 billion in 1996, $140.5 billion in 1997, $217.1 billion in 1998, and increased to $331.5 billion in 1999 or 3.7% of GDP - up from 1.8% in 1990.

Since the merchandise trade balance comprises the greater part of the current account, the two tend to track each other. Unlike the merchandise trade balance, however, the services account has been in surplus since 1975. In 1998, the United States enjoyed a $79.6 billion surplus with the world services trade. Since Americans are such large investors in foreign economies, the United States traditionally has had a surplus in its investment income. This surplus on income from investments, which reached as high as $32.9 billion in 1981, however, dropped to a deficit of $18.5 billion in 1999, down from a $6.2 billion deficit in 1998. The U.S. deficit in unilateral transfers at $48.0 billion is up from $44.0 billion in 1998, and has been growing in recent years – partially offsetting the U.S. surplus in services. In 1991, payments by Japan and European nations in support of the Gulf War brought the balance for unilateral transfers into surplus and, combined with the 1990-91 recession, brought the current account into surplus at $6.6 billion.

FORECASTS

According to DRI (Standard & Poor's Data Resources Inc.) and WEFA, two leading U.S. economic forecasting firms, in 2000 the U.S. merchandise trade deficit is expected to rise to about $450 billion on a balance-of –payment basis (see Figure 5.) In 2001, the deficit is expected to rise between $480 billion and $500 billion.

Figure 5. U.S. Merchandise Trade Deficit, Actual from 1996 and Forecast to 2002 (in current dollars)

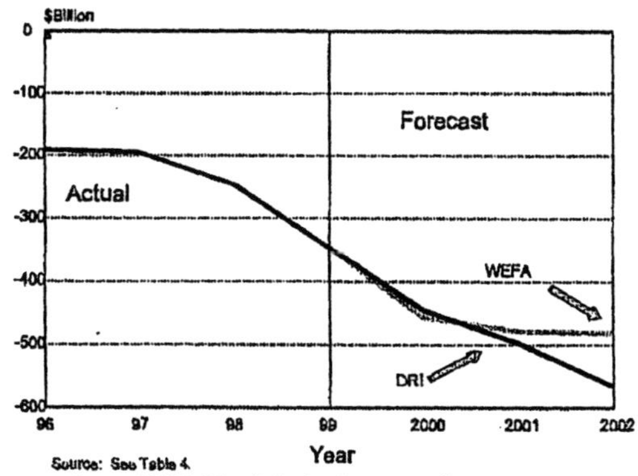

Table 4 includes these published forecasts. As for the U.S. current account deficit, the two firms project it to rise to between $430-$450 billion in 2000 and again to about $540 billion in 2001 (see Figure 6).

Figure 6. U.S. Current Account Deficit Actual from 1996 and Forecast to 2002 (in current dollars)

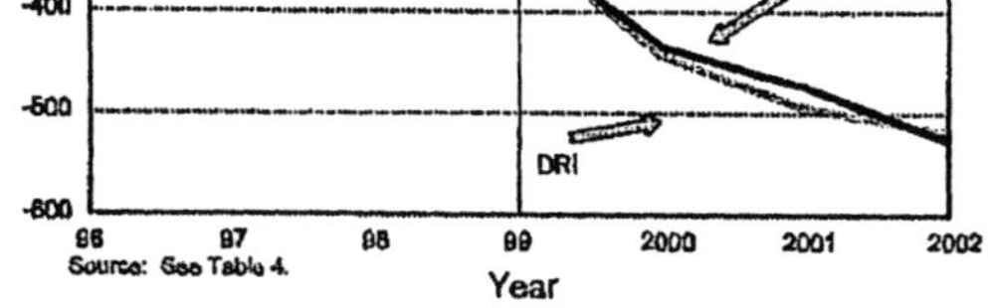

U.S. BILATERAL TRADE BALANCES

The overall U.S. merchandise trade balance consists of deficits or surpluses with all trading partners. Although no country attempts to balance its trade with each nation, abnormally large or rapidly increasing trade deficits with particular countries can indicate that underlying problems may exist with market access, the competitiveness of particular industries, currency misalignment, or macroeconomic adjustment. Table 5 shows U.S. trade balances with selected nations.

Most of the U.S. trade deficit can be accounted for by trade with Japan, China, Canada, Germany, Mexico, and Taiwan. Trade with the oil exporting countries also is in deficit. U.S. trade surpluses occur in trade with the Netherlands, Australia, Brazil, Belgium, Hong Kong, and other countries including Argentina and the United Kingdom. In 1998, Canada was America's largest trading partner, followed by Mexico, Japan, China, and Germany. Table 6 lists the United States' top 20 trading partners ranked by trade turnover (imports plus exports). Trade with Canada accounts for approximately one-fifth of total U.S. trade. Canada is the largest supplier of U.S. imports and the top purchaser of U.S. exports. Trade with Mexico accounts for 11.4%, and trade with Japan accounts for 11% of total U.S. trade.

Table 7 lists the U.S. top 10 deficit trading partners. Japan is at the top, but China is closing the gap quickly. The next highest deficit trading partners are Canada, Germany, Mexico, and Taiwan. Table 8 lists trade balances on goods, services, and income, net unilateral transfers and current account balances for selected U.S. trading partners in 1997.

Table 9 shows U.S. trade in advanced technology products. This includes about 500 commodity codes representing products whose technology is from a recognized high technology field (e.g., biotechnology) or that represent the leading technology in a field. The United States had been running a surplus in these products, but that surplus declined from 1991-195 but recovered somewhat in 1996-1997. It dropped from \$27.2 billion in 1993 to \$22.6 billion in 1994 and fell further in 1995 to \$13.6 billion. In 1997, the surplus rose to \$32.2 billion but has dropped again to \$29.6 billion in 1998 and again in 1999 to \$19.1 billion.

Table 10 provides data on trade in passenger cars with major automobile producing nations for May 1999. This does not include foreign cars assembled in the United States. The United States incurs deficits in this trade with Canada, Japan, Germany, Mexico, and the United Kingdom.

Figure 7. U.S. Trade Balances with Selected Nations, 1999

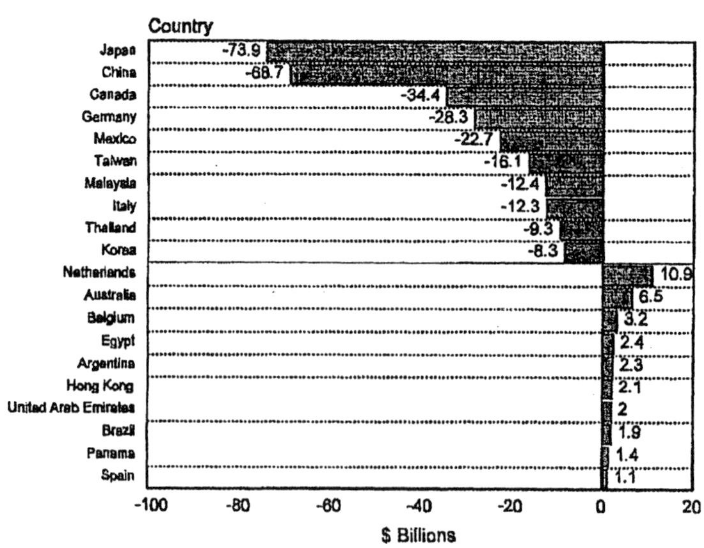

Source: Data from U.S. Department of Commerce

Table 1. U.S. Exports, Imports, and Merchandise Trade Balances, 1978-1999 (Census Basis, billions of U. S. dollars)

Year	Exports f.a.s. [a]	Imports, Customs	Trade Balance
1978	145.8	173.3	-27.5
1979	186.3	207.1	-20.8
1980	225.5	241.3	-15.8
1981	238.7	261.0	-22.3
1982	216.4	244.0	-27.6
1983	207.6	258.0	-50.4
1984	223.1	325.7	-102.6
1985	219.2	345.3	-126.1
1986	227.5	370.0	-142.5
1987	252.9	405.9	-153.0
1988	322.7	441.3	-118.6
1989	363.8	473.4	-109.6
1990	393.0	496.0	-103.0
1991	421.9	488.9	-67.0
1992	447.5	532.0	-84.5
1993	464.9	580.5	-115.6
1994	512.4	663.8	-151.4
1995	583.0	743.5	-160.5
1996	622.8	791.3	-168.5
1997	689.2	869.7	-180.5
1998	682.1	911.9	-229.8
1999	695.8	1.025.3	-328.8

Source: Compiled from official statistics of the U.S. Department of Commerce by CRS using the International Trade Administration's *Trade Policy Information of System* database, [http://www.ita.doc.gov/td/industry/otea/tpis/].

[a]Exports are valued on the f.a.s. basis, which refers to the free-alongside-ship value at the port of export and generally includes inland freight, insurance, and other charges incurred in placing the goods alongside the carrier at the port of exportation.

[b]Imports are valued as reported by the U.S. Customs Service. (Excludes import duties, the cost of freight, insurance, and other charges incurred in bringing merchandise to the United States.)

Note: For trade data on a balance-of-payments basis, see Tables 3 and 4.

Figure 8. U.S. Balance of Trade in Goods and Services by Month, 1999-2000 (in billions of current dollars)

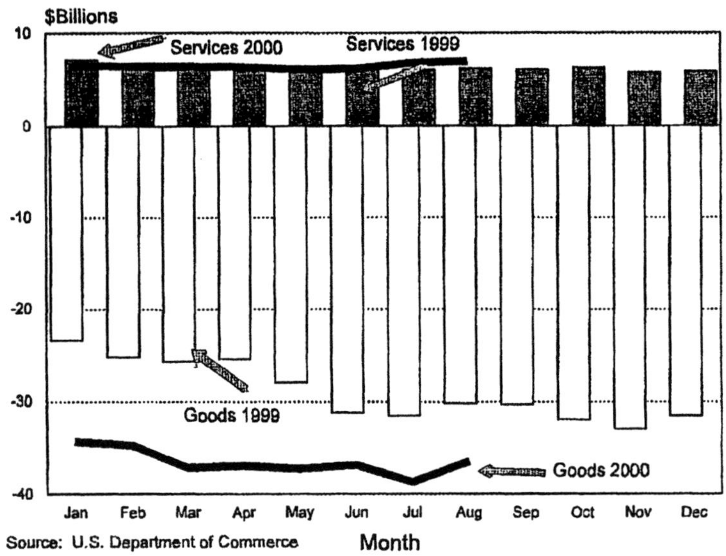

Table 2. U.S. Merchandise Trade in Volume Terms, 1990-1999 (billions of chained 1999 dollars)

Year	Exports	Export Growth	Imports	Import Growth	Net Exports
1990	393.2	8.3	497.9	3.0	-104.7
1991	421.1	7.1	497.6	6.2	-76.5
1992	449.8	6.8	543.7	9.3	-93.9
1993	463.4	3.0	598.4	10.1	-135.9
1994	508.2	9.7	677.9	13.3	-169.7
1995	568.8	11.9	739.1	9.0	-170.3
1996	618.4	8.7	808.3	9.4	-189.1
1997	708.1	14.5	923.2	14.2	-215.1
1998	722.8	2.1	1031.6	11.7	-313.3
1999	750.3	3.8	1162.7	12.7	-412.4

Source: Council of Economic Advisers, *Economic Report of the President,* April 2000

Table 3. U. S. Current Account Balances: 1982 to 1999
(billions of U.S. dollars)

Calendar Year	Merchandise Trade Balance[a]	Service Balance[b]	Investment Income Balance[c]	Net Unilateral Transfers[d]	Current Account Balance[e]
1982	-36.5	12.3	35.2	-16.5	-5.5
1983	-67.1	9.3	36.3	-17.3	-38.7
1984	-112.5	3.4	35.1	-20.3	-94.3
1985	-122.2	0.3	25.7	-22.0	-118.2
1986	-145.1	6.5	15.5	-24.1	-147.2
1987	-159.6	7.9	14.3	-23.3	-160.7
1988	-127.0	12.4	18.7	-25.3	-121.2
1989	-115.2	24.6	19.8	-26.2	-97.0
1990	-109.0	30.2	28.6	-26.7	-77.0
1991	-74.1	45.8	24.1	10.8	6.6
1992	-96.1	60.4	23.0	-35.0	-47.7
1993	-132.6	63.7	23.9	-37.6	-82.7
1994	-166.2	69.1	16.7	-38.3	-118.6
1995	-173.7	77.8	20.5	-34.0	-109.5
1996	-191.3	89.2	18.9	-40.1	-123.3
1997	-196.7	90.7	6.2	-40.8	-140.5
1998	-246.9	80.0	-6.2	-44.0	-217.1
1999	-347.1	80.6	-18.5	-48.0	-331.5

Source: U.S. Bureau of Economic Analysis. Also in U.S. Department of Commerce, *Survey of Current Business*, International Transactions Tables, May 2000.

[a]On a balance-of-payment basis.

[b]Includes travel, transportation, fees and royalties, insurance payments, other government and private services, and investment income.

[c]Income receipts on U.S. assets abroad minus income payments on foreign assets in the United States.

[d]International transfers of funds, such as private gifts, pension payments, and government grants for which there is no *quid pro quo.*

[e]The trade balance plus the service balance plus investment income balance plus net unilateral transfers, although conceptually equal to the current account balance, may differ slightly as a result of rounding errors.

Table 4. U.S. Merchandise and Current Account Trade: Actual and Forecasts (billions of U.S. dollars)

	Actual				Forecast		
	1996	1997	1998	1999	2000	2001	2002
Merchandise Trade							
Exports							
Actual	618.4	688.9	670.3	684.4	--	--	--
DRI[a]	--	--	--	--	775.8	832.0	877.0
WEFA[b]	--	--	--	--	792.5	88.4	973.7
Imports							
Actual	808.3	885.1	917.2	102.9	--	--	--
DRI[a]	--	--	--	--	122.2	1328.8	1442.8
WEFA[b]	--	--	--	--	1250.5	1367.4	1456.4
Trade Balance							
Actual	-190.0	-196.1	-246.2	-345.6	--	--	--
DRI[a]	--	--	--	--	-446.5	-496.8	-565.8
WEFA[b]	--	--	--	--	-458.0	-479.1	-482.7
Current Account Balance							
Actual	-123.3	-140.5	-217.1	-331.4	--	--	--
DRI[a]	--	--	--	--	-428.7	-469.1	-536.0
WEFA[b]	--	--	--	--	-450.8	-511.0	-537.0

Sources: U.S. Bureau of Economic Analysis, *Survey of Current Business,* Data Resources, Inc., *Review of the U.S. Economy* September 2000; WEFA Group, *U.S. Economic Outlook 1998-2005,* September 2000. All figures on a balance-of-payment basis.

[a]DRI: Standard & Poor's Data Resources, Inc.

[b]WEFA: The WEFA Group.

Table 5. U.S. Trade Balances with Selected Nations: 1995-1999 (millions of U.S. dollars, Census basis)

Country	1995	1996	1997	1998	1999
Total	-151,415	-160,473	-168,400	-229,758	-330,022
North America	-34,489	-74,613	-31,790	-32,509	-54,936
Canada	-19,095	-23,922	-17,926	-16,653	-32,095
Mexico	-15,394	-16,202	-14,494	-15,856	-22,841
Western Europe	10,458	14,463	-16,061	-25,857	-42,442
European Union	-8,311	-15,208	-16,741	-27,346	-43,723
United Kingdom	1,936	2,024	3,746	4,220	-853
Germany	-14,470	-15,469	-18,602	-23,185	-23,305
France	-2,937	-4,202	-4,743	-6,287	-7,071
Italy	-7,635	-9,437	-10,387	-11,968	-12,344
Netherlands	10,180	9,997	12,543	11,378	10,939
European Free Trade Association (EFTA)	-7,509	-5,596	-7,269	-7,748	-9,551
Former Soviet Republics	-1,100	402	-284	-2,116	-4,123
Eastern Europe	-395	-258	-531	-1,506	-2,064
Pacific Rim Countries	-108,317	-102,055	-121,101	-160,395	-186,684
Japan	59,280	47,683	55,687	-64,014	-73,920
China	-33,807	-39,517	-49,747	-56,927	-68,668
Newly Industrialized Countries (NICS)	-7,770	-7,149	-7,770	-22,691	-24,211
Singapore	-3,246	-3,655	-2,340	-2,662	-1,941
Hong Kong	3,926	4,008	4,818	2,387	2,116
Taiwan	-9,680	-11,498	-12,236	-14,960	-16,077
Republic of Korea	1,230	3,916	1,908	-7,456	-8,308
South/Central American Countries	4,568	1,693	7,119	9,218	-4,257
Argentina	2,430	2,337	3,595	3,655	2,340
Brazil	-590	2,628	6,283	5,040	1,935
Colombia	873	435	474	160	-2,744
OEPC	-12,696	-14,332	-17,976	-8,771	-21,707
Venezuela	-5,070	-8,162	-6,841	-2,666	-5,896
Indonesia	-4,081	-4,249	-4,659	-7,042	-7,575
Saudi Arabia	-2,148	-1,486	-1,113	4,279	-336
Nigeria	-4,173	-5,033	-3,375	-3,375	-3,733

Trade Balance equals Total Exports (f.a.s value) minus General Imports (Customs value).
Source: Compiled from official statistics of the U.S. Department of Commerce by CRS using the International Commission's (ITC) Dataweb [http://dataweb.usite.gov].

Table 6. Top 30 U.S. Trading Partners Ranked by Total Trade (Exports + Imports) in 1999 (billions of U.S. dollars)

Country	Exports(f.a.s)	Imports(customs)	Trade Balance	Total Trade
World total	692.8	1,024.8	-322.0	1,717.6
Canada	163.9	198.3	-34.4	362.2
Mexico	87.0	109.7	-22.7	196.7
Japan	57.5	131.4	-73.9	188.9
China	13.1	81.8	-68.7	94.9
Germany	26.8	55.1	-28.3	81.9
United Kingdom	38.3	39.2	-0.9	77.5
Taiwan	19.1	35.2	-16.1	54.3
Korea	23.0	31.3	-8.3	54.3
France	18.8	25.9	-7.1	44.7
Singapore	16.2	18.2	-2.0	34.4
Italy	10.1	22.4	-12.3	32.5
Malaysia	9.1	21.4	-12.3	30.5
Netherlands	19.4	8.5	10.9	27.9
Brazil	13.2	11.3	1.9	24.5
Hong Kong	12.6	10.5	2.1	23.1
Belgium	12.4	9.2	3.2	21.6
Philippines	7.2	12.4	-5.2	19.6
Thailand	5.0	14.3	-9.3	19.3
Switzerland	8.4	9.6	-1.2	18.0
Israel	7.7	9.9	-2.2	17.6
Ireland	6.4	11.0	-4.6	17.4
Australia	11.8	5.3	6.5	17.1
Venezuela	5.4	11.3	-5.9	16.7
Saudi Arabia	7.9	8.2	-0.3	16.1
India	3.7	9.1	-5.4	12.8
Sweden	4.2	8.1	-3.9	12.3
Indonesia	1.9	9.5	-7.6	11.4
Spain	6.1	5.1	1.0	11.2
Colombia	3.5	6.3	-2.8	9.8
Russia	1.8	5.8	-4.0	7.6

Source: Compiled from official statistics of the U.S. Department of Commerce by CRS using the International Trade Commission's (ITC) Dataweb [http://dataweb.usite.gov].

Table 7. Top 10 U.S. Deficit Trading Partners: 1999 (billions of U.S. dollars, Customs basis)

Country	U.S. Exports (f.a.s)	U.S. Imports (customs)	Trade Balance
Japan	57.5	131.4	-73.9
China	13.1	81.8	-68.7
Canada	87.0	198.3	-111.3
Germany	26.8	55.1	-28.3
Mexico	87.0	109.7	-22.7
Taiwan	19.1	35.2	-16.1
Malaysia	9.1	21.4	-12.3
Italy	0.1	22.4	-12.3
Thailand	5.0	14.3	-9.3
South Korea	23.0	31.3	-8.3

Source: Compiled from official statistics of the U.S. Department of Commerce by CRS using the International Trade Commission's (ITC) Dataweb [http://dataweb.usite.gov].

Table 8. U.S. Current Account Balances With Selected U.S. Trading Partners, 1999 (billions of U.S. dollars)

Country	Merchandise Trade Balance[a]	Services Balance[b]	Investment Income Balance[c]	Net Unilateral Transfers[d]	Current Account Balance[e]
All Countries	-345.6	80.6	-18.4	-48.0	-331.4
Canada	-34.7	5.8	14.4	-0.6	-15.1
Japan	-74.5	14.6	-27.6	-0.2	-15.1
United Kingdom	-1.5	3.2	-36.2	1.5	-33.1
European Union	-45.6	17.7	-32.7	0.3	-60.4
Eastern Europe	-6.3	1.3	1.0	-4.1	-8.3
Latin America	-27.8	17.5	7.6	-14.7	-17.4

Source: U.S. Department of Commerce, *Survey of Current Business*, July 2000.
[a]On a balance-of-payments basis.
[b]Includes, travel, transportation, fees and royalties, insurance payments, other government and private services, and investment income.
[c]Income receipts on U.S. assets abroad minus income payments of foreign assets in the United States
[d]International transfers of funds, such as private gifts, pension payments, and government grants for which there is no *quid pro quo*.
[e]The trade balance plus the service balance plus investment income balance plus net unilateral transfers, although conceptually equal to the current account balance, may differ slightly as a result of rounding errors.

Table 9. U.S. Trade in Advanced Technology Products (billions of U.S. dollars)

Year	U.S. Exports	U.S. Imports	Trade Balance
1989	83.4	56.4	7.0
1990	93.4	59.3	4.1
1991	101.6	63.3	8.3
1992	107.1	71.9	5.2
1993	108.4	81.2	7.2
1994	120.7	98.1	2.6
1995	138.4	124.8	3.6
1996	154.9	130.4	4.5
1997	179.5	147.3	2.2
1998	186.4	156.8	9.6
1999	200.0	180.6	9.4
August 1999	16.6	15.5	1.1
August 2000	18.1	20.1	-0.4

Source: U.S. Bureau of the Census. *U.S. International Trade in Goods and Services.* FT-900, issued monthly. Includes about 500 of some 22,000 commodity classification codes that meet the following criteria: (1) contains products whose technology is from a recognized high technology field (e.g., biotechnology), (2) represent leading edge technology in that field, and (3) constitute a significant part of all items covered in the selected classification code.

Table 10. U.S. Trade in Passenger Automobiles by Selected Countries, August 2000 (millions of U.S. dollars)

Trading Partner	U.S. Exports	U.S. Imports	Trade Balance
Total World	1,095	9,052	-7,957
Canada	556	2,907	-2,351
Germany	101	1,158	-1,057
Japan	62	2,902	-2,840
Mexico	164	1,404	-1,240
United Kingdom	22	215	-193

Source: U.S. Bureau of the Census. *U.S. International Trade in Goods and Services.* FT-900, issued monthly.

U.S. FOREIGN-TRADE ZONES: CURRENT ISSUES

Mary Jane Bolle

ABSTRACT

This report provides an overview of the U.S. foreign-trade zone system which has evolved under the U.S. Foreign-Trade Zones Act of 1934 [P.L. 73-397, 19 U.S.C. 81(a)-81(u)]. The report covers what zones are and how they function, the history of the U.S. zone system, how the zone system has evolved from its original intent, and policy issues and legislative issues relating to zones. Twelve tables and figures provide a list of zones and subzones by state, and information on zone or subzone application, cost savings available to zone users, winners and losers from zone use, and major zone legislation in the 105th and 106th Congresses. While this report mentions specific bills, it is not intended as a bill-tracking device. It will be updated periodically, as needed.

SUMMARY

Foreign-trade zones are the U.S. version of *free trade zones* scattered around the world. Free trade zones are geographic areas which primarily facilitate economic development, and *co-production*- the joint production of a single good through the efforts of workers in two or more countries. All zones are geographic areas which are physically located *inside* the boundaries of the country, but treated as if they were located *outside* the country for customs purposes. Thus, for goods or materials which are imported, processed, and later re-exported, no tariffs are payable and customs procedures are streamlined.

The 253 U.S. zones are among nearly 850 zones world-wide, but different from them in two major ways. First, two-thirds of the world's zones are in developing countries, producing primarily for *export*, while U.S. zones produce primarily for *import*. Second, whereas many foreign zones are exempt from customs oversight, taxes, and regulations, U.S. zones are subject to customs control as well as most other federal, state and local laws and taxes.

Most goods enter the United States through customs at the port of entry and then travel to their ultimate destination. Imports which are not yet complete, needed, or allowed to enter the United States (for quota reasons, for example) after being unloaded at ports of entry, may be taken to a nearby foreign-trade *general purpose zone* (for warehousing or further processing) or to a *special purpose subzone* (a manufacturing site which is separate from but linked to a zone.)

They system of U.S. foreign-trade zones evolved greatly over its 65-year history since it was set up by the U.S. Foreign-Trade Zones (FTZ) Act in 1934 [P.L. 73-397, 19 U.S.C. 81 (a)-81(u)]. Envisioned by some as an engine of export growth, it has become largely a system for avoiding *inverted tariff structures* on imports (higher duties on components than on finished products.)

Policy questions relating to zones today are similar to those of a decade ago; however, the answers are different, largely because of the evolution of the U.S. and world economies. Issues today are: Is the Act fulfilling its original intent? (No. The intent has evolved.) Have U.S. foreign trade zones helped or hurt U.S. workers? (The question has been eclipsed by the perceived effects of NAFTA and other trade influences). Do U.S. foreign-trade zones set U.S. trade policy by circumventing Congress and U.S. trade negotiators?" (Perhaps, but the issue has dimmed as tariffs and trade barriers decline, and since new regulations went into effect in 1991.)

Legislative issues pertaining to zones have moved from the macro to the micro level. P.L. 106-36 (S. Report 106-2), approved June 25, 1999, provides that commercial importation data for foreign-trade zones shall be included under the National Customs Automation Program under construction. In addition, H.R. 975 (H. Report 106-52), which passed the House on March 17, 1999. provides for a reduction in the volume of steel imports, and requires a steel notification certificate for any steel entering through a foreign-trade zone. Other bills, instead of being focused on how zones affect the U.S. economy, are now focused more on whether zone policy should be used to help specific industries and specific localities.

*****

Foreign-trade zones are the U.S. version of *free trade zones* scattered around the world. Free trade zones are geographic areas which primarily facilitate economic development, and *co-production*-the joint production of a single good through the efforts of workers in two or more countries.[1] In the United States, this means that zones are places where some foreign components are typically mixed with U.S. components in the manufacturing process.

Current policy issues reflect the impact of U.S. zones relative to other influences on the U.S. economy. Many current legislative proposals tend to focus on fine-tuning the

---

[1] The difference between *free trade zones* and *free trade areas* is this: *Free trade areas* involve agreement to reduce or eliminate certain trade barriers to all members of the group, while each county is free to negotiate its own barriers with countries outside the group. *Free trade zones*, on the other hand, do not affect a country's trade barriers. Rather, they set up secure locations (often fenced) which are inside the boundaries of the country but which are considered to be outside the country for tariff purposes. Hence, the trade barriers do not apply as long as the good is within the zone. When the good exits the zone, only if it then enters the country in which the zone is located, do normal trade barriers apply.

workings of the zone system or reflect the difference that zone status can make in promoting economic development for a community and improving competitiveness of a company in a specific industry.

First, however, this report examines what the U.S. zone system is, how it relates to zones abroad, and how the U.S. foreign-trade zone program has changed from its original intent. Tables detail trade zone legislation in the 105th and 106th Congresses, provide information on application methods and requirements for zone status, and list zones and subzones, by state.[2]

U.S. ZONES IN A WORLD CONTEXT

Zones all over the world have an important characteristic in common: They are geographic areas which are physically *inside* the boundaries of a country, but which are treated as if they were located *outside* the country for customs purposes – that is, zones are declared to be outside the customs territory of a country.

This separation from the country for customs purposes links world zones together into a type of international "no-man's-land," which has two important traits. First, no tariffs (taxes on imported goods), and in many cases, (including the United States) no other taxes (sales, excise, or other) are payable on goods so long as they remain in the zone system. Only when they leave the system and enter a country are tariffs, payable on the imported value of the product and are sales taxes payable on imported goods sold. If the goods are re-exported, no duties are payable.

Second, customs procedures are streamlined for all goods entering and leaving the zone system. As a result, if buttons from Indonesia and fabric from India are sent to a trade zone in the Philippines for assembly into a shirt, which is then exported to the United States, *no tariffs* are payable in the Philippines, and *all customs procedures are streamlined* until the completed shirt enters the United States for consumption. At that time, tariffs are payable on the import value, and the shirt goes through normal customs procedures.

The 235 U.S. zones are part of the world system of 850 zones.[3] Two thirds of these zones are in developing countries, which produce primarily for export. In these

---

2 While this report mentions a number of specific bills, it is not intended as a bill-tracking device. It will be updated periodically as needed.

3 Zones around the world are called by at least 19 different names, depending on the country in which they are located or the author or organization referring to them. Among these are the following: Generically they are often called *free trade zones*. Those in the United States are called *foreign-trade zones*. Those in developing countries producing specifically for export are typically called *export processing zones*. They are also called *maquiladoras* in Mexico, *special economic zones* in China, *industrial free zones* or *export free zones* in Ireland, *free zones* in the United Arab Emirates, and *duty free export processing zones* in the Republic of Korea. In addition they are called *tax free zones* or *tax free trade zones* by Walter H. and Dorothy B. Diamond, authors of *Tax-Free Trade Zones of the World*. They have been called *free export processing zones* by the Organization for Economic Cooperation and Development. Source: International Labor Organization. *Economic and Social Effects of Multinational Enterprises in Export Processing Zones*. Geneva, 1988, p. 5.

countries, zones are often used as an economic development tool. Production takes place in *export processing zones* which are typically islands of modernization, located at ports, in countries which lack extensive infrastructure. Supplies which are unloaded from container ships travel a short distance to be manufactured into components or completed goods, which are then reloaded on ships for export. Multinational corporations in developed countries may view these zones as low-cost offshore production sites.

CHARACTERISTICS OF U.S. ZONES

U.S. zones, in contrast with the export emphasis of zones in developing countries, are primarily for warehousing or processing of *imports* prior to going through customs at the port of entry.

U.S. zones differ from other zones around the world in other ways as well. U.S. imports which are not complete, not yet needed, or not allowed to enter the United States (for quota reasons, for example) after being unloaded at ports of entry, prior to facing full customs procedures, may be taken to a nearby foreign-trade *general purpose zone* for warehousing or further processing, or to a subzone – a unique U.S. invention. The 235 zones include seaports, airports, and fenced industrial parks with warehousing and processing facilities , which are run by public corporations as if they were utilities – with published rates. *Subzones*, of which there are about 427, are manufacturing operations which are administratively linked to a zone, but physically separated from it. They are typically pre-existing operations which have applied for and been granted subzone status. However, businesses may also apply for zone status before beginning construction on a new manufacturing operation.[4]

U.S. zones and subzones, like other zones around the world, are viewed, in part, as an economic development tool. They allow businesses to save money on *imports* through duty (tariff) deferral, duty exemption, elimination of the need for duty drawback, and tax avoidance. They also allow U.S. businesses to save small amounts through quota storage, zone-to zone-transfer, and customs and inventory efficiencies. (See table 1 for details.) Most importantly, however, *subzones* in particular, allow businesses to save money, in part because they are places where inverted tariff structures can be changed to uniform rate structures (explained below). The Foreign-Trade Zones Board estimates that slightly less than 50% of all foreign merchandise entering through trade zones is being used in the inverted tariff situation.

---

[4] Another difference is that many foreign zones allow companies to operate under special or relaxed rules with respect to taxes and customs oversight. Certain foreign zones require neither customs documentation or supervision of merchandise while materials are admitted, stored, or processed in the zone. Some allow significant tax exemptions, including income and property taxes. U.S. foreign –trade zones, on the other hand, are fully subject to all federal, state and local laws and taxes, except for federal excise taxes and local inventory taxes. They are also subject to full customs supervision throughout while materials are admitted, processed, and shipped, and to customs penalties for failure to adhere to requirements, and to customs penalties for failure to adhere to requirements. In addition, prohibited goods (including illegal products) are not allowed into U.S. zones.

What is an Inverted Tariff Structure?

An *inverted tariff structure* means that the tariff rate on a product used as a component of a finished product is higher than the tariff rate on the finished good containing the component. When imported components are combined with domestic supplies in subzones, importers can effectively reduce the tariff rate on components of the same level as those levied on a completed good.[5]

Thus, if a zone manufacturer applies for and is granted subzone status, he can use his zone status to eliminate the adverse cost effect of the inverted tariff in the industry in which he produces. This is because customs provisions allow zone users to choose (when the component enters the zone) between paying, (when the component leaves the zone system as part of a completed good) the tariff on the component itself or the tariff on the component as if it were incorporated into the completed good.[6] Industries where there may be inverted tariffs include oil refining, auto manufacturing, electronics, chemicals, food products, pharmaceuticals, apparel and textiles, steel, and machinery. Not all zone applicants in these industries have been granted zone status. The granting of zone status by the Foreign-Trade Zones Board means that zone status has been deemed in the "public interest." The determination is based, in part, on the cause of the inverted tariff structure.

Inverted tariffs have arisen in the very extensive Harmonized Tariff Schedule in two ways: *inadvertently*, and *by design.* When an industry has an inverted tariff by design, it is generally to protect the component industry from import competition. In such cases, application for zone status may be denied or limitation may be placed on zone status. Inverted tariff structures are the major reason for zone application in the United States, and the greatest source of benefit to users (with duty deferral second). In recent year, tariff levels generally have been negotiated to very low levels, and typically the differences between tariffs on components and tariffs on finished products have become smaller and smaller.

---

[5] World Wide Shipping. *Economic Impact Analysis*, by Dennis Puccinelli, August, 1985, p. 71.

[6] The procedure the zone manufacturer follows to change the tariff rate is as follows; When the duty rate on the imported component is lower than that on the end product into which the component is to be incorporated, the zone manufacturer must file a formal application for the component to receive 'privileged foreign status." If such status is approved, the component, when it leaves the zone, is dutied at its own rate—typically that applicable to the product of which it will make an integral part.

Table 1. Possible Cost Savings Available to U.S. Foreign-Trade Zone Users

Benefit	How Costs Can Be Saved
Duty Reduction(on Inverted Tariff Situations)	Zone users may choose the lower duty rate when a product is entered into customs territory (for importation) in inverted situations (when the rate of the foreign inputs is higher than the rate applied to the finished product produced in the zone. Zone status, however, is granted by the FTZ Board when it determines that such status will result in a public benefit (typically a net positive effect for U.S. businesses and workers).
Duty Deferral	Cash flow savings can result because customs duties are paid only when and if the goods are transferred from the zone to a U.S. customs territory for import.
Duty Exemption	No duty is payable on goods which are exported from a zone, or which are consumed, scrapped, or destroyed in a zone.
Drawback Elimination	Zones eliminate the need for duty drawback. That is, the refunding of duties previously paid on imported and then re-exported merchandise.
Tax Savings	Goods stored in zones and goods exported are not subject to state and local ad valorem taxes, such as personal property and sales taxes.
Quota Storage	Cash flow savings and savings from buying in bulk can be made because U.S. quota restrictions do not apply to merchandise admitted to a zone until is entered into customs territory. When the quota opens, the goods may be immediately entered into U.S. customs territory for importation.
Zone to Zone Transfer	Zones can transfer merchandise "in-bond" from one zone to another. Customs duties may be deferred until the product's eventual entry into U.S. customs territory.
Customs and Inventory Efficiencies	Cost savings (especially cash-flow savings) can occur from zone efficiencies affecting inventory control. These efficiencies include customs procedures such as direct delivery and weekly entries.

Source of table data: U.S. Foreign-Trade Zones Board.

HOW TO ACHIEVE ZONE STATUS

The primary constituent interest relating to zones is how to achieve zone status, as quickly as possible. Appendix table 4, 20, includes information on how to apply for zone or subzone status and requirements for applications, together with telephone and website contracts.[7] While new zones are approved when the Board finds that existing or authorized zones do not adequately serve the "convenience of commerce,"[8] subzones can be approved only when a "public benefit" – (i.e., increased employment without detrimental effects on other competitors) can be clearly demonstrated.[9]

Zone or subzone status is achieved by applying to the U.S. Foreign-Trade Zones Board in the Import Administration of the U.S. Department of Commerce in Washington, D. C. (202) 482-2862. The Board is a committee of two, made up of the Secretaries of Commerce and the Treasury, whose agencies each play a role in the approval and oversight of foreign-trade zones.[10]

The U.S. Foreign-Trade Zones Board is supported by a professional staff of 11, under the leadership of an executive director. It is responsible for reviewing applications for zone approval and making recommendations to the Board. Regulations covering zone application may be found at 15 CFR Part 400. The general purpose zone applications process takes about 18 months, and the subzone application process takes about 12 months. Zones are operated by public or public-type corporations, which may contract out operations. Zones are operated like utilities with published rates.

Day-to-Day supervision of goods into and out of zones is the responsibility of the U.S. Customs Service in the Treasury Department. Customs Service regulations relating to zones are included at 19 CFR Part 146. Overhead costs for zones include reimbursement to Customs for services rendered.

HOW DID THE U.S. FOREIGN-TRADE ZONES PROGRAM BEING?

The Foreign-Trade Zones Board was created by the *U.S. Foreign-Trade Zones Act* in 1934 [P.L. 73-397, 19 U.S.C. 81(a)-81(u)][11] It was given the power to approve

---

[7] Most successful zone applicants use general purpose zones for storage, manipulation, and manufacturing, and special purpose subzones for specific larger scale manufacturing. However, some creative uses of zones are also emerging. The International Wildlife Recovery Center has set up an operation in the Medford-Oregon FTZ. The Center specializes in the decontamination and rehabilitation of wildlife affected by oil and other hazardous material spills around the world. By locating the center in a foreign-trade zone, in a pollution event involving 250 birds, for example, the IWRC can save $500,000 in customs duties associated with food imports for the animals.

[8] Foreign-Trade Zones Act. P.L. 73-397, sec. 2(b).

[9] Da Ponte, John J., Jr. United States *Foreign-Trade Zones: Adapting to Time and Space.* The Maritime Lawyer, Fall, 1980, p. 211.

[10] Authority is typically delegated to the Assistant Secretary of Commerce for Import Administration, and the Deputy Assistant Secretary of the Treasury for Enforcement.

[11] Regulations issued by the U.S. Foreign-Trade Zones Board for establishing and maintaining a foreign-trade zone can be found at 15 CFR 400.

applications by public corporations for zone status. The act itself was fairly short-less than six pages in length. It entitled each U.S. port of entry to at least one zone, and prescribed physical conditions and standards for each zone, requirements for operation, record keeping, and goods being moved into and out of zones, activities permissible in zones, and the applicability of all U.S. laws to zones.

When the U.S. foreign trade zones program began in 1934, it was a program designed to help accelerate U.S. trade in the wake of the restrictive impact of the Smoot-Hawley Tariff bill of 1930. Which raised U.S. tariffs on imported goods as high as 53%.[12] Some have argued that zones were designed originally to be way stations where goods coming in from one foreign port could be *transshipped (reloaded* for export to another foreign port) or *re-exported (processed* for subsequent export).[13]

The foreign-trade zones legislation was controversial, however, because there was some fear that it would promote imports of cheaper components used in the manufacturing process, and thereby put domestic components manufacturers at risk. To make sure this would not happen, the Act prohibited manufacturing in zones.

CHANGES TO THE FTZ ACT[14]

After the Foreign-Trade Zone Act was passed, it proved restrictive enough to be very little used. It did not encourage U.S. exports as some had expected. Even sixteen years after the Act was passed, in 1950, there were till fewer than ten zones.[15] Intense lobbying by manufacturing trade groups to make the zone concept more useful led Congress to permit manufacturing in zones. Many reasoned that zones were too small for much manufacturing to occur there.

The Foreign-Trade Zones Board took the amendment one step further. This one step led the zone system on a course which eventually made it successful in a way that was very different form what some originally intended the program to be. Two years after Congress passed the amendment permitting manufacturing in zones, the years after Congress passed the amendment permitting manufacturing in zones, the Foreign-Trade Zones Board issued regulations creating the concept of *subzones.* Those regulations

---

12 Yarborough, Beth V., and Robert M. *The World Economy: Trade and Finance.* Harcourt Brace, 1991, p. 368.

13 U.S. General Accounting Office. *Foreign-Trade Zone Growth Primarily Benefits Users who Import For Domestic Commerce.* GAO/GGD 84-52, March 2, 1984, p. 3, 5.

14 Historical material in this and the following two sections is taken from: U.S. General Accounting Office. *Foreign-Trade Zone Growth Primarily Benefits Users Who Import for Domestic Commerce.* GAO/GGD 84-52. March 2, 1984, and *Foreign-Trade Zones Program Needs Clarified.* GAO/NSIAD 89-85; U.S. International Trade Commission. *The Implications of Foreign-Trade Zones for U.S. Industries and for Competitive Conditions Between U.S. and Foreign Firms.* USITC Publication 1496, February, 1984, and *The Implications of Foreign-Trade Zones for U.S. Industries and for Competitive Conditions Between U.S.> and Foreign Firms.* USITC Publication 2059, February, 1988.

15 In fact, even as recently as 1970, there were still fewer than ten cities with zones. All of these were ocean or Great Lakes ports. Source: Da Ponte, John J., Jr. United States *Foreign-Trade Zones: Adapting to Time and Space.* The Maritime Lawyer, Fall, 1980, p. 202.

declared that when a zone was of insufficient size to accommodate manufacturing, an employer could apply for subzone status, and thereby have access to full zone benefits without having to relocate.

Two administrative decisions by the U.S. Treasury Department served to make zone status even more attractive for manufacturing operations. These decisions- one in 1980 (U.S. Treasury decision 80-87) and another in 1982, modifying the first decision, clarified that manufacturers need not pay duty either on *value added* or on *brokerage* or *transportation fees* connected with imported goods.[16]

1980s: The Zone System Began Expanding Rapidly

Once the second Treasury decision was handed down in 1982, the zone program began growing very rapidly and changing in nature, for a number of reasons. Among these were that the world-wide technological support system (communications, transportation, merchandise tracking, etc.) was at last ready to handle the huge demands of expanded international trade. Second, increased international price competition led U.S. businesses to seek new ways of shaving costs.

In addition, the value of the dollar was quite high in the 1980s, making cheaper imports even more attractive.[17] On top of this, the Tariff Schedule of the United States (TSUS, replaced by the Harmonized Tariff Schedule in 1989) contained a number of *inverted tariffs*. Many inverted tariffs were later reduced or eliminated by the Uruguay Round of negotiations under the General Agreement on Tariffs and Trade (GATT) in 1994.

Soon businesses figured out that, if they could achieve zone status, they could import components in industries with inverted tariff structures, assemble them together with domestic inputs in zones, and import from U.S. zones products that were less expensive to produce by the amount saved in customs costs on each item times the number of items. Word of how to take advantage of the inverted tariff structure and other cost-saving means afforded by zones (reported in table 1) spread through trade organizations. Zone use and zone employment accelerated dramatically. (see figure 1.)

---

[16] GAO Report, 1984, op. Cit., p. 12.

[17] U.S. Congress House Committee on Government Operations. *Foreign-Trade Zones (FTZ) Program Needs Restructuring.* House Report 101-363. November 16, 1989, p. 11.

Figure 1. Growth in Number of and Employment in Zones, 1978-1997

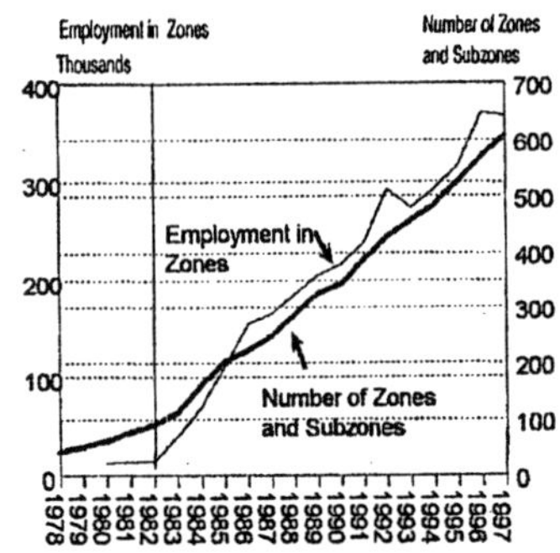

Source of data: U.S. Foreign Trade Zones Board

Congressional Oversight of Zone Growth

The House Ways and Means Committee, concerned about the potential impact that zone status was having on U.S. industries (especially domestic components industries), employment, communities, tariff and tax revenues, competitiveness abroad, and the U.S. economy in general, asked both the General Accounting Office (GAO) and the International Trade Commission (ITC) to examine the economic impact of U.S. foreign-trade zones, in 1983 and again in 1987. Primary findings of these agencies were that the zone program, while growing rapidly, was having only a small (but difficult to measure) effect on U.S. revenue collection, employment, and the economy in general, and a somewhat larger effect on the U.S. components industry, particularly in the auto sector. Not only did the auto sector have an inverted tariff, but application for zone status there was reportedly met with relatively little objection from components manufacturers.[18]

One of the most important ITC findings, however, was that the U.S. foreign-trade zones program was doing the opposite of what it was originally intended to do: The International Trade Commission found that: "While a stated intention of the 1934 Act was to increase the competitiveness of U.S. products in *foreign* markets, zone status (particularly subzone status) is being used to maintain or improve the competitive

---

[18] Quantitative findings included the following: **Effect of Zones on Tariff Revenues**: International Trade Commission (ITC) reports (referred to in footnote 13) found that the net effect of zone operations on customs revenue was small-0.04% of total customs duties collected in 1982 and 0.3% of the total customs duties collected in 1986. (ITC Report 1984, p. xi) and (ITC Report 1988, p. xix-xx).

Per-auto savings by manufacturing in zones: In addition, in 1986, autos accounted for 87% of all shipments from subzones, seven zones accounting for 76% of total zone employment. (ITC Report 1988, p. xiv) and (ITC Report 1988, p. 5-2). For auto plants, the average duty savings per car in 1986-87 was small-about $8.67, down from $9.91 in 1983 and up from $5.54 in 1985 (ITC Report 1988, p. xix).

Employment effect from zones, in the auto industry: Overall, the ITC found a 3.5% decline in employment in the auto parts sector for new vehicles, and a 1.6% increase in employment in the auto assembly industry, between 1983 and 1987. (ITC Report 1988, p. 8-7).

posture of firms in *domestic* markets (emphasis added)."[19] The U.S. Foreign-Trade Zones Board points out, however, that this statement is not entirely correct. In fact, the Act itself stated as its purpose "to expedite and encourage foreign commerce," favoring neither exports nor imports over the other.[20]

In 1989, subsequent to the GAO and ITC studies, subcommittees of the House Ways and Means Committee and the House Government Operations Committee held hearings on foreign-trade zones.[21] In addition, the House Government Operations Committee issued an independent report on the Foreign-Trade Zones Program. Its findings were compatible with those reported by GAO and ITC, but went a step further. It found that the Foreign-Trade Zones Act and program were in need of extensive revision for failing to carry out what it referred to as "the original intent of the Act." The committee report, like the GAO and ITC reports, criticized the program for promoting instead of exports, domestic competitiveness and imports for domestic consumption.

The House Government Operations Committee report also criticized the Foreign-Trade Zones Board, among other things, for poorly conceived and inefficiently administered processes, for overly general regulations, which failed to list and use a single set of criteria for granting zone or subzone status, for maintaining regulations no longer consistent with Board practice, for relying on improperly conducted economic analyses, for failing to set time limits for states in the application process, for failing to certify that operations continue to function in the public interest, and for failing to operate in a manner consistent with trade policy.[22] The Committee made a number of recommendations to address these perceived weaknesses. Ultimately, in October 1991, in consultation with congressional committees, the Board issued new regulations aimed at codifying its existing practice and meeting congressional criticisms.

In addition to congressional requests to the GAO and the ITC, hearings, and the report mentioned above, continuing periodic congressional interest in foreign-trade zones has been part of a broader focus on trade issues. Zone issues have been addressed by minor amendments to the Foreign-Trade Zones Act and been included in a number of more inclusive hearings and trade laws over the years. Some of the amendments have increased the benefits of zone imports and exports.

---

19 U.S.> International Trade Commission. *The Implications of Foreign-Trade Zones for U.S. Industries and for Competitive Conditions Between U.S. and Foreign Firms.* USITC Publication 1496, February, 1984, p. viii.

20 Notes received from Dennis Puccinelli, Executive Director of the U.S. Foreign-Trade Zones Board, July 16, 1999.

21 U.S. House. Committee on Ways and Means. Subcommittee on Trade. October 24, 1989. *Operations of the Foreign-Trade Zones Program of the United States and its Implications for the U.S. Economy and U.S. International Trade.* Serial 101-56. 442 p. and U.S. House Committee on Government Operations. Subcommittee on Commerce, Consumer, and Monetary Affairs. March 7, 1989. *Foreign-Trade Zones.* 343 p.

22 *Foreign-Trade Zones (FTZ) Program Needs Restructuring,* p. 19-24.

THE ZONE SYSTEM TODAY

Today, as during the 1980s, zones are predominantly instruments for changing inverted tariff structures into uniform rate structures. This is the case even though subzone users may save money in a variety of other ways (listed in table 1) and even though tariffs overall have declined considerably in the past 15 years, from an average rate of 5.5% in 1984 to an average rate of 2.0% in 1998.[23] Today, instead of being places where relatively large tariff savings-(i.e., 5-10% per car, for example) can be made on a few major components, zones are now more typically places where small savings (i.e., $1-3 per car, using the same industry example, according to the Foreign-Trade-Zones Board) can be made on a larger volume of components.[24] While the auto industry is still a prime beneficiary of zone status, the petroleum industry is the primary user now, accounting for 64% of the value of all goods entering zones (see figure 6), with motor vehicles accounting for another 23%. Some of the auto production operations have moved offshore, and large numbers of petroleum operations are still applying for zone status.

The importance of trade zones today is evidenced by the following statistics: Since 1970, the total number of trade zones and subzones combined has grown from 10 to 662, and employment in them has increased from 7,000 to 367,000 as was shown in figure 1. Nevertheless, zones (including subzones) represent only a small part of the U.S. economy. The total zone employment accounts for only 0.2% of total U.S. employment. In addition, all zone inputs (both domestic and foreign-a total of $178 billion in 1997) represent only a small part-2% of U.S. gross domestic product ($8,111 billion in 1997). While the world-wide zone system plays a large role in international trade, it should be noted that very few imported zone inputs in these industries enter the U.A. zone system from other zones around the world. In addition, only a small part of *all* U.S. imports (6%) enter the United States through zones in other countries.[25]

The map in figure 2 shows the states in which zone and subzone use is concentrated (darker shading). Zone and subzone use is concentrated primarily in traditionally heavy industrialized states where there is considerable auto manufacturing and in coastal states where there is considerable oil importing.

---

[23] Data for 1984 from U.S. Department of Commerce, Bureau of the Census. Highlights of U.S. Export and Import Trade, FT900/December, 1984, Table 9, p. C-31. Data for 1998 from http[://dataweb.usitc.gov.]

[24] Savings on a particular item may result from the rationalization of inverted tariffs together with other savings of the types detailed in figure 1.

[25] Zone data are taken from U.S. Department of commerce. Foreign-Trade Zones Board. *The 59th Annual Report of the Foreign-Trade Zones Board.* Employment data are taken from U.S. Department of Labor. *Employment and Earnings* (any issue), table B-1. U.S. GDP data are taken from *Economic Report of the President, 1999,* p. 342.

Figure 2. Concentrations of U.S. Foreign-Trade Zones and Subzones Among States

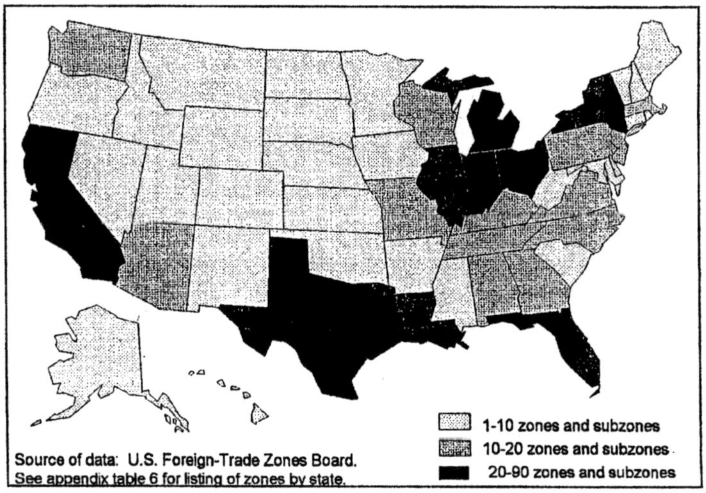

Zones Today are Functionally Import Rather Than Export Zones

Zones today are primarily import zones, rather than export zones as some observers believe Congress originally anticipated. They are *import* zones in terms of both zone *inputs* and zone *outputs*, even though both the Act itself and the Foreign-Trade Zones Board are currently neutral on this issue. In addition, the fact that most U.S. zones are functionally import zones reflects both the economic maturity (in comparison to developing countries) and the relative strength of the U.S. economy.

Figure 3. Extent to Which *Imports* Entering Zones are Subsequently Re-Exported, 1978-1997

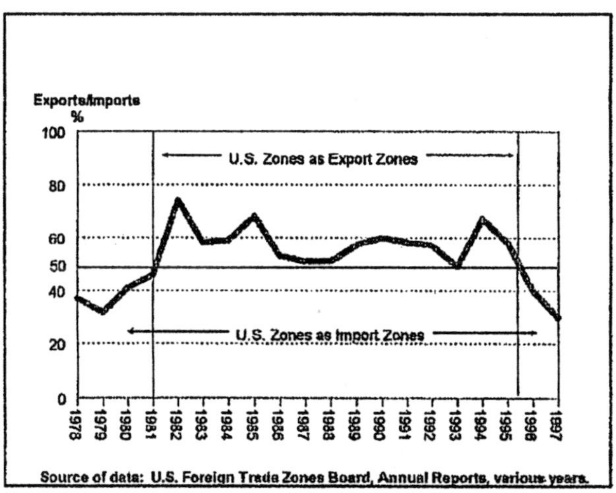

In terms of zone inputs, today's zones have lately become "import" zones in that, in recent years, more goods *entering* the zones have been subsequently imported into the United States than exported. In figure 3, export years 91981-95) are those in which the thick black line remains above the 50% line. Import years (1978-91) and 1996-97) are represented where the line dips below the 50% line. (See appendix table 6 for data supporting figures 3, 4, and 5.)

In terms of zone outputs, today's zones are import zones rather than export zones in that the majority of zone *output* is imported into the United States, and very little is exported. Figure 2 shows that since 1984, the proportion of total zone output that is exported has averaged about 10-15%.

Figures 3 and 4 both show that 1982 is the year when zones reached their pinnacle as export zones.

Figure 4. Extent to Which Total Zone *Output* is Consumed Domestically or Exported 1978-1997

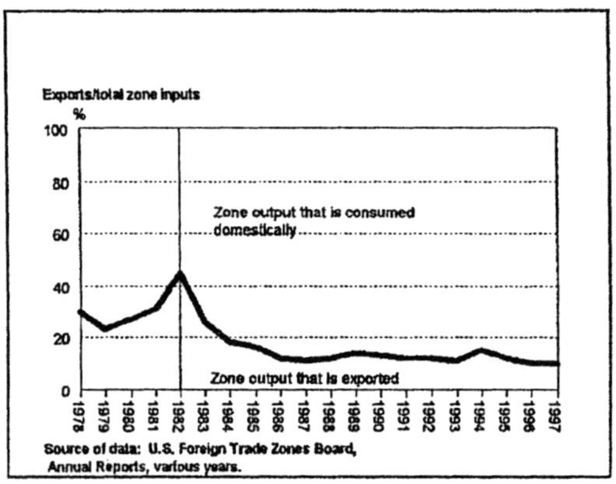

Zones Today are Primarily "Domestic-Trade" Rather Than "Foreign-Trade" Zones

Zones can also be classified today as being functionally "domestic-trade" zones rather than "foreign-trade" zones. This is because most of the *inputs* into the zones are of *domestic* origin, even though the *gains* to be made from zone status stem from *imports*. (See table 1 for a listing of the type of gains to be made from zone status.) Since 1983, zone inputs sourced domestically have accounted for more than half, and since 1985 they have accounted for about 75-80% of al zone inputs. (See figure 5). The fact that the percentage of domestically sourced zone inputs has declined somewhat in the last few years reflects a greater presence in zones of oil refining, which uses primarily imported crude, compared to auto assembly, which uses mostly domestic components.

Figure 5. Source of Zone Inputs (Domestic or Foreign) 1978-1997

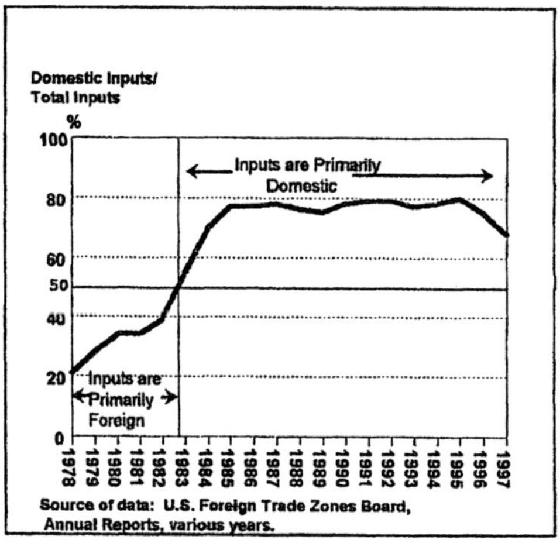

Calling zones "import" zones rather than "export" zones, and "domestic" zones rather than "foreign" zones is another way of reiterating what the ITC found in the 1980s: Instead of increasing the competitiveness of *U.S.* products in *foreign* markets, zone status is still being used (with the support of the Act) to maintain or improve the competitive posture of firms in domestic markets.

Figure 6. Industry Concentrations of Imports in Zones, 1984 and 1987

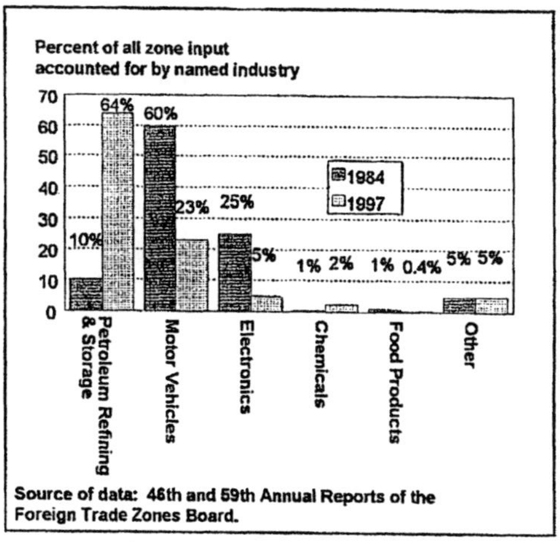

Industry Concentrations in Zones Have Changed

Industry concentrations in zones have changed since the mid-1980s, as mentioned previously. Figure 6 shows that in 1984, motor vehicle assembly plants accounted for 60% of all imports into zones, and electronics companies were the second greatest users of zones. By 1997, many electronics and auto assembly plants had relocated abroad, and petroleum refining had become the dominant zone user. Today, the two industries account for 87% of all zone inputs.

The Future of Zones

Overall, most tariffs have continued to be reduced to very low levels in the Untied States, through numerous trade agreements or establishment of free-trade areas. This would arguably point to an accompanying reduction in the use of trade zones. Inverted tariffs will lose their significance when all duties are near the same level. In addition, the nominal cost savings of duty deferral in a country with low tariff rates, like the United States, would make zone status an unnecessary administrative burden in addition to its reduced effect as a protectionist device.[26] Similarly, the gradual phasing out of quotas will also diminish demand for zone use.

However, at the same time, computers are facilitating zone use by making it easier for corporations to search through tariffs on all imported parts that potentially go into making a certain item, in order to identify those that represent an inverted tariff structure. Computers also make it easier to keep track of quota fulfillment and to calculate final tariffs owed on a large and diverse array of small imported components. Thus, smaller savings from zone use, including logistical and administrative savings, may be relatively more important than they once were.

Applications for zone or subzone status are still being approved. In 1997, the U.S. Foreign-Trade Zones Board approved 8 new general-purpose zones and 37 new subzones-consistent with the rate over the past several years-increasing the total number of zones by 3.5% and subzones by 9.5%.

Thus, even though businesses may be reaping smaller savings per imported item used in zones, they may be able in some cases to expand the number of items on which they save money. In addition, international competition has become sufficiently great in recent years that even very small savings from zone status, through duty reduction, deferred duty payment, duty exemption, tax savings, quota storage, or other means outlined in table 1 can make important contributions to U.S. competitiveness.

POLICY ISSUES RELATING TO ZONES

Many of the zone-related policy issues that were prominent ten years ago are less important today, because the circumstances that surround them have changed.[27]
In the 10 years since the GAO, ITC, and congressional studies were conducted, foreign-trade zones have become much less an issue of congressional focus than they were. This has occurred, in part because congressional interest has shifted from the employment and competitive effects of zone status to increased importation of manufactured goods and the effect this is having on U.S. jobs and the U.S. economy in the long run. Economists

---

[26] Kanellis, William G. *Reining in the Foreign-Trade Zones Board: Making Foreign-Trade Zone Decisions Reflect the Legislative Intent of the Foreign-Trade Zones Act of 1934.* Northwestern Journal of International Law and Business, Spring 1995, p. 635.

[27] The major issues of the late 1980s were documented in the GAO and ITC reports previously mentioned, and also in U.S. Library of Congress. *Foreign-Trade Zones and the U.S. Automobile Industry*, by Gwenell L. Bass, and Lenore Sek. CRS Report 88-659E, October 14, 1988

argue that with increased trade, everybody wins; however, dislocation of workers in various sectors has become an important congressional concern.

Is the Congressional Intent of the Foreign-Trade Zones Program Being Met

The answer to a question on whether the congressional intent on zones is being met depends on whether one judges congressional intent at the time of passage of U.S. Foreign-Trade Zones Act, or as it has evolved over the past 65 years.

Some of the pre-passage debate suggested hope that the zones would boost exports rather than imports. In addition, while the preamble of the act emphasized the promotion of trade without reference to either exports or imports, section 3 of the Act did strictly prohibit manufacturing was prohibited in order to discourage the importation of cheaper components which would compete with domestically produced components.

Amendments to the Act over the years, however, have reflected a gradual shift in congressional intent toward greater acceptance of zones for handling imports. The 195-amendment permitted manufacturing in zones, thus reversing the original exclusion. In addition certain other amendments, including a 1990s amendment providing for evaluation of products upon importation from a zone, make specific reference to imports (sec. 81 c, of title 19 of the U.S. Code)[28].

Therefore, one could conclude that the congressional intent as it has evolved over the years is being met. In addition, the shifting of congressional focus on the zone issue from major oversight and evaluation to minor tinkering reflects an apparent acceptance of the U.S. zone system as it stands today.

Have Foreign-Trade Zones Helped or Hurt U.S. Workers and Businesses?

The questions about whether zones have helped or hurt U.S. *workers* is seen differently in the 1990s than in the 1980s. Some employment effects from trade with Mexico and Canada since the North American Free Trade Agreement (NAFTA) went into effect and from trade with developing countries generally and under the General System of Preferences (GSP),[29] have shifted the perspective on the effects of trade zones on U.S. jobs.

By way of comparison, in the 1980s, there was some alarm that increased use of U.S. foreign-trade zones was leading to the loss of U.S. jobs . The International Trade Commission estimated that for the four-year period 1983-1987, trade zones reduced the overall employment in the auto industry by a net 1.9%. This represents a gain in the auto assembly sector and a loss in the auto parts sector.[30] Concern over the effect of *zones* on

---

[28] Any program that specifically promoted exports to the detriment of imports could violate WTO rules against export subsidies.

[29] The General System of Preferences provides duty-free treatment under specific conditions for 142 developing countries.

[30] A FTZ Board letter to the file documenting a March 3, 1988 meeting with the ITC economist who developed the economic model which was the basis for the ITC findings indicates that the

employment, however, has been eclipsed in recent years by concern over the effect of *trade agreements* [especially the North American Free Trade Agreement (NAFTA)] on employment. A difference in the order of magnitude on a particular industry is shown in the following example: In the 1990s, over a five and one-half year time period after NAFTA went into effect increased trade with Mexico and Canada led to a 5.3% job loss in the apparel sector.[31]

Thus, small benefits from avoiding the higher tariff rates in industries with inverted tariffs (differentials which are continually shrinking) may seem less important today than they did a decade ago. In addition, in the 1980s, trade zones were viewed as a way of encouraging U.S. manufacturing plants to remain in the United States rather than relocate abroad. Today, the potential cost savings from using zone status to avoid the penalties of an inverted tariff (which may be only a percent or two) seem small compared to the potential cost savings which some businesses can obtain by relocating a labor-intensive plant to Mexico or some other country with a preferential system (i. E., GSP. CBERA, or Andean), and thus saving large amounts from wage differentials.[32]

model was meant to provide estimates rather than definitive numbers on jobs gained or lost as a result of zone procedures.

31 For 1983-87 data for the motor vehicle transportation sector (SIC 37), see ITC Report, 1988, p. 8-7, and U.S. Department of Labor, Bureau of Labor Statistics. *Employment, Hour, and Earnings United States 1981-93*, bulletin 2429. For data on the apparel sector (SIC 23), see *NAFTA: Estimates of Job Effects and Industry Trade Trends After 4 _ years,* by Mary Jane Bolle. CRS Report 98-783E, p. 8, and *Employment, Hours, and Earnings Untied States 1990-95,* Bulletin 2465.

32 The Caribbean Basin Economic Recovery Act (CBERA), applying to 27 Caribbean nations, and the Andean Initiative (applicable to imports from Bolivia, Ecuador, Colombia, and Peru) are similar to the GSP in that they offer duty-free treatment under specific conditions.

Table 2. Potential Winners and Losers From Zone Use[33]

	Potential Winners	Potential Losers
Manufacturers	**Final assemblers** could win to the Extent that righting an inverted tariff lets them get components at a lower cost. **Components manufacturers** could win to the extent that they can automate, become more competitive with imports, and thereby save on production costs.	**Components manufacturers** could lose to the extent that the product becomes less competitive with imported components.
Workers	Workers in assembly operations could win to the extent that FTZ status results in greater profits which may be passed along to workers Workers in "losing" industries could win to the extent that job loss encourages them to upgrade skills, which could lead to higher paying jobs.	Either automation, or plant closings, in components industries from losing sales to importers operating in zones, could put workers out of jobs.
Community	Any zone effects, could have ripple effects on the community. Communities with new zones may benefit because zones can attract new business into the area	Communities with component manufacturing operations that close may suffer.
Consumers	To the extent that FTZs help manufacturers reduce prices and those prices are passed along to consumers, consumers could benefit.	Consumers may suffer from reduced choices or reduction in quality to the extent that foreign-trade zones encourage the substitution of cheaper imported components or goods for domestically produced ones.
Tariff Revenues	Total U.S. tariff revenues increase to the extent that increased zone use results in an increased demand for the imported components.	Tariff revenues decline by the difference between the tariff on the component and the tariff on the finished product for each item imported into a zone, times the number of items.[a]
Tax Revenues	Total U.S. tax revenues increase to the Extent that increased zone use results in an increased demand for the product and in greater earnings for each worker producing goods in zones. Increased tax revenues would come from increases in u.s. income tax collections brought about by increased profits and wages, federal excise taxes, and state and local taxes of the types affected by increased business.	

[a]An example showing the potential magnitude of such tariff revenue loss is an ITC finding that zone use reduced overall tariff revenues by 3% for 1986. Overall customs duties of $1,216 million represented an overall duty savings of nearly $39 million on the U.S. economy from foreign-trade zone use in 1986. This represents a total loss of about 3% of tariff revenues for 1986. Sources of duty savings: 1988 ITC report, op. Cit. Source of overall duties; Highlights of U.S. Export and Import Trade, op. Cit., 1986.

[33] These arguments were largely drawn from GAO and ITC reports

In addition, the question of whether zones have helped or hurt U.S. *businesses* invites a mixed response. Table 2 shows typical winners and losers form zone use. Certainly businesses that have applied for and achieved zone status have benefited. On the other hand, once one business in an industry achieves zone status, others are forced to follow suit to remain competitive. As a result, once auto assembly plants started getting zone status, virtually all others in the industry followed suit.[34] Today, this is occurring in the oil refining industry.

On the other hand, zone regulations require that U.S. zone activity have a net positive effect for U.S. businesses and workers. In addition, the 1991 regulations applicable to the Foreign-Trade Zones Board specifically require that the Board disallow any actions that would circumvent U.S. trade policy or programs developed by the administration and Congress. In keeping with this policy, the Board has disapproved applications that proposed to use the Foreign-Trade Zones program to circumvent sugar, milk, textile and apparel quota programs in an attempt to prevent situations where there are "losers" (business or workers).

Does the Zone System Set U.S. Trade Policy by Circumventing Congress and U.S. Trade Negotiators?

It can be argued that the U.S. zone system sets trade policy by circumventing Congress and U.S. trade negotiators. The decision to lower tariffs is thus shifted from the traditional method involving Congress and U.S. negotiators to an alternative method involving the U.S. Foreign-Trade Zones Board and its approval of the use of zones by representatives of various industries. However, as mentioned, the gradual decline of tariffs from an average rate of 5.5% to 2.0% between 1984 and 1998 has somewhat diminished the influence of the Foreign-Trade Zones Board on U.S. effective tariff rates.

In addition, the Foreign-Trade Zones Board is adamant that if it perceives that zone status in an industry (usually the assembly sector) will harm the components sector, it will deny or limit zone status. Industries where zone status has been denied or limited for this reason include textiles, steel, pigments, TV tubes, ink, ethanol, chain saws, lawn mowers and agricultural products (e. g. dairy and sugar, and orange juice.)[35]

In the last ten years, legislative issues relating to zones have shifted from the macro to the micro level. Instead of being focused on how zones affect the U.S. economy, they are now more focused on whether zone policy should be used to help specific industries.

Nor does foreign-trade zone legislation in the 105th and 106th Congresses attempt to reverse the evolutionary changes which have affected the U.S. foreign-trade zones. The current legislative proposals are much more narrowly focused on changing trade policy for various industries and promoting economic development. Bills relating to the foreign-trade zone system fall into four categories: technical corrections relating to zones; bills to help achieve trade objectives through zones (i. E. legislation relating to steel, peanut butter, or tobacco products); legislation to assist zone expansion or promote

---

[34] Bass and Sek, op. Cit., p.11.

[35] From a telephone conversation with Dennis Puccinelli, Executive Director of the U.S. Foreign-Trade Zones Board on may 21, 1999.

economic development; and legislation to support specific programs (i. E., space exploration). (See table 3 on major zone legislation).

P.L. 105-303, enacted in the 105th Congress, included a foreign-trade zone provision to further encourage the development of the commercial space industry. It clarifies that payloads launched from trade zones shall be considered exports (not imports) with regards to customs entry.

Technical Corrections Relating to Zones

In the 106th Congress, Sec. 2405 of P.L. 36, signed by the President on June 25, 1999 (S. Report 106-2) makes technical corrections to various trade laws. It provides, among other things, that the Secretary of the Treasury shall include commercial importation data for foreign-trade zones in the new program automating customs procedures (the National Customs Automation Program)-which is currently undergoing both construction and funding difficulties.

Legislation to Achieve Trade Objectives For Specific Industries

A number of bills relating to U.S. foreign-trade zones in the 106th Congress, would accomplish trade objectives by affecting the way certain imports are treated. H.R. 975, passed by the House on March 17, 1999, (H. Report 106-52) provides for a reduction in steel imports. It requires a steel notification certificate before steel is entered into the U.S. customs territory of the United States.

Other legislation in the 105th Congress would have related to the tobacco industry by providing for an increase in taxes on tobacco products which enter the United States through a foreign-trade zone (H.R. 1229), and prohibiting the manufacturing of tobacco products in or forwarding them through foreign-trade zones, or selling them in or to duty-free shops (H. R. 3738).

Also in the 105th Congress H.R. 1875 would have allowed the entry of peanut butter and paste from Mexican peanuts through foreign-trade zones without being subject to the tariff rate quota.

Legislation to Assist Zone Expansion or Promote Economic Development

Other bills would aim to promote economic development by directing the U.S. Foreign-Trade Zones Board to grant approval for new or expanded zones. In the 106th Congress, H.R. 465 would direct the Board on behalf of the municipal airport of Chico, California. H.R. 5401 would make this direction for zones on Indian territory.

Table 3. Some Major Zone Legislation of the 106th and 105th Congresses

106th Congress

P.L. 106-36: H. R. 435/S. 262 (S. Report 106-2) made technical changes to various trade laws. It also included a provision (Sec. 2405) which stated that not later than Jan. 1, 2000, the Secretary of the Treasury shall provide for the inclusion of commercial importation data for foreign-trade zones under the national Customs Automation Program. On June 7, 1999, the House agreed to Senate amendment, roll call #168.

Passed the House March 17, 1999: H.R. 975 (Visclosky). H. R. Report 106-52 provides for a reduction in the volume of steel imports. For steel brought into the United States through a foreign-trade zone, requires a steel notification certificate before the merchandise is entered into the customs territory of the United States.

Other Bills:
H.R. 465 (Herger) directs the Foreign-Trade Zones Board to expand Foreign-Trade Zone No. 143 to include an area of the municipal airport of Chico, California.
S. 401 (Campbell, Nighthorse), Sec. 205 provides for business development and trade promotion for Native Americans. Directs the U.S. Foreign-Trade Zones Board to consider on a priority basis and expedite processing of any application aiming to establish a foreign-trade zone on Indian territory, including any designated an empowerment zone or enterprise community.

105th Congress

Enacted H. R. 1702 (Sensenbrenner, P.L. 105-303, Oct 28, 1998: To encourage the development of a commercial space industry in the United States, and for other purposes. Sec. 102: Clarifies that a launch vehicle is not, because of launch or reentry, an export or import. However, payloads launched pursuant to foreign-trade zone procedures shall be considered exports with regard to customs entry. This means that if any part of the launch vehicle or its payload is imported (for example part of the fuel), no tariffs are payable.

Other Bills:
H.R. 1875 (Crane) would amend the U.S. Harmonized Tariff Schedule to allow entry of peanut butter and paste from Mexican peanuts in foreign-trade zones with out being subject to the tariff rate quota.
H.R. 1319 (Royce), Sec. 204 would abolish the Department of Commerce and transfer the U.S. Foreign-Trade Zones Board to the Department of Treasury. The U.S. Trade Representative would replace the Secretary of Commerce on the Foreign-Trade Zones Board.
H.R. 1229 (Ackerman), Sec. 301 provides for an increase in taxes on tobacco products, cigarette papers, or cigarette tubes entered into a customs territory from a foreign-trade zone.

H.R. 3738 (Doggett), Sec. 407: prohibits against the sale of tobacco products in or to duty-free shops or forwarding through or manufacturing in foreign-trade zones.
S. 1415 (McCain): Section 1147 is similar to the provision in H.R. 3738.

APPENDIX

The appendix includes information on how to apply for zone status, data supporting figures 3, 4, and 5, and lists, zones and subzones, by state.

Appendix Table 4. Information Pertaining to Zone or Subzone Application

How to Apply for Zone or Subzone Status

- Apply to the U.S. Foreign-Trade Zones Board, Import Administration, U.S. Department of Commerce, Washington, D. C. 20230 (202) 482-2862.
- Basic requirements for foreign – trade zone applications are found in 15 CFR Part 400, available at the U.S. Foreign-Trade Zones Board website: http://ita. Doc.gov/import_admn/records/ftzpage/ftzhome.html.
- Applications are rather involved, and the approval process is somewhat lengthy. General Purpose Zone applications take about 18 and Subzone applications take about 12 months.
- After application approval is granted by the Foreign-Trade Zones Board, before operations can take place, approval to activate the zone must be obtained from the Customs Port Director.

Zone Status

- Zone status is typically granted to state or local agencies or public type corporations (I. E., port authorities or economic development agencies), which may contract out operations.
- Zone sites must be in or near U.S. Customs ports of entry (listed at 19 CFR Part 101).
- Zones are operated under the day-to-day supervision of the U.S. Customs Service. Overhead costs include reimbursement to Customs for services. See regulations at 19 CFR Part 146.
- Operations are conducted as public utilities, with published rates.
- Zone projects should be coordinated at the state level for consistency with economic development plans.
- Applicants must have a suitable plan including provisions for facilities and financing
- Need for the proposed zone must be shown in terms of the local economy and overall economic development objectives.
- Zone manufacturing is reviewed under "public interest" criteria for consistency with trade policy and net positive economic effects.
- Zones should help create, not just divert employment from region to another.

- There must be convincing evidence of a need for zone services. Letters of intent from firms expecting to be the first zone users should be included in the application.

Subzone Status:

- Subzones are normally private plant sites that usually cannot be accommodated within an existing general-purpose zone.
- Subzones can be approved only when a "public benefit" resulting in a "positive economic effect" is demonstrated.
- Subzone applications include company background, product description, industry background, zone benefits to the company and public, impact on the domestic industry and environment.

Sources of the above information: websites of the U.S. Foreign-Trade Zones Board (listed above), the U.S. Customs Service: http://www.customs.ustreas.gov/imp-exp2/comm-imp/ftstart.htm, and the National Association of Foreign-Trade Zones: http://www.imex.com/naftz.html.

Appendix Table 5. Data Supporting Figures 3, 4, and 5 (In $billions, and percent)

	Mdse Received in Zone ($billions)	Domestic Inputs ($billions)	Foreign Inputs ($billions)	Exports ($billions)	Data for Figure 4 Exports as % of Mdse. Received in Zones (%)	Data for Figure 3 Exports From Zones/ Imports Into Zones (%)	Data for Figure 5 Domestic Inputs/Total Inputs (%)
1978	0.81	0.17	0.63	0.24	30	38	21
1979	1.52	0.43	1.09	0.35	23	32	28
1980	2.60	0.89	1.71	0.69	27	40	34
1981	3.02	1.03	1.99	0.93	31	47	34
1982	3.40	1.32	2.08	1.54	45	74	39
1983	6.51	3.61	2.90	1.67	26	58	55
1984	15.00	10.50	4.50	2.65	18	59	70
1985	24.75	19.01	5.74	3.89	16	68	77
1986	40.19	31.07	9.12	4.87	12	53	77
1987	48.95	38.42	10.52	5.40	11	51	78
1988	58.65	44.56	14.10	7.22	12	51	76
1989	76.27	57.51	18.76	10.75	14	57	75
1990	90.06	70.64	19.42	11.59	13	60	78
1991	84.44	66.42	18.02	10.48	12	58	79
1992	98.69	78.39	20.30	11.65	12	57	79
1993	103.97	80.16	23.81	11.65	11	49	77
1994	119.57	93.61	25.96	17.37	15	67	78
1995	143.51	114.37	29.14	16.94	12	58	80
1996	168.62	125.68	42.94	17.09	10	40	75
1997	177.85	121.16	56.69	16.93	10	30	68

Source of data: U.S. Foreign-Trade Zones Board.

Appendix Table 6. List of Zones and Subzones, by State

STATE	ZONE#	SUBZONE #	LOCATION	BUSINESS	INDUSTRY	YEAR APPROVED	STATUS: (Active unless otherwise indicated)
ALABAMA							
	82		Mobile				
	83		Huntsville				
	98		Birmingham				
	211		Anniston				
	222		Montgomery				
	233		Dothan				
		116	Mobile	ADDSCO	shipbuilding	88	
		137	Huntsville	Chrysler	auto electronics	88	
		159	Mobile	Degussa	methhionine	89	
		293	Foley	Peavey	electronics	95	
		329	Tuscaloosa	Mercedes-Benz	motor vehicles	96	
		334	Dothan	Sony	magnetic & battery	96	
		336	Madison	MagneTec	lighting ballasts	96	
		351	Mobile .	Zeneca	ag. chemicals	96	
		368	Tuscaloosa.	ZFIndustries	auto axles	97	
		382	Mobile Cnty.	Coastal Refining	oil refining	97	
		392	Tuscaloosa	JVC America	videotape prds.	97	
ALASKA							
	108		Valdez				
	159		St. Paul				
	160		Anchorage				
	195		Fairbanks				
	232		Kodiak				
		256	Fairbanks	Flowline	pipeline insulation	93	
ARIZONA							
	48		Pima County				
	60		Nogales				
	75		Phoenix				
	139		Sierra Vista				
	174		Pima County				
	219		Yuma				
	221		Mesa				
		197	Glendale	Conair	small appliance	91	
		250	Buckeye	Wal-Mart	distribution	93	
		269	Chandler	Intel	semiconductors	94	
		323	Phoenix	SGS-Thompson	semiconductors	96	
		353	Casa Grande	Abbott Mfg.	infant formula	96	
		354	Phoenix	PETsMART	warehouse/distributio	96	
		375	Phoenix	Sumitomo Sitix	semionductor wafers	97	
		420	Chandler/Tem	Microchip	semiconductors	98	
		427	Yuma County	Meadowcraft	patio furniture	98	
ARKANSAS							
	14		Little Rock				
		16	Forrest City	Sanyo	microwave ovens	82	
		350	West Helena	Cedar Chemical	ag. chemicals	96	
		376	El Dorado	Mid States Pipe	steel pipe fab.	97	
CALIFORNIA							
	3		San Francisco				
	18		San Jose				
	50		Long Beach				
	56		Oakland				
	143		W. Sacramen.				
	153		San Diego				
	191		Palmdale				
	202		Los Angeles				
	205		Port Hueneme				
	226		Merced				
	230		Stockton				
		1	San Francisco	Lilli Ann	aparel	63	
		25	Long Beach	Toyota	truck beds	83	

STATE	ZONE#	SUBZONE #	LOCATION	BUSINESS	INDUSTRY	YEAR APPROVED	STATUS: (Active unless otherwise indicated)
		30	San Jose	Olympus	med. equip.	83	
		54	San Diego	National Steel &	shipyard	84	
		66	Fremont	NUMMI	auto	84	
		147	Benecia	Mazda	auto	89	
		178	Perris	National RV	motor home/RV	90	
		233	Pasadena	Datatape	tape recording equip	92	
		276	Garden Grove	Alps Mfg.	computer etc. parts	94	
		332	Auburn	C. Ceronix	video monitors	98	
		380	Los Angeles	MMM	pharmaceuticals	97	
		385	Sacramento	Hewlett-Packard	computer-related	97	
		398	Dixon	Gymboree	apparel/toys	98	
		400	El Segundo	Checron	oil refining98	98	
		408	Richmond	Chevron	oil refining	98	
		412	Fremont	Cirrus Logic	integrated circuit	98	
		419	San Jose	Hewlett-Packard	computer etc. parts	98	
COLORADO							
	112		El Paso				
	123		Denver				
		226	Fountain	Apple	data proc. equip	92	
		234	Boulder	Storage	electronic storage	92	
		415	Broomfield	Artesym	elec. power supplies	98	
CONNECTICUT							
	71		Windsor Lake				
	75		Bridgeport				
	162		North Haven				
	208		New London				
		174	West Haven	Miles	pharmaceuticals	90	
DELAWARE							
	99		Wilimington				
		41	Wilmington	J. Schoeneman	apparel	84	
		42	Newark	Chrysler	auto	84	
		47	Wilmington	Ge. Motorsauto	–	84	
		286	Newark	Zeneca	pharmaceuticals	94	
		340	Newastle	Star Enterprise	oil refinery	96	
FLORIDA							
	25		Broward				
	32		Miami				
	43		Orlando				
	64		Jacksonville				
	65		Panama City				
	79		Tampa				
	135		Palm Beach				
	136		Brevard				
	166		Homestead				
	169		Manatee				
	180		Miami				
	193		Pinellas				
	198		Volusia & Flagler Counties				
	209		Palm Beach County				
	213		Fort Myers				
	215		Sebring				
	217		Oscala				
	218		St. Lucie County				
		204	Cocoa	Flite Technology	machinery	91	
		231	Melbourne	American Digital	telecom./computer	92	
		277	Tampa	Reilly Dairy	dairy prds.	94	
		281	Tampa	Group	electronics	94	
		355	Ft. Lauderdale	Federal-Mogul	vehicle parts dist.	97	
		407	Miani	Hewlett-Packard	computer etc.	98	
		411	Broward Cty.	CITGO	petrol. storage	98	
		426	BrevardCount	Harris Corp	telecommunications	98	
GEORGIA							
	26		Atlanta				

STATE	ZONE#	SUBZONE #	LOCATION	BUSINESS	INDUSTRY	YEAR APPROVED	STATUS: (Active unless otherwise indicated)
	104		Savannah				
	144		Brunswick				
		24	Atlanta	GM	auto	83	
		46	La Grange	Goetze Gasket	auto gaskets	84	Lapsed
		70	Hapeville	Ford	auto	85	
		149	Coweta	Yamaha	golf carts/water	98	
		296	Dougherty	Merck	pharmaceuticals	95	
		299	Bulloch	Wal-Mart	distribution	95	
		330	Chatham	CITGO	oil refining	96	
		346	Columbus	Pratt& Whitney	United Technologies	96	
		347	Columbus	Precision	aircraft engine	96	
HAWAII							
	9		Honolulu				
		2	Oahu	Tesoro Hawaii	refinery	70	
		57	Honolulu	Kerr Pacific Corp	–	95	
		95	Kahului	Maui pineapple	food	86	
		72	Honolulu	Dole	food	85	
		138	Oahu	Chevron	oil refining	88	
		364	Oahu	Gasco	oil refining	97	
IDAHO							
	192		Meridian				
ILLINOIS							
	22		Chicago				
	31		Granite City				
	114		Peoria				
	133		Milan				
	146		Lawrenceville				
	176		Rockford				
		22	Chicago	UNR-Leavitt	steel pipe fab.83	83	Lapsed
		60	Peoria	Caterpillar Tractor	tractor	85	
		89	Chicago	Ford	auto	86	
		98	Du Page	Power Packaging	packaging	87	expired 91
		99	Du Page	Power Packaging	packaging	87	expired 91
		100	Kane	Power Packaging	packaging	87	expired 91
		104	Belvidere	Chrysler	auto	87	transferred 93
		112	Flora	N. Am. Lighting	auto components	88	
		113	Salem	N. Am. Lighting	auto components	88	
		114	Peoria	Mitsubishi Motor	auto	88	
		154	Galesburg	Maytag	appliances	89	lapsed
		155	Herrin	Maytag	appliances	89	
		220	Effingham	Fedders	room air conditioners	92	
		222	Dundee	Milk Specialities	animal feed	92	
		224	Loves Park	Clinton	cathode ray tubes	92	
		243	N. Chicago	Abbott	pharmaceuticals	92	
		275	Des Plaines	Sanofi Winthrop	pharmaceuticals	94	
		306	Manhattan	Amoco	crude storage	96	
		312	Will County	UNO-VEN	oil refining	95	
		314	Robinson	Marathon Ashland	oil refining	95	
		361	Madison	Shell	oil refining97386	97	
		386	Marengo	Nissan	engines	97	
		401	Will County	Mobil Oil	oil refining	98	
		403	obile County	Shell	oil refining989	89	
		405	Kankakee	Henkel	vitamin E	98	
INDIANA							
	22		Indianapolis				
	31		South Bend				
	114		Burns Harbor				
	133		Clark County				
	146		Evansville				
	176		Fort Wayne				
		60	Kokomo	GM	auto electronics	84	
		73	Indianapolis	Eli Lilly	pharmaceuticals	85	
		74	Lafayette	Eli Lilly	pharmaceuticals	85	
		75	Clinton	Eli Lilly	pharmaceuticals	85	

STATE	ZONE#	SUBZONE #	LOCATION	BUSINESS	INDUSTRY	YEAR APPROVED	STATUS: (Active unless otherwise indicated)
		90	Indianapolis	Chrysler	auto components86	86	lapsed
		91	Kokomo	Chrysler	auto components	86	
		92	New Castle	Chrysler	auto components86	86	
		127	Lafayette	Caterpillar	tractor engines	88	
		148	Lafayette	Subaru-Isuzu	auto	89	
		179	Indianapolis	Alpine	audio equip.	90	
		180	South Bend	EWI	auto parts	90	
		239	Midlebury	Coachmen	vehicles	92	
		244	Greenwood	Endress& Hauser	instruments	92	
		246	Evansville	Mead Johnson	pharmaceuticals	92	
		249	Elkhart	Fairmont Homes	manufactured	93	
		252	Bartholomew	POnkyo America	accoustical prods.	93	
		305	Whiting	Amoco	oil refining	95	
		333	Indianapolis	Thompson	electronics	96	
		379	Rushville	Fugitsu	auto audio	97	
IOWA							
	107		Polk County				
	133		Davenport				
	175		Cedar Rapids				
		55	Forest City	Winnebago	auto	84	
		156	Newton	Maytag	appliances	89	lapsed
KANSAS							
	17		Kansas City				
	161		Sedgwick				
		84	Kansas		auto	85	
		274	McPherson	Abbott Labs	pharmaceuticals	94	
		356	Butler County	Equilon	oil refining	97	
KENTUCKY							
	29		Jefferson County				
	47		Campbell				
		37	Georgetown	Clark	lift trucks	84	lapsed
		43	Louisville	Ford	auto	84	
		86	Jefferson	GE	home appliances	85	
		87	Jefferson	Lexmark	typewriters & printers	86	
		111	Scott County	Toyota	auto	87	
		177	Walton	Clarion	auto audio	90	
		182	Harrodsburg	Hitachi	auto parts	90	
		359	Boyd	Marathan	oil refining	97	
		365	Campton	Ascent	elec./electronic	97	
LOUISIANA							
	2		New Orleans				
	87		Calcasieu Parish				
	124		St. Charles				
	145		Shreveport				
	154		Baton Rouge				
		120	Gramercy	Trans-American	oil refining 88	88	
		134	Lake Charles	Conoco	oil refining 88	88	
		150	Lake Charles	Citgo	oil refining	89	
		193	Avondale	Avondale	shipbuilding	91	
		194	Westwego	Avondale	shipbuilding	91	
		195	Harvey	Avondale	shipbuilding	91	
		196	New Orleans	Avondale	shipbuilding	91	
		210	Lafourche	N.Am.Shipbuildin	shipbuilding	91	
		212	Shreveport	AT&T	telecommunications	91	
		223	New Orleans	Equitable	shipbuilding	93	
		261	Convent	Star Enterprise	oil refining	94	
		297	Lafourche	LOOP	crude oil	95	
		310	Garyville	Marathon	oil refining	95	
		318	St. Bernard	Chalmette	oil refining	95	
		337	Plaquemines	BP	oil refining	96	
		343	St. Charles	Shell Oil	oil refining	96	
		348	Baton Rouge	Exxon	oil refining	96	
		373	St. Bernard	Murphy Oil	oil refining	97	
		404	Lockport	Halter Marine	shipbuilding	98	

STATE	ZONE#	SUBZONE #	LOCATION	BUSINESS	INDUSTRY	YEAR APPROVED	STATUS: (Active unless otherwise indicated)
		418	Lockport	Bollinger	shipbuilding	98	
MAINE							
	58		Bangor				
	179		Madawaska				
	186		Waterville				
		202	Madawaska	Northern Trading	cosmetics	91	
MARYLAND							
	63		Prince Geoge's County				
	73		BWI Airport				
	74		Baltimore				
		61	Sparrow's	Bethlehem	steel	85	
		307	Walkersville	Rotorex	rotary compressors	95	
MASSACHUSETTS							
	27		Boston				
	28		New Bedford				
	201		Holyoke				
		7	Fall River	Sterlingwale	apparel	80	terminated 89
		31	Quincy	General Dynamics	shipyard	89	
		32	Lawrenceville	Lawrence Textiles	textiles	84	
		105	Framingham	GM	auto	87	
		117	New Bedford	Codman &Shur.	surgical instrumenrs	88	
		118	Avondale	Codman & Shur.	surgical instrumenrs	88	
		119	Randolph	Codman & Shur.	surgical instrumenrs	88	
		183	Norwood	Polaroid	camera	91	
		184	Needham	Polaroid	camera	91	
		185	New Bedford	Polaroid	camera	91	
		186	Waltham	Polaroid	camera	91	
		187	Freetown	Polaroid	camera	91	
		188	Boston	Polaroid	camera	91	
		189	Cambridge	Polaroid	camera	91	lapsed
		410	Quincy	Mass. Heavy Inds.	shipbuilding	98	
MICHIGAN							
	16		Sault Ste. Marie				
	43		Battle Creek				
	70		Detroit				
	140		Flint				
	189		Kent/Ottawa/Muskegon				
	210		St. Clair				
		10	Romeo	Ford	tractor	81	
		13	Detroit	Chrysler	auto	82	
		19	Wayne	Ford	auto	83	
		28	Wixom	Ford	auto	83	
		29	Dearborn	Ford	auto	83	
		36	Springfield	Clark	lift trucks	84	terminated 91
		48	Ypsilanti	GM	auto	84	
		49	Pontiac	GM	auto	84	
		67	Sterling	Chrysler	auto	85	
		94	Flat Rock	Mazda	auto	86	
		101	Flint	GM	auto	87	
		103	Trenton	Chrysler	auto	87	
		123	Midland	Dow	chemical	88	lapsed
		129	Detroit	GM	auto	88	
		130	Orion	GM	auto	88	
		131	Lansing	GM	auto	88	
		161	Detroit	Chrysler	auto	89	
		162	Trenton	Chrysler	auto	89	terminated 92
		163	Detroit	Chrysler	auto	89	
		164	Detroit	Chrysler	auto	89	
		165	Detroit	Chrysler	auto	89	
		216	Zeeland	Mead Johnson	--	92	
		303	Wyandotte	BASF	vitamins/plastics	95	
		362	Detroit	Marathon	oil refining	97	
		377	Sturgis	Abbott	infant formula	97	
		390	Kentwood	Diesel Technology	fuel injection	97	

STATE	ZONE#	SUBZONE #	LOCATION	BUSINESS	INDUSTRY	YEAR APPROVED	STATUS: (Active unless otherwise indicated)
MINNESOTA							
	51		Duluth				
	119		Minneapolis/St. Paul				
		248	St. Peter	Davisco	dairy prds.	93	
		251	Apple Valley	Wirsbo	polyethylene tubing	93	
		255	Howard Lake	Am. Feeds &	animal feeds	93	
		264	Preston	Wisconsin Dairies	infant formula	94	
		345	Lindstrom	Plastic Products	in-line skates	96	
		414	Redwood Falls	Artesyn	elec. power supplies	98	
MISSISSIPPI							
	92		Harrison				
	158		Vicksburg/Jackson				
		115	Escatawpa	Moss Pt. Marine	shipbuilding	88	
		190	Pascagoula	Ingalis	shipbuilding	91	
		237	Harrison	Avondale Ent.	shipbuilding	92	
		271	Corinth	Cortelo USA	phone & computer	94	
		279	Meridian	Peavey Elec.	audio/acoustical	94	
		300	Pascagoula	Chevron	oil refining	95	
MISSOURI							
	15		Kansas City				
	102		St. Louis				
	225		Springfield				
		20	St.Louis	Chrysler	auto	83	
		23	Claycomo	Ford	auto	83	
		48	Hazelwood	Ford	auto	84	
		64	Kansas	--	auto	93	
		132	Wentzville	GM	auto	88	
		151	Kirksville	Ortech	auto components	89	
		152	Kansas City	Bayer	ag. chemicals	89	
		160	Kansas City	Kawasaki	engine parts	89	
		181	Grandview	Metcals	sink processing	90	lapsed
		278	Jefferson City	Florsheim	shoes	94	
MONTANA							
	88		Great Falls				
	187		Toole County				
	190		Butte-Silver Bow				
NEBRASKA							
	19		Omaha				
	59		Lincoln				
		8	Lincoln	Kawasaki	motorcycles & robots	80	
NEVADA							
	89		Clark County				
	126		Sparks				
		52	Reno	Porsche	auto	84	
NEW HAMPSHIRE							
	81		Portsmouth				
		18	Portsmouth	Nashua	office equip	83	
		33	Colebrook	Manchester Mfg.	apparel	84	
		232	Newington	ABB Combustion	industrial/nuclear	92	
NEW JERSEY							
	44		Morris County				
	49		Newark/Elizabeth				
	142		Salem/Millville				
	200		Mercer				
	235		Lakewood				
		36	Edison	Ford	auto	84	
		85	Linden	GM	auto	85	
		107	Hazlet	Int'l Flavors	--	87	lapsed
		108	Union Beach	Int'l Flavors	--	87	lapsed
		109	S. Brunswick	Int'l Flavors	--	87	lapsed

STATE	ZONE#	SUBZONE #	LOCATION	BUSINESS	INDUSTRY	YEAR APPROVED	STATUS: (Active unless otherwise indicated)
		153	N. Brunswick	Squibb	pharmaceuticals	89	
		298	Rahway	Merck	pharmaceuticals	95	
		319	Linden	Bayway	oil refining	95	
		321	Gloucester	Mobil Oil	oil refining	95	
		331	Gloucester	CITGO	oil refining	96	
		363	Perth Amboy	Chevron	oil refining	97	
		372	Gloucester	Coastal Eagle Pt.	Oil refining	97	
		383	East Windsor	Conair	warehouse/distributio	97	
		416	Bridgewater	Hewlett-Packard	computer-related	98	
NEW MEXICO							
	110		Albuquerque				
	194		Rio Rancho				
	197		Dona Ana				
		58	Albuquerque	SP	pharmaceuticals	84	
NEW YORK							
	1		NY City				
	23		Buffalo				
	34		Niagara				
	37		Orange				
	52		Suffolk				
	54		Clinton				
	90		Onondaga				
	109		Jefferson County				
	111		JFK Intl. Airport				
	118		Ogdensburg				
	121		Albany				
	141		Monroe				
	172		Oneida				
		26	Webster	Xerox	office equip	90	
		59	Waltertown	NYAirbrake	–	84	lapsed
		63	Cortland Cnty.	Smith-Carona	electronics	85	
		66	N. Tarrytown	GM	auto	85	
		93	NY City	Jack Young	–	86	lapsed
		96	Chatauqua	CPS Corp.	–	86	expired 96
		106	Onodaga	Chrysler	auto transmissions	87	lapsed
		133	Rochester	Eastman Kodak	photography	88	
		213	Rochester	ITT	auto electronics	91	lapsed
		258	New Rochelle	Bally	shoes	93	
		273	Rensselaer	Sanophi Winthrop	pharmaceuticals	94	
		292	Rochester	Gleason Corp.	gear production	95	
		302	Sherrill &	Oneida	tableware	95	
		322	Rensselaer	BASF	chem. pigments/dyes	95	
NORTH CAROLINA							
	57		Mecklenburg County				
	66		Wilmington				
	67		Morehead City				
	93		Raleigh				
	214		Lenoir County				
	230		Fuilford, Forsuth,, etc.				
		88	Mecklenburg	IBM	electronics	86	
		173	Alamance	Honda	lawnmowers	90	
		219	Kernersville	Deere-Hitachi	hydraulic excavators	92	
		227	Raleigh/Durha	IBM	info processing equip	92	
		230	Wake County	Mallinckrodt	pharmaceuticals	92	
		283	Wilson	Merck	pharmaceuticals	94	
		328	Goldsboro	R.G. Barry	footwear & thermal	96	
		336	Whitsett	Lucent	telecommunications	96	
		378	Yadkinville	Unifi	polyester yarn	97	
NORTH DAKOTA							
	103		Grand Forks				
OHIO							

STATE	ZONE#	SUBZONE #	LOCATION	BUSINESS	INDUSTRY	YEAR APPROVED	STATUS: (Active unless otherwise indicated)
	8		Toledo				
	40		Cleveland				
	46		Butler County				
	100		Dayton				
	101		Clinton				
	138		Franklin				
	151		Findlay				
	181		Akron/Canton				
		5	Hamilton Cty.	GE	jet engines	79	
		6	Union City	Honda	motorcycles	79	
		34	Toledo	Jeep	auto	84	
		44	Lorain	Ford	auto	84	
		65	Lordstown	GM	auto	85	
		102	Norwood	GM	auto	87	
		110	Shelby	Honda	car/motorcycle	87	
		121	Findlay	Cooper Tire &	tires	88	
		128	Cincinnati	Nine West	shoes	88	
		157	Dayton	GM	electric motors	89	
		158	Kettering	GM	auto parts	89	
		166	Dayton	Chrysler	auto parts	89	
		167	Perrysburg	Chrysler	auto parts	89	
		168	Sandusky	Chrysler	auto parts	89	
		169	Van Wert	Chrysler	auto parts	89	
		170	Toledo	Giant Products	industrial pumps	90	
		203	Richwood	Wascator Mfg.	washing machines	91	
		236	Ottawa	W.C. Wood	freezers	92	
		254	Avon Lake	Ford	motor vehicles	93	
		257	Euclid/Mentor	Lincoln Electric	arc welding equip.	93	
		259	McComb	Consolidated	food	93	
		268	Bedford	Mr. Coffee	small appliance	94	
		280	Valley View	Picker	medical disgnostics	94	
		325	Grove City	Pier 1	distribution	96	
		326	Bedford	Ben Venue	pharmaceuticals	96	
		338	Toledo	BP Oil	oil refining	96	
		344	Euclid	Motch	machinery	96	
		358	Stark/Allen	Marathon	oil refining	97	
		366	Springboro	pioneer	auto audio	97	
		387	Columbus	Abbott	infant formula	97	
		417	Beverly	Globe	ferroalloys	98	
		424	Columbus	Lucent	telecommunications	98	
		425	Lima	Clark USA	oil refining	98	
OKLAHOMA							
	53		Rogers				
	106		Oklahome City				
	164		Muskogee				
	227		Durant				
		51	Oklahome City	GM	auto	84	
		240	Oklahome City	Ted Davis Mfg.	voice aoil motors	92	
		394	Lincoln	ARCO Pipe Line	crude oil	98	
OREGON							
	45		Portland				
	132		Coos County				
	184		Klamath Falls				
	206		Medford-Jackson County				
		9	Multnomah	Beall Pipe		80	deactivated 83
		171	Portland	AIM		90	lapsed
		207	Portland	Alcatel Submarine	fiberoptic cable	91	
		221	Pendleton	Continental Mills	food	92	
		247	Tualatin	Tofle USA	stainless steal tubing	92	
PENNSYLVANIA							
	24		Pittston				
	33		Allegheny County				
	35		Philadelphia				
	147		Berks County				
		3	Westmoreland	VW	auto	77	

STATE	ZONE#	SUBZONE #	LOCATION	BUSINESS	INDUSTRY	YEAR APPROVED	STATUS: (Active unless otherwise indicated)
		4	Harrisburg	Olivetti	typewriters, printers	78	deactivated 81
		21	Landsdale	Ford	auto	83	
		142	Allegheny	Verosol USA	window shade fabric	89	
		282	West Point	Merck	pharmaceuticals	94	
		285	Riverside	Merck	pharmaceuticals	94	
		342	Philadelphia	Sun Company	oil refining	96	
		369	Delaware	Tosco	oil refining	97	
PUERTO RICO							
	7		Mayaguez				
	61		Guyanabo				
	163		Ponce				
		15	Penuelas	CORCO	oil refining	82	
		217	Humacao	Bristol-Myers	pharmaceuticals	92	
		218	Barceloneta	Bristol-Myers	pharmaceuticals	82	
		245	Caguas	Searle	pharmaceuticals	92	
		266	Barceloneta	Searle	pharmaceuticals	94	
		267	Cidra	SB Pharmco	pharmaceuticals	94	
		294	Arecibo	Merck	pharmaceuticals	95	
		295	Barceloneta	Merck	pharmaceuticals	95	
		316	Guayama	IPR	pharmaceuticals	95	
		317	Carolina	IPR	pharmaceuticals	95	
		360	San Juan	Baxter Caribe	pharmaceuticals	97	
		371	Skagit Cnty.	PR Sun oil	oil refining	97	
		384	Cidra	PepsiCo	concentrate	97	
		423	San Juan	Pfizer	pharmaceuticals	98	
RHODE ISLAND							
	105		Providence				
SOUTH CAROLINA							
	21		Dorchester Cnty				
	38		Spartanburg Cnty				
	127		West				
		53	Charleston	Porsche	auto	84	
		208	Anderson	AUTECS	auto electronics	91	
		235	Goose Creek	Haarmann &	chemicals	92	
		272	Spartanburg	BMW	auto	94	
		399	Goose Creek	Bayer Corp	rubber	98	
SOUTH DAKOTA							
	220		Sioux Falls				
TENNESSEE							
	77		Memphis				
	78		Nashville				
	134		Chattanooga				
	148		Knoxville				
	204		Tri-City				
	223		Memphis				
		14	Symnra	Nissan	truck/auto	82	
		27	Lebanon	Toshiba	microwave ovens	83	
		38	Hartsville	TVA Nuclear Plant	energy	84	
		39	Phipps Bend	Global Power	energy	84	
		45	Memphis	Sharp	microwave ovens	84	
		175	Maury Cnty.	Saturn	auto	90	
		192	Hawkins Cnty.	Form Rite	–	91	
		289	Bristol	SmithKline	pharmaceuticals	95	
		301	Carter Cnty.	Soemens Energy	industrial automation	95	
		308	Bartlett	Brother Ind.	typewriters/word	95	
		311	Columbia	Columbia	room	95	
		413	Ripley	Komatsu America	equip. parts dist.	98	
TEXAS							
	12		McAllen				
	36		Galveston				
	39		Dallas/Fort Worth				
	62		Brownsville				

STATE	ZONE#	SUBZONE #	LOCATION	BUSINESS	INDUSTRY	YEAR APPROVED	STATUS: (Active unless otherwise indicated)
	68		El Paso				
	80		San Antonio				
	84		Harris County				
	94		Webb County				
	95		Starr County				
	96		Maverick				
	97		Val Verde County				
	113		Ellis County				
	115		Beaumont				
	116		Jefferson County				
	117		Orange				
	122		Corpus Christi				
	149		Freeport				
	150		El Paso				
	155		Victoria & CalhounCounties				
	156		Weslaco				
	165		Midland				
	168		Dallas/Fort Worth				
	171		Liberty				
	178		Presidio				
	183		Austin				
	196		Fort Worth				
	199		Texas City				
	234		Gregg County				
		62	Jefferson City	Bethlehem Steel		85	
		76	Corpus Ch.	Coastal St. Petr.	oil refining		
		77	Corpus Ch.	Koch Refining	oil refining	95	
		78	Corpus Ch.	Trifinery	oil refining	85	
		79	Corpus Ch.	Gulf Marine	oil refininh	85	
		80	Corpus Ch.	Berry Contracting	–	85	
		81	Corpus Ch.	CC Distributing	–	85	expired 91
		82	Corpus Ch.	Compressors	–	85	expired 91
		83	Corpus Ch.	Hitox	–	85	
		122	Athens	Harvey Inds.	TVs	88	
		124	Victoria	Safety Railway	freight car repair	88	lapsed
		125	Victoria	Safety Steel	freight car repair	88	lapsed
		135	Corpus Christi	Citgo	oil refining	88	
		136	Nueces Cnty.	Valero	oil refining	88	
		139	Weslaco	McManus	food processing	88	
		140	Weslaco	FGulf De Bruyn	food processing	88	
		141	Weslaco	Sundor	food processing	89	
		143	Corpus Ch.	Reynolds Metals	alumina	88	
		144	Houston	Hughes Tool	drilling tools	89	
		145	Houston	Texas Steel	heat-treat oil	89	
		176	LaPorte	DuPont	hydrofluoric acid	90	
		198	Houston	United General	hand tools	91	
		199	San Antonio	Bausch & Lomb	sunglasses	91	lapsed
		200	San Antonio	Colin Medical Inst.	medical equip,	91	
		201	San Antonio	Friedrich A/C &	air conditioners	91	
		205	Calhoun Cnty.	Alcoa	alumina/aluminum	91	
		206	Houston	Gulf Coast	oil refining	91	
		209	Nueces Cnty.	Koch Refining	oil refining	91	
		211	Arlington	GM	auto	91	
		214	Houston	Calero Refining	oil refining	91	
		215	Houston	Goodman Mfg.	–	91	
		225	Harris County	Shaffer	oil drilling equip.	92	
		241	Austin	Dell Computer	electronics	92	
		242	Harris County	Tuboscope Vetco	steel tube prds.	92	
		260	Harris County	Shell Oil	oil refining	93	
		262	Port Arthur	Star Enterprise	oil refining	93	
		263	Wylie	Sanden Internatl.	auto a/c components	93	
		265	Houston	Dril-Quip	oil field equip	94	
		287	Houston	Hydril	oil field equip	95	
		288	Houston	Tadiran	telecom. prds.	95	
		290	Tx City	Amoco	oil refining	95	
		291	Freeport	BASF	chemicals	95	
		309	Jefferson City	Fina	oil refining	95	
		313	Jefferson/Libe	Mobil Oil	oil refining	95	

STATE	ZONE#	SUBZONE #	LOCATION	BUSINESS	INDUSTRY	YEAR APPROVED	STATUS: (Active unless otherwise indicated)
		315	Freeport	JHoffnam-LaRoch	pharmaceuticals	95	
		320	Harris County	Crown Central	oil refining	95	
		324	Mansfield	Pier1	distribution	96	
		327	San Angelo	R.G. Barry	footwear & thermal	96	
		339	Texas City	Marathon	oil refining	96	
		341	Harris County	Exxon	oil refining	96	
		349	Jefferson	Clark	oil refining	96	
		367	Texas City	Valero	oil refining	97	
		374	Jefferson	USDOE Oil	crude oil shortage	97	
		381	Brazoria Cnty.	Phillips	oil refining	97	
		388	Richardson	Fossil Partners	watches, etc.	97	
		389	Dallas	B&F System	consumer prds.	97	
		395	Brazoria Cnty.	Seaway Pipeline	crude oil transship.	98	
		396	Texas City	Seaway Pipeline	crude oil transship.	98	
		402	Harris County	Lyondell-Citgo	oil refining	98	
		409	Harris County	Equistar	petrochemicals	98	
		421	Lewisville	Ultrak	closed circuit TV	98	
		422	Brazoria Cnty.	Amoco	petrochemicals	98	
UTAH							
	30		Salt Lake City				
VERMONT							
	55		Burlington				
	91		Newport				
		17	St. Albans	Pedigree	apparel	82	
		172	Georgia	Wyeth Nutritionals		90	
VIRGINIA							
	20		Suffolk				
	137		Wash. Dulles Intl. Airport				
	185		Culpeper				
	207		Richmond				
		146	Va. Beach	Stihl	chain saw/power	89	lapsed
		228	Culpeper	ITT Teves	auto brake comp.	92	
		229	Culpeper	Rochester Corp.	cable	92	
		253	Newport News	NN Shipbuilding &	shipbuilding	93	
		284	Elkton	Merck & Co	pharmaceuticals	94	
		305	Whiting	Amoco	oil refining	95	
		367	Altavista	Abbott	formula/nutritional	97	
		406	Richmond	Hewlett-Packard	computer-related	98	
WASHINGTON							
	5		Seattle				
	85		Everett				
	86		Tacoma				
	120		Cowlitz				
	128		Whatcom				
	129		Whatcom				
	130		Whatcom				
	131		Whatcom				
	173		Grays Harbor				
	188		Yakima				
	203		Moses Lake				
	212		Tacoma				
	216		Olympia				
	224		Spokane				
		126	Tacoma	Tacoma Boat.	shipbuilding	88	
		191	Hoquiam	Lamb-Grays	--	91	
		270	Arlington	West-Coast Forest	wood building	94	
		370	Skagit Cnty.	Equilon	oil refining	97	
WEST VIRGINIA							
	228		Wood/Jackson Counties				
	229		Charleston				
		397	Buffalo	Toyota	auto engines	98	
WISCONSIN							

STATE	ZONE#	SUBZONE #	LOCATION	BUSINESS	INDUSTRY	YEAR APPROVED	STATUS: (Active unless otherwise indicated)
	41		Milwaukee				
	167		Brown County				
		11	Kenosha	Chrysler	auto	81	
		12	Manitowac	Muskegon	piston rings	81	
		68	Janesville	GM	auto	85	
		69	Oak Creek	GM	auto electronics	85	lapsed
		71	Sturgeon Bay	Bay Shipbuilding	shipbuilding	85	
		97	Milwaukee	Ambrosia	--	87	expired 91
		238	Blue Mounds	Stauffer CHeese	cheese prods	92	
		352	Hudson	Robin Mfg.	small engines	96	
		391	Osceola	Polaris Industries	small engines	97	
		393	Plymouth	Sargento Foods	cheese prcessing	98	
WYOMING							
	157		Casper				

TRADE, TRADE BARRIERS, AND TRADE DEFICITS: IMPLICATIONS FOR U.S. ECONOMIC WELFARE

Craig Elwell

ABSTRACT

Trade has become an ever more important activity for the U.S. economy. In economics trade is viewed as a means to raising overall economic well-being, but like other market forces it can be disruptive, imposing significant costs on some sectors of the economy. This report provides an overview of the economic reasons supporting free trade among nations. It also examines the major arguments for restricting trade and provides a general economic assessment of their merit. Finally, the report provides an analysis of the U.S. trade deficit. Policy issues are also highlighted. This report will be updated if developments warrant.

SUMMARY

International trade is a means to a higher standard of living for all trading nations. The post-war era has seen a rapid expansion of trade and the U.S. has been a major participant in this process both as a trading nation and as a leader in the steady lowering of barriers to trade worldwide. The significant benefit of trade does not come without disruption and cost, however. Gaining the benefit of trade and also treating those hurt by trade equitably is often a difficult public policy issue. There is recurring congressional concern about the effect of trade on U.S. economic welfare. Current issues include: "fast-track", steel dumping, export controls, and the rapidly growing trade deficit. This report provides a brief overview of the economic case for free trade, the economic perspective on common arguments for trade barriers, and the cause and economic significance of persistent large trade deficits. The economic benefit of specialization and trade is a fundamental aspect of economic life whether for the individual, region, or nation. Arguments for trade barriers come in many forms but none is on economic grounds greatly compelling. The trade deficit is not a necessary aspect of trade, nor is it caused by foreign trade barriers. The deficit is a means for the nation to spend beyond current production. It can confer significant benefits but at some level of cost. This report will be updated if developments warrant.

THE GROWING IMPORTANCE OF TRADE TO THE U.S. ECONOMY

In the post World-War II era the American economy has experienced steady and substantial growth of international trade. Total trade (the combined value of exports and imports) as a share of output (GDP) has risen from 9% in 1950 to 25% in 1998, with sizable gains in the last decade. Even this large increase may understate the rising impact of trade on the economy because of the large share of services output, much of which is *non-tradable*, in U.S. GDP. For example, looking at merchandise exports as a share of total *tradable* output for the U.S. we see growth from near 4% in 1950 to about 40% in 1998.

The rising integration of the American economy with the world economy has been facilitated by technical advances that have reduced the natural barriers of time and space that separate national economies, as well as policy actions that have steadily lowered various man-made barriers to international exchange. As natural and man-made barriers have fallen, the considerable economic advantages of trade have induced large increases I the international exchange of goods.

WHY DO COUNTRIES TRADE?[1]

Trade occurs because it is *mutually enriching*, with a positive economic effect like that caused by technological change, whereby economic efficiency is increased, allowing greater output and consumption from the same endowment of productive resources. But, like technological change and other market forces, international trade creates wealth by inducing a reallocation of the economy's scarce resources (capital and labor) into relatively more efficient activities and away from less efficient activities. Such reallocation while beneficial to the overall economy can be disruptive and costly to some workers and industries to the relatively less efficient activities. They will likely bear significant adjustment costs and find a diminished market value for their economic services. The economy-wide gains exceed the costs; however the perennially tough policy issue is how to secure the gains from trade for the wider community while dealing with equitably with those who are hurt by the process.

The importance of the *gains from trade* is clearly evident in our individual economic behavior. Rather than build our own automobile, provide our own medical services, or produce our own food, we find it far more efficient to specialize in the production of some good or service we are good at and trade these (indirectly with the use of money) for most other goods or services that we want. Such specialization and trade clearly allow each of us to consume far more than we could if we tried to be completely self-sufficient. The same is true for a country, albeit to a less extensive degree in most cases (i. e., U.S. imports amount to only about 12% of GDP).

What is also important to understand about the gains from specialization and trade is that they are mutual, occurring even if the trading parties have an absolute advantage or disadvantage in the efficiency with which they produce all tradable goods. All that is

[1] For a fuller discussion see: Mankiw, N. Gregory. *Principles of Economics.* Dryden Press. New York. 1997. m Pp. 45-47.

required is a difference in relative efficiency, that is, a difference among countries in the rate at which the output of one good must be curtailed to expand production of another good. If these rates are different, then a comparative advantage exists creating the potential for gains from trade. This principle would explain, for example, why Michael Jordan, the basketball star, despite being able to mow his lawn faster then anyone else, would still find it more efficient to employ a lawn service for that job. The income gained from other uses of the time he would spend lawn mowing will likely more than compensate for the cost of the lawn service. Similarly, the hired lawn mower gains by spending more time cutting grass and less time playing basketball.

Differences in comparative advantage will arise between countries because of differences in the relative abundance or scarcity of the factors of production. Comparative advantage will be found in those activities that make intensive use of the abundant factor. For example, compared to other countries the U.S. with a relative abundance of high-skilled labor and a relative scarcity of low-skilled labor will find that specialization in the production of goods that use high-skilled labor intensively will, with trade, raise national income. In contrast, China which has a relative abundance of low-skilled labor and relative scarcity of high-skilled labor would find that specialization in the production of goods that use low-skilled workers intensively would, with trade, raise that country's real income. (Differences in productive technology among countries could also create differences in relative efficiency and form a basis for trade.) In addition to specialization the gains from trade can also emerge due to fuller realization of economies of scale, increased competitive pressures, and a raised incentive for innovation.

THE ECONOMIC EFFECT OF TRADE BARRIERS[2]

If international trade is economically enriching, imposing barriers to such exchanges will prevent the nation from fully realizing the economic gains from trade and must reduce real income. Protection of import-competing industries with tariffs, quotas, and non-tariff barriers will lead to an over-allocation of the nation's scarce resources in the protected sectors and an under-allocation of resources in the unprotected tradeable goods industries. This distortion reduces trade, national income, and overall economic welfare.

The U.S. and other nations have made great progress in the post-war era in reducing trade barriers, but significant impediments still exist. A 1994 estimate of the economic cost of existing. U.S. barriers was $60 billion per year with an average cost per protected job of about $170,000.[3] The issue, however, is not just whether to continue

[2] Man-made trade barriers come in several forms. Two common manifestations are tariffs and quotas. Tariffs area tax on imported goods. Quotas are a limit on the quantity of a good that can be imported. A variant of the quota is the voluntary export restraint (VER), where the exporting country imposes the restriction. Other forms of barriers (often called non-tariff barriers) include: local content requirements, national procurement policies, and unduly protracted health, safety, and customs procedures. The magnitude of the negative effect on economic welfare will likely vary with the type of barrier used. In general, for a given level of protection quota-like restrictions carry a greater potential for reducing welfare than do tariffs.

[3] See Hufbauer, Gary Clyde, and Kimberly Ann Eliott. *Measuring the Costs of Protection in the United States,* Washington, Institute for International Economics, 1994.

removing barriers but whether to resist the erection of new barriers. It is important to remember that during most of the first half of this century trade barriers grew sharply, reversing the substantial trade liberalization achieved in the previous century. Therefore, much of the effort towards free trade in the post-war era has involved reversing protectionist structures erected in the first half of the century.

Arguments for trade barriers come in several forms, but none is greatly compelling on economic grounds alone.

- Jobs are destroyed by trade. The reality is that trade creates and destroys jobs just as other market forces do. Trade creates jobs in industries that have comparative advantage and destroys jobs in industries that have a comparative disadvantage. The economy has had no net loss of jobs. There is a short-run hardship for some, but the whole economy's living standard is raised. These effects are qualitatively the same as those induced by purely domestic disruptions such as shifting consumer demand or technological change. In that context, easing adjustment of those harmed is economically more fruitful than protection given the net economic benefit of trade to the total economy.

- Worker wages are hurt by trade. There is no doubt that international trade can have strong effects, good and bad, on the wages of American workers. The plight of the worker adversely affected by imports comes quickly to mind. But it is also true that workers in export industries will benefit from trade. Moreover, all workers are consumers and benefit from the expanded market choices and lower prices that trade brings. It is true that real wages of American workers have grown slower over the last 25 years than in the earlier post-war period, and it is also true that there has occurred a sharply rising inequality of wages between the skilled and less skilled. But, economic analyses indicate it is very unlikely that growing international trade has had much to do with the slowdown in real wage growth and very unlikely that trade has caused more than a minor share of rising wage inequality. Slow productivity growth and the bias toward high skill in recent technological change have likely played a much larger role than trade in explaining poor wage performance.[4]

- Infant-industries that are so important to our future economic welfare that they need temporary protection to assure their eventual maturity. This is another argument for protection that could, in concept, be valid. But, it is also a policy that would be very hard to implement in practice. The difficulty is that it would require the

---

[4] For further discussion see: U.S. Library of Congress. Congressional Research Service. *Is Globalization the Force Behind Recent Poor U.S. Wage Performance?: An Analysis. By Craig Elwell.*

government to evaluate future profitability, to in effect pick economic "winners." This is not a task that government is likely to be very good at and therefore invites significant inefficiency. One might ask, if the case for long-run profitability of an emergent industry is so compelling, why is the private market overlooking this prospect. Recent manifestations of this argument for trade barriers have been called *industrial policy* and *strategic industries policy.*

- Unfair competition undermines the benefits of trade. Can trade be beneficial if all parties don't abide by the same rules and regulations? Yes it can. If another country chooses to give a subsidy to an exporting industry, buying those now cheaper exports will hurt domestic industries that compete with those foreign goods, but it will benefit the domestic consumers who purchase them. The gain to consumers will typically exceed the loss to producers and workers. Therefore, from the standpoint of overall economic welfare, a prudent economic response may be to accept the gain in real income offered by the subsidized foreign goods and facilitate the adjustment of the adversely affected home workers to more efficient endeavors. Similarly, many economists see a possible economic advantage of buying foreign goods produced under different labor and environmental standards. They view differences in such standards as a basis for creating comparative advantage and realizing mutual gains from trade. In addition to the economic benefit to the U.S. economy, for any poor nations the ability to use such small advantages to produce a tradeable good today, may offer the best vehicle to increased productivity and a steadily rising living standard in the future. Despite the economic gain to the U.S., trade on this basis can undermine long held domestic norms of "fair" market conduct. If deviation from these norms is unacceptable in domestic transactions it may be hard to justify them in international exchanges. Another common activity widely seen as an unfair trade practice is foreign dumping of exports. Dumping can hurt particular workers and firms. But, for total economic welfare to be reduce by dumping one has to accept the premise that there can be a price that is too low. Price cutting is a basic element of competition, widely practiced in the domestic economy, that leads to greater efficiency and economic gain to consumers. Actions to prevent dumping curtail the benefit of such competition in international commerce. A possible exception would be instances of dumping that are "predatory" and in part of a plan to establish monopoly power. Such predatory practices reduce economic welfare and preventing them is in our economic interest. Because predatory pricing is rare economists place little merit in the claimed unfairness of most instances of dumping. In general, most concerns with unfair trade reflect a conflict between the goal of increasing economic welfare and some other public policy goals such as distributional equity,

> environmental quality, or human rights. The tough policy question is finding the most efficient reconciliation of these conflicting goals without necessarily resorting to protection from trade. Policies to compensate for loss and to provide temporary adjustment assistance can be helpful in this regard.[5]

Despite their lack of economic merit trade barriers persist. This most likely occurs because they have very focused benefits accruing to a well defined and politically influential group, while the barriers costs are often widely dispersed over the population among people with less natural cohesion and a more diluted political voice. The protected groups gain, however, is at the greater expense of the wider community.

THE TRADE DEFICIT[6]

The U.S. trade deficit has risen steadily since 1992. It exceeded $233 billion in 1998 and has increased nearly $100 billion since 1996. The trade imbalance has grown despite good export sales in recent years, as a strong economic expansion has brought a tremendous increase in the demand for imports. But, it is not necessary that an economic expansion generate a large trade deficit.

A trade deficit does not occur because U.S. exports may face high foreign trade barriers or because foreign exports are being "dumped" in the U.S. market. Nor does the trade deficit exist because American industry and workers are unable to produce world class goods. The global trade deficit is largely reflective of underlying macroeconomic conditions at home requiring more imports than exports to meet current domestic demand. In effect, the economy spends more than it produces, and the excess of demand is sated by a net inflow of goods and services—a trade deficit. Of course, for this to occur there must be at least one other economy that produces more than it spends at home, and that excess supply becomes a net outflow of goods and services-a trade surplus. For the U.S. this phenomenon has its roots in changes over recent decades in both private and government spending/saving behavior. In this recent period, strong rates of domestic investment spending have far exceeded he flow of domestic saving available to finance it. A net inflow of foreign savings, relatively abundant due to economic weakness abroad, has filled this gap. But, the necessary counterpart of that inflow is a net inflow of foreign goods—the trade deficit.[7]

So long as domestic saving in the U.S. falls short of domestic investment and an inflow of foreign saving is available to fill all or part of the gap, the United States will run a trade deficit. The saving-investment balance suggest two ways the trade gap can be closed. One, the supply of foreign savings dwindles, forcing domestic investment down

[5] For a discussion of striking a balance between fairness and free trade see: Rodrik, Dani. *Has Globalization Gone too Far?* Institute For International Economics. Washington. 1997.

[6] For a fuller discussion see: U.S. Library of Congress. Congressional Research Service. *U.S. Trade Balance: An Analysis of Recent Trends and Policy Options. CRS Report 98-508E. Washington, 1998.*

[7] See also: U.S. Library of Congress Congressional Research Service. *U.S. Trade Balance: An Analysis of Recent Trends and Policy Options. CRS Report 98-508 E by Craig Elwell.*

toward the level of domestic savings. Or two, the level of domestic savings rises and curtails the attraction of foreign savings and shrinks the associated trade deficit. A lower rate of domestic investment is not desirable, but would follow if foreign investors become less willing to invest in the United States. The alternative of raising domestic savings has more economic merit, but is problematic. Large budget surpluses have raised public saving inflows but are unlikely to continue to push higher. The private saving rate is low, not easy to influence by policy leers, and not a highly probable source of accelerated domestic saving flows.

A trade deficit is not necessarily undesirable. Increasing current spending beyond current means need not be imprudent behavior. Borrowing is widely and usefully done by individuals and businesses and so too by countries. Of course borrowing carries a cost as the lender at least demands that interest be paid on the borrowings. This "debt" service cost" is a burden the borrower must carry tomorrow for living beyond his means today. One's judgment about the desirability or undesirability of the trade deficit will hinge on the benefits gained from that added spending relative to the debt service burden that is also incurred. The current debt service burden of Americas stock of foreign debt can be roughly judged from the net investment income component of the current account balance. From a surplus of near $33 billion in 1981, U.S. net foreign investment income has fallen steadily to a deficit in 1998 of $23 billion.[8] A payment of this magnitude certainly does not suggest insolvency, but it is a significant decrement to the annual rate of advance of the nation's living standard and a decrement that can get larger.

CONCLUSION

For economists the case for free trade is strong and compelling. A reduction of impediments to the flow of goods among nations will raise each trading nation's economic welfare. This conclusion has been repeatedly validated by studies of trade liberalization policies such as the Uruguay Round Agreement and NAFTA.[9] However, public debate over such initiatives makes very clear that many Americas do not share economists' optimism about the virtues of free trade. Some of this antipathy might arise from economic concerns that U.S. workers and industries hurt by trade do not receive equitable compensation and other adjustment assistance. Allying this concern, economists argue, is best achieved by efforts to augment and refine the various U.S.

---

[8] Two common indictments of the trade deficit-deindustrialization and net job loss-are not macroeconomic issues. The first largely did not happen and the second could not happen. For a discussion of deindustrialization see: U.S. Library of Congress. Congressional Research Service. *Is Globalization De-Industrializing the U.S. Economy?: An Analysis. CRS Report 98-440 E by Craig Elwell.*

[9] For example see: U.S. Library of Congress. Congressional Research Service. *The Uruguay Round: A Macroeconomic Assessment.* CRS Report 95-529 E, by Craig Elwell and Alfred Reifman. Washington, 1995; and Lustig, Nora, Barry Bosworth and Robert Lawrence. *Assessing the Impact of North American Free Trade. Washington, Brookings Institution, 1992.*

trade adjustment assistance programs.[10] Others, may simply doubt that trade is beneficial. If unconvinced by the numerous technical studies, they might consider that the United States *itself* gives clear evidence of the virtue for free trade. This country is comprised of fifty separate political entities that under the Constitution are required to allow unfettered trade among themselves. Specialization has occurred, interstate trade has grown, and national economic welfare has benefited. Certainly U.S. economic welfare would be reduced if barriers to interstate trade were erected. The benefit of interstate trade are of the same nature as the benefit of international trade. In policy deliberations, of course, national economic welfare, will be considered in conjunction with political, social, and national defense issues that will also influence trade policy.

[10] See: Lawrence, Robert Z. and Robert Litan. Globaphobia: The Wrong Debate over Trade Policy. The Brookings Institution. Washington, DC. 1998

THE U.S. TRADE DEFICIT: TRENDS, THEORY, POLICY AND SUSTAINABILITY

Dick K. Nanto

ABSTRACT

This report briefly surveys recent rends in the U.S. trade deficit and the economic theory and policies surrounding it. The Federal Trade Deficit Review Commission was organized in June 1999 to develop trade policy recommendations. This report points out some problems with and recent advances in traditional economic approaches to trade theory and policy, the twin deficits, the exchange rate, and intertemporal savings and investment. It also examines the sustainability of the trade deficit and its relationship to employment. This report will be updated as conditions warrant.

SUMMARY

This report briefly surveys recent trends in the U.S. trade deficit and the economic theory and policies surrounding it. After dropping to $74 billion in 1991, the U.S. merchandise trade deficit increased by $49 billion in 1998 to a record high of $248 billion. Even though the reasons for the rising deficit seem apparent, it raises questions about the theoretical analysis that underlies U.S. policies to deal with it and its sustainability and effect on the U.S. economy.

The Federal Trade Deficit Review Commission was organized on June 10, 1999, and is responsible for developing trade policy recommendations by examining the economic, trade, tax, and investment policies and laws, and other incentives and restrictions that are relevant to addressing the causes and consequences of the U.S. merchandise and current account deficits.

Economic theory is evolving with respect to the international trade side of the U.S. economy and the relevant policy implications. The standard macroeconomic approach to explaining the trade deficit is encountering some obstacles. First, the savings and investment equality is an *ex post* identity, a framework for analysis, and not a behavioral equation. Second, the linkage between macroeconomic conditions and a nation's exchange rate has not been established; exchange rate changes do not translate completely into price changes for imports and exports, and exchange rates tend to overshoot the equilibrium rates. This brings other inefficiencies into an economy. Government policy may also affect exchange rates. Recent weakness in the Japanese yen, for example, has been exacerbated by Japanese government policy. The United States does not seem to have a transparent method of determining if and when it should intervene in currency markets.

A third issue is that a focus on the savings-investment relationship in the economy can lead to dubious policy prescriptions-such as the assertion in the 1980s that eliminating the federal budget deficit would do the same for the trade deficit. A fourth problem is that a static macroeconomic approach does not account for why the United States may be borrowing from abroad and how those funds are being used. There may be an optimal level for a nation's current account deficit, and borrowing may be justified if it is used to increase productivity. Recent U.S. trade data indicate that a rising share of U.S. imports has been for capital goods that should raise U.S. productivity and economic growth.

The policy implications with respect to trade still center on the belief that free trade is optimal, but extensions of the theory now allow for a strategic trade policy aimed at assisting certain industries. The conventional economic conclusion that all intervention into trade flows has no effect on the trade deficit, however, is yet to be demonstrated empirically. In terms of sustainability, if the recent large capital inflows reaching nearly $200 billion per year continue into the next century, a U.S. foreign debt would develop equivalent to a quarter of GDP and foreigners may end up owning more than half the U.S. federal debt. If the capital inflows do not continue, the U.S. trade and current account deficits of today will be unsustainable.

*****

After dropping to $74 billion in 1991, the U.S. merchandise trade deficit increased from $199 billion in 1997 to $248 billion (balance-of-payments basis) in 1998. This surge in the U.S. trade deficit can be explained primarily by the strong U.S. economy (which is buying more of almost everything-including imports), the Asian financial crisis (which has reduced U.S. exports to Asian countries and lowered prices of Asian exports to the U.S.), and inflows of capital (which drive up the value of the dollar and make imports into the United States cheaper and American exports more expensive). Even thought the reasons for the rising deficit are apparent, it raises questions about the long-term implications of this imbalance, the economic analysis that underlies U.S. policies to deal with it, and its sustainability.

In concert with the rising U.S. trade deficit, the exchange value of the dollar has been rising, particularly with respect to the currencies of Asian countries (except for China and Hong Kong). The strength of the dollar in the late 1990s bears a strong resemblance to the strong dollar in the first half of the 1980s. This was the period when the U.S. trade deficit grew by six times. In 1998, the dollar gained so much strength with respect to the yen that on June 17, 1998, both the United States and Japan intervened in currency markets to support the yen.

This report first provides an overview of trends in the U.S. trade deficit. It then examines the economic theory for analyzing the trade deficit and formulating policy implications. This section is somewhat technical and touches only on the major points in the theoretical debate. It is intended to point out some of the pitfalls of the standard interpretations of the trade deficit. It includes both a discussion of the traditional comparative advantage and macroeconomic approaches to the deficit and a brief review of exchange rates, the sustainability of the trade deficit, and the effect of trade on jobs. This report will be updated as major events warrant.

As for legislative activity, in the 105th Congress, H.R. 3579 (Livingston, Supplemental Appropriations) included a provision to establish an Emergency Trade Deficit Review Commission to study the causes and consequences of the U.S. merchandise trade and current account deficits and develop trade policy recommendations for the 21st century. Although this measure passed the Senate, the provision was removed in Conference.[1] It then was inserted into the Legislative Branch FY99 Appropriations bill (S. 2137) and became the Trade Deficit Review Commission Act of 1998 (19 USC 2213). The Federal Trade Deficit Review commission is responsible for developing trade policy recommendations by examining the economic, trade, tax, and investment policies and laws, and other incentives and restrictions that are relevant to addressing the causes and consequences of the U.S. merchandise and current account deficits. The Commission is composed of twelve members appointed by the Senate and House and is to submit a final report to the President and Congress not later than twelve months after the date of its initial meeting on June 10, 1999. In the 106th Congress, Section 312 of the Legislative Branch Appropriations Act, 2000 (S. 1206, Bennett, reported by the Senate Appropriations Committee on June 10, 1999) would make some changes to the Trade Deficit Review Commission. It would extend funding for the Commission and its termination day to 90 days after the Commission submits its final report. It also would exempt Commission members from certain pay authorities and provision of the Federal Advisory Committee Act. Other legislation related to the U.S. trade deficit includes trade provisions aimed at specific countries, such as Japan and China,[2] and legislation dealing with fast-track trade negotiating authority.[3]

---

1 U.S. Congress. House of Representatives Report to accompany H.R. 3579, 105th Congress, 2nd Session. (Emergency Supplemental Appropriations bill for the fiscal year Ending September 30, 1998, and for other purposes."

2 See: CRS Issue Brief 97015, *U.S. Japan Economic Ties: Status and Outlook*, by William H. Cooper , and CRS Issue Brief 91121, *China-U.S. Trade Issues*, by Wayne M. Morrison.

3 See: CRS Issue Brief 97016, *Trade Agreements: Renewing the Negotiating and Fast-track Implementing Authority*, by Valdimir N. Pregelj.

RECENT TRENDS IN THE U.S. TRADE DEFICIT

Figure 1. U.S. Merchandise Imports, Exports, and Balance of Trade (balance-of-payments basis), 1980-98

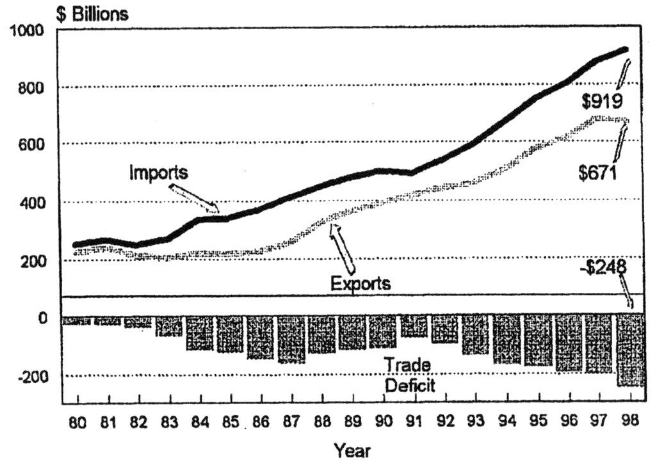

As shown in Figure 1, the U.S. trade deficit grew from $25 billion in 1980 to a peak of $160 billion in 1987 as the burgeoning Federal budget deficit along with rising U.S. interest rates drew in international capital, appreciated the dollar, and hampered U.S. net exports. The deficit then declined to $74 billion during the U.S. recession of 1991 but rose to $199 billion in 1997 and further to $248 billion in 1998 despite significant shrinkage in the Federal budget deficit. U.S. export growth had been strong until 1998 when exports declined. Imports have continued to increase.

Standard and Poor's Data Resources, Inc., a major economic forecasting firm. Projects that for 1999, the U.S. merchandise trade deficit (balance-of-payments basis) may reach 327 billion.[4] Much of the deterioration is occurring because the Asian financial crisis has cut U.S. exports to countries in difficulty, such as South Korea, Japan, Indonesia, and Thailand, and has driven capital from Asian markets to higher quality investments in the United States. Prices of imports from Asia also are lower because of their weakened currencies.

[4] Standard & Poor's. *Review of the U.S. Economy,* May 1999.

Figure 2. U.S. Balance on Current Account, Merchandise Trade, Unilateral Transfers, and Investment Income, 1992-1998

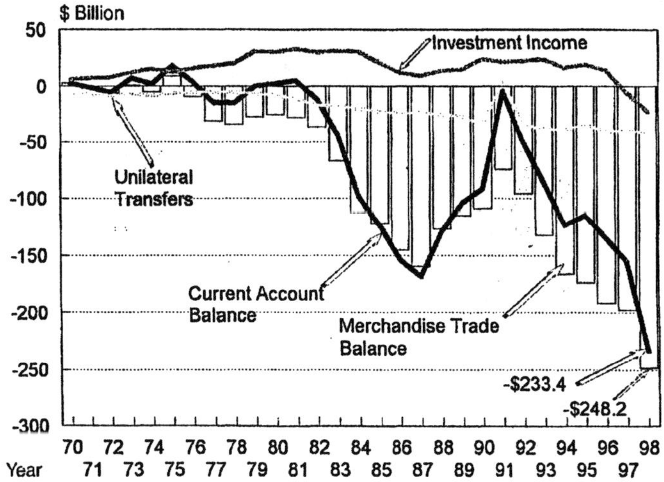

In terms of the U.S. current account (which includes trade in merchandise and services, investment income, and unilateral transfers), the picture is similar-primarily because the deficit in merchandise trade dominates the other balances. (See Figure 2). In services trade, however, the United States ran a surplus of $78.9 billion in 1998-down somewhat from 1997. Net unilateral transfers (transfers of money not in return for goods or services performed, e.g. remittances, private gifts, pension payments, and government grants) have been fairly stable at about -$40 billion. In 1998 it was $-41.9 billion. A significant change in the U.S. current account has been in the balance on investment income. This is the balance of income received on U.S. investments abroad less income paid on foreign assets in the United States. This balance dropped from a surplus of around $30 billion in the early 1980s, to $20 billion in the early 1990s, to a deficit of -$5.3 billion in 1997, and -$22.5 billion in 1998. The switch from surplus to deficit in this balance largely reflects the net inflow of investment into the United States. This inward investment is the functional equivalent of foreign borrowing and has pushed the net investment position of the United States to a negative $1.545 trillion in 1998. The United States has become the world's largest debtor nation, and the servicing of that debt has increased the U.S. deficit on current account.

Figure 3. U.S. Bilateral Merchandise Trade Balances with Selected Trading Partners, 1998

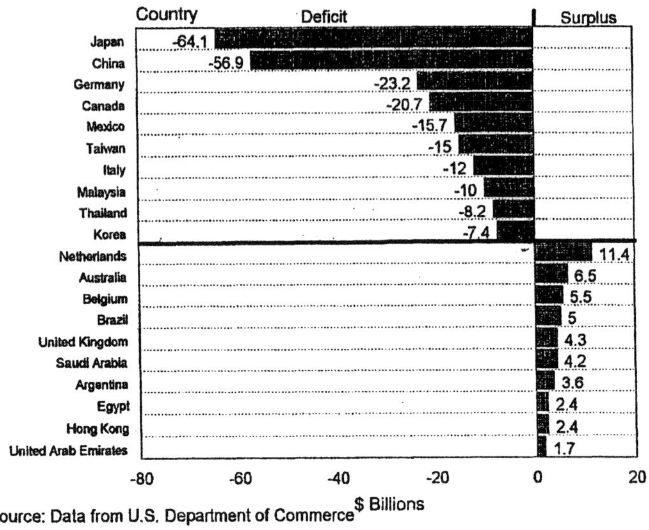

Source: Data from U.S. Department of Commerce

The rising overall U.S. merchandise trade deficit is reflected in bilateral trade with specific countries. (See Figure 3) In 1997, U.S. trade deficits with Japan and China accounted for nearly two-thirds of the total U.S. deficit. Trade with Canada and Mexico, the two NAFTA (North American Free Trade Agreement) trading partners, also remained in deficit. With Japan, after declining from a peak of $66 billion in 1994, the U.S. deficit fell to $48 billion in 1996 before rising to $64 billion in 1998. The U.S. deficit with China has surged from $30 billion in 1994, to $39 billion in 1996, and to $57 billion in 1998. With NAFTA, the U.S. deficit has shrunk somewhat as it eased from $39 billion in 1996 to $36 billion in 1998.[5]

Although there is no economic reason that bilateral trade with any particular trading partner should be in balance, the chronic U.S. deficit with Japan and the rising imbalance with China have attracted criticism, raised political tensions, and have induced calls for changes in U.S. trade policy. Trade barriers and market-opening measures, moreover, clearly affect trade with individual nations. The continual trade deficit with Japan combined with that nation's weak-yen policy and capital outflows from Japanese financial deregulation along with trade barriers in China have arguably contributed to the rising U.S. trade deficit.[6]

---

[5] See: CRS Report 970183, *The U.S. Trade Deficit in Manufacturers:* The Rise of China and NAFTA, by Dick K. Nanto.

[6] In July 1998, a senior official of the U.S. Department of Commerce stated before the House Committee on International Relations, Subcommittee on International Economic Policy and Trade, that the U.S.> trade deficit is largely due to distortions in the trading relationship with Japan and China. See: Trade Imbalance with China and Japan Priority in Reducing Trade Deficit. *Inside U.S. Trade,* July 31, 1998. Internet edition available at <www.insidetrade.com>.

TRADE THEORY AND POLICY

International trade theory takes two basic tracks in analyzing aggregate trade flows. The first harkens back to the theory of comparative advantage along with neoclassical economics and the second focuses in the macroeconomic foundations of trade flows. Although the theory of comparative advantage and neoclassical economic theory do not focus on the trade deficit, *per se*, we discuss this briefly in order to provide a picture of how various aspects of trade theory and policy are evolving.

The theory of comparative advantage and traditional trade policy analysis conclude that under certain idealized conditions, a country maximizes its well-being by specializing in producing those goods and services in which it has a comparative advantage and importing those in which other nations have advantage. The policy implication of the comparative advantage arguments is that barriers to trade reduce national welfare and free trade brings optimal benefits for the economy as a whole. Import competition may hurt some domestic competitors and impose some adjustment costs on certain actors in the economy, but, in the long run, free trade tends to lower prices and provide benefits to consumers that should offset the negative effects on industries that are hurt. For the economy as a whole, therefore, national well-being is increased. It is up to the political system to determine whether income is then transferred to the industries that are hurt. According to this analysis, protectionism is self defeating. It benefits certain trade interests but at a cost to the rest of society.

Criticism of this model for trade policy based on comparative advantage and traditional trade theory comes both from some policymakers and theoretical economists. Somė decision-makers assert that the policy implication that free trade is always optimal is too broad-brushed and unidimensional and does not account for the complexities of the real world. Adjustment costs from free trade may be too high, or, in some cases, other countries may pursue industrial and trade policies that are "unfair." Governments may subsidize certain industries, maintain trade barriers, or allow companies to engage in dumping or other unfair trade practices. Most economists content, however, that retaliation for trade barriers and protectionism abroad usually ends up hurting U.S. consumers rather than solving the problem.

Economists acknowledge, however, that traditional trade models do not describe or predict accurately trade flows in the real world, particularly in terms of manufactured products. The models either ignore or provide unsatisfactory treatment of five major deviations between the real world and the theoretical models. These include: (1) increasing returns to scale (larger firms can produce goods at a lower per unit cost than smaller firms), (2) learning-by-doing (comparative advantage can be created as economies learn how to produce certain products and entry costs are high for latecomers), (3) external effects (benefits exist from research and development and technological change that cannot be captured solely b those directly involved, plus a concentration of industrial processes-such as in Silicon Valley or Detroit- produces benefits for other firms and society at later), (4) inter-firm strategic rivalries (in contrast to the pure competition economic model in which all firms are small and produce identical products, in the real world, the actions of one firm in an industry can affect the operations of others), and (5) the existence of abnormal profits or losses by firms for systematic reasons (i.e. for reasons beyond simple randomness or "luck") which government policies can influence greatly.[7] The comparative advantage approach also does not account for trade barriers, exchange rate manipulation, or business subsidies by individual countries that may alter the competitiveness of certain firms.

A large body of economic literature has been developed to study these deviations form the pure theory of international trade. This literature is summarized in *the Handbook of International Economics*, edited by G. Grossman and K. Rogoff. An important conclusion of this literature is that international trade theory is not repudiated, rather it is being extended. The critical question is whether or not the above problems with the pure theory are significant enough to invalidate the analysis. So far, most economists retain their support of the position that as a rule of thumb, free trade is most beneficial, but acknowledge that in certain industries the deviations between the model and the real world are significant enough to alter the standard policy prescriptions.

A complete review of the literature on how trade theory and policy are evolving is beyond the purview of this paper. Here we examine two areas in which deviations from the standard model bring new insights into real policymaking. They are intra-industry trade and strategic trade.

Intra-industry Trade

The theory of comparative advantage goes a long way in explaining why one country specializes in producing one product which it then trades for another. Saudi Arabia, for example, trades petroleum for aircraft. What the theory of comparative advantage does not explain, however, is why Europe buys aircraft, automobiles, and machine tools from the United States, while the United States buys the same products from Europe. This is **intra**-industry trade or trade in products within the same industry (e.g., American Jeeps for German BMWs) and contrasts with **inter**-industry trade which is trade between countries for products of different industries (e.g., American power generators for Chinese-made shoes).

Intra-industry trade arises partly because of economies of scale in production. The average cost of manufactured products tends to fall as the units produced increase. If one country tries to produce the full variety of products that consumers demand, it will be able to do so only at relatively high costs. Companies often need extensive production runs to be competitive with respect to price. They produce large quantities of certain product lines for sale in both domestic and export markets, but they are not able to produce each type of the product (intellectual property rights also come into play). The conclusion of traditional comparative advantage analysis that, for example, Europe could produce all high-fashion goods, the United States all automobiles, and Japan all consumer electronics makes way for a more complex system of intra-industry trade in which all three economies produce and trade with each other for all three products. This is the two-way trade of products within the same industry, and it counters the idea that countries should abandon entire industries that may appear uncompetitive at some time.

This intra-industry analysis may provide, for example, a framework to analyze whether a government-backed loan to a company (i.e. the Chrysler corporation in the

[7] Brander, Ja,es A. Strategic Trade Policy. In *Handbook of International Economics,* Vol. III, Edited by G. Grossman and K. Rogoff. New York, Elsevier Science, 1995. p. 197-98, 1447.

1970s) is economically efficient. This extension of trade theory, however, does not address the size of the U.S. trade deficit.

Strategic Trade Theory

Another response to the criticisms of the traditional approach to trade has been to develop a theory of "strategic trade" in which governments play a role in fostering the development of strategic industries and pursue trade policies that condition or alter strategic relationships among firms. The primary strategic relationship in which government intervention might be justified is interdependence: the profits of one firm are directly affected by the individual strategy choices of other firms. In economic models, one way to account for this interdependence is to introduce oligopolies (industries dominated by a few firms producing differentiated products) or imperfect competition into trade policy analysis. The appeal of this approach is that it allows trade theory to address some of the practical concerns that dominate the political debate over actual trade policy.

The policy implications of the strategic trade approach tend to justify government intervention in favor of "strategic industries." Intervention might include subsidies for research and development, military contracts to develop dual-use technology, or export support for commercial aircraft. The strategic approach also helps to understand how apparently modest government intervention can have large effects. If a comparatively small subsidy determines whether a foreign or domestic firm enters an industry in which there are significant learning requirements and economies of large-scale production, a sizable long-run impact can arise if the domestic industry eventually becomes viable. The approach also helps explain how trade and industrial policies have had a major role in influencing the current international pattern of specialization and trade. It further provides a theoretical rationale for deviating from the policy of free trade.[8]

Strategic trade policy prescriptions, however, pose problems of their own. Many economists still are not convinced that the risks involved in implementing them justify the deviation from free trade. Selecting a strategic industry is difficult in a political system in which traditional industries (such as steel, automobiles, petroleum, and textiles) have major influence on national economic policy. A true strategic industry may be small and not represented well in political power centers. Strategic trade also can be used as a rationale for protection of industries that may be strategic primarily in terms of size or political clout but not with respect to the economic definition of the term.

Studies of strategic trade also indicate that even nationally successful strategic trade policies have a "beggar-thy-neighbor" aspect; that is, one country's strategic industries may advance at the expense of those of another. This may induce other countries to retaliate and attempt to neutralize the gain. Also, countries that compete with each other with strategic trade policies tend to make agreements to ameliorate or prevent such rivalries. The United States and other industrialized nations, for example, have multilateral trade agreements curbing excessive use of subsidies and other government assistance to industries.

---

[8] *Ibid.*, 1446-1447.

Strategic trade policies, moreover, are not aimed directly at the U.S. trade deficit. Whether a deficit exists or not does not change the rationale for a strategic trade policy.

Macroeconomic Theory

Macroeconomics deals primarily with aggregate flows in an economy. It is largely separate from considerations of comparative advantage or the actions of particular microeconomic actors, such as business production or consumer choice. It is in macroeconomics that the problem of the level of the trade deficit is addressed.

The macroeconomic interpretation of trade and current account deficits is that they are caused by an imbalance in domestic saving and investment. Businesses, consumers, or governments do not save enough to finance domestic investment, so they use foreign capital to bridge that gap. They borrow from abroad to finance investments or deficit spending.[9] This implies that the relative level of trade flows is determined outside of specific trade policies that are aimed at imports or exports - including strategic trade policy. Trade policies may change particular product flows but are unlikely to change their aggregate level.

According to macroeconomic theory, for example, a policy to restrict imports of steel may cause foreign steel inflows to decline, but the overall balance of trade would not change. An important barrier causing a fall in U.S. imports of steel would have two major effects: exchange rate appreciation and a multiplier effect on the domestic economy. A decline in steel imports would first push up the value of the dollar as fewer Japanese yen, Korean won, and other foreign currencies were required to buy foreign steel. This dollar appreciation would make imports into the United States relatively cheaper and U.S. exports more expensive for foreign buyers. The second effect would be a domestic demand stimulus as steel consumers bought less steel from abroad and more from local producers. This would be multiplied through the domestic economy raising incomes and economic activity. Higher economic activity would induce more imports. The combination of these two effects would eventually bring international trade flows back to the previous level determined by the balance of savings and investment.

The same logic applies to export promotion or even an increase in exports that may occur for any of a variety of reasons. Paul Krugman, one of the foremost international trade economists, for example, states the following:

> ...[C]onsider a national economy that finds one of its major exports growing rapidly...[T]here will be strong negative feedbacks from the growth of that export to employment and exports in other industries. Indeed, those negative feedbacks will ordinarily be so strong that they

---

[9] The accounting identity that produces this result is derived as follows: Income(Y)=Consumption (C) + Business Investment (I) + Government Expenditures (G)+ Net Exports (Exports [X] – Imports [M]) or: Y=C + I + G + (X-M). By an alternate definition, Income (Y) = Consumption (C) + Taxes (T) + Household savings (S) or: Y = C + T + S. Solving the above two equations yields: T + S = I + G + (X-M). Rearranging the equation yields: (X-M) = (S-I) + (T-G), or the **trade deficit** equals the **savings-investment shortfall** plus the **budget deficit**.

will more or less completely eliminate any improvements in overall employment or the trade balance.[10]

The policy implications of a macroeconomic approach to the trade deficit, therefore, is that trade policy measures have no effect on the overall balance of trade, although they can influence specific flows of imports or exports or change the distribution of the trade deficit among trading partners or among specific traded goods. According to this approach, trade policy may do many things, but it is unlikely to alter the aggregate size of the nation's trade deficit.

This macroeconomic approach to the trade deficit is reflected in policy conclusions, such as the following from the Cato Institute:

Contrary to popular conception, the trade deficit is not caused by unfair trade practices abroad or declining industrial competitiveness at home. Trade deficits reflect the flow of capital across international borders, flows that are determined by national rates of savings and investment. This renders trade policy an ineffective tool for reducing a nation's trade deficit.[11]

In recent years, this basic approach to the trade deficit and trade policy has been extended. Economists have developed new models that attempt to deal with some shortcomings of traditional analysis such as: (1) the inability of macroeconomic models to explain movements in actual data, such as the exchange rate, (2) the inability of macroeconomic models to indicate when exchange rates are over- or undervalued, and (3) the static nature of macroeconomic models which do not consider dynamic and intertemporal effects on variables such as productivity and consumption at different time periods. Recently, the Asian financial crisis has raised the issue of the sustainability of the trade deficit. The macroeconomic approach also pays little attention to the time necessary for adjustment, the adjustment path, or whether the adjustment is partial or complete.[12]

Problems with the Basic Macroeconomic Approach

The accounting identity underlying the macroeconomic approach to the trade deficit relies heavily on the equality of savings and investment. The problem with this is that while the savings-investment identity always holds *ex post* (with an adjustment for errors and omissions of several billion dollars), it is less useful in determining policy and in forecasting future changes.

The economic profession agrees that "savings-investment" is an accounting identity and not a behavioral equation. The identity captures a final result but does not show how to get there. It is a framework for analysis, a macroeconomic relationship that overlays a

10 Krugman, Paul. A Country is Not a Company. *Harvard Business Review*, v. 74, January/February 1996. p. 40-51. Krugman assumes the economy is at full employment

11 Griswold, Daniel T. America's Maligned and Misunderstood Trade Deficit. Cato Trade Policy Analysis No. 2, April 20, 1998. On Internet at ,http://www.freetrade.org/pubs/pas/tpa-0002.html>.

12 For a simulation of some macroeconomic effects, see: CRS Report 96-301, *Effects of Trade Policies on the U.S. Trade Deficit and Other Macroeconomic Variables.* By Dick K. Nanto.

microeconomic world. It provides a way to sort out the many forces in an economy that affect trade and to highlight relationships that might be difficult to grasp otherwise. It also is useful in categorizing the sources of a savings-investment gap in a country. The identity, however, does not show the direction of causality. Do levels of savings affect trade savings? It also does not provide a mechanism to show exactly how a domestic savings-investment gap determines international capital flows and the trade deficit.

A survey of the state of macroeconomic theory with respect to trade policy is beyond the purview of this report.[13] To catch a flavor of the debate and the policy implications of it, however, we will examine three issues that seem pertinent today. These are foreign exchange rates, the so-called twin deficits, and then the trade deficit over time.

Exchange Rate Effects and Determination. Exchange rates and the role they play in equilibrating imbalances in trade flows among nations are a key to macroeconomic trade analysis. Exchange rates are like international prices among countries. They are a central part of the mechanism by which macroeconomic flows of goods, services, and capital are brought into balance. In theory, by allowing exchange rates to adjust, countries can bring their international accounts into balance.

Exchange rates also play a key role in linking capital flows to trade flows. Consider, for instance, an inflow of capital which is usually considered to cause an offsetting increase in a country's trade deficit. How does the process work. The standard interpretation is that the capital influx increases demand for a country's currency which causes the nation's exchange value to appreciate. The higher value for the currency makes imports cheaper and exports more expensive to foreign buyers. The net effect is that imports rise, exports decline, and the trade deficit increases. (The inflow of capital, if not offset by actions by monetary authorities, also may lower interest rates which then stimulates demand for products-including imports.)

In the real world, however, exchange rates do not always determine the prices of traded goods and services. The problem is that international markets tend to be segmented: a product may have different domestic prices in different countries. The "law of one price" does not hold in most cases.[14] Prices for commodities, such as petroleum and coal, tend to be the most similar across countries, while prices for sophisticated manufactures or for services tend to be the leas similar. If different prices for the same product can be charged in various countries, then an exchange rate change will not necessarily induce the expected response in import (and export) flows. On brand-name products, in particular, the pass-through of exchange rate changes is usually incomplete.

For example, between January 5, 1994 and April 19, 1995, the Japanese yen appreciated by 34% against the dollar as it rose from 113 to 80 yen per dollar. Prices for exported products from Japan to the United States should have risen significantly, but, for example, the U.S. sticker price of a Toyota Celica ST Coup rose by only 2% (it went from \$16, 968 to \$17, 285), while the suggested retail price of a large-screen Sony Trinitron television receiver actually fell by 15%. Between 1982 and 1985, the dollar

---

[13] For more detail, see: Grossman, G. and K. Rogoff, eds. *Handbook of International Economics*, Vol. III, New York, Elsevier Science, 1995.

[14] The law of one price states that under perfect competition (and ignoring transportation costs) the price of an identical product must be the same across markets.

appreciated by 21%, but U.S. import prices fell by only 4%. Between 1985 and 1988, the dollar depreciated by 44%, while U.S. import prices rose by only 10%.[15]

For shipments to the United States, economic studies have found that, on average, an exchange rate change induces a price response equal to one-half the amount, although it varies by industry. Measures of trade barriers, moreover, tend to play no role in explaining the differences in prices across markets.[16] An implication of this lack of response of domestic prices to exchange rate changes is that a currency depreciation will not necessarily eliminate a nation's trade deficit,[17] although empirical studies indicate that for most countries over the long run, a real depreciation (adjusting for domestic inflation) is likely to improve a nation's current account balance while a real appreciation is likely to worsen it. In the short-run, however, the opposite is likely to occur.[18]

For practical purposes, the lack of response in flows of imports and exports to an exchange rate change means that the exchange rate will often overshoot the amount of change necessary to bring trade and capital flows back into balance. This introduces more distortions and inefficiencies into the economy. An extreme case would be the situation in Indonesia in which its trade gap was not closed despite a drop in the value of its currency from 2,500 rupiah per dollar in July 1997 to about 14,000 per dollar in July 1998.

A further problem with exchange rates and the macroeconomy is that the link between the two still has not been sufficiently quantified. If the savings-investment relationship determines the trade deficit, and one of the mechanisms by which the trade deficit changes in response to macroeconomic variables is through the exchange rate, then economists should be able to establish linkages between exchange rate movements and underlying macroeconomic conditions such as relative interest rates and the money supply.

The economic literature on this point, however, is less than persuasive. Several economic models have been estimated that seek to explain or forecast monthly or quarterly exchange rates with traditional observable macroeconomic fundamentals but have generated few encouraging results. In the words of a reviewer of this literature for the *Handbook of International Economics,*

> "The dispiriting conclusion is that relatively little explanatory power is found, and the models contain little forecasting ability compared to very simple alternatives. Existing structural models have little in their

---

15 Krugman, Paul R. and Maurice Obstfeld. *International Economics, Theory and Policy*, 2nd edition. New York, Harper Collins Publishers, 1991. p. 454.

16 Goldberg, Pinelopi Koujianou and Michael M. Knetter. Goods Prices and Exchange Rates: What Have We Learned? *Journal of Economic Literature*, Vol. 35, September 1997. p. 1244, 1270. Note: Two national markets are segmented if buyers in those markets face systematically different common currency prices for the same product (p. 1245)

17 *Ibid.* p. 1248.

18 In order for a real depreciation to improve the current account, exports and imports must be sufficiently elastic respect to the real exchange rate. This condition holds for most industrialized countries for trade in manufactured goods in the long run but not in the short run. Krugman and Obstfeld, *International Economics*, p. 450, 468.

favor beyond theoretical coherence. Positive results, when they are found, are often either fragile or unconvincing in that they rely on implausible theoretical or empirical models. For these reasons, we, like much of the profession, are doubtful of the value of further time-series modeling of exchange rates at high or medium frequencies using macroeconomic models."[19]

In commenting on another study, the same reviewers concluded that "macroeconomic variables cannot be very important determinants of exchange rate volatility...There appears to be a growing general consensus for this conclusion; it is the rule rather than the exception that large movements in exchange rates occur in the absence of plausible or detectable macroeconomic events.[20] The theory, however, appears to do better with annual changes and in predicting long-term trends.

In view of volatility in exchange rates in the 1997-99 Asian financial crisis, more work on exchange rate determination is being conducted. The current trend is to view exchange rates in terms of microeconomic analysis-not unlike that used to analyze stock prices-but this approach is still primarily a research agenda.[21] What everyone does seem to agree upon is that exchange values (for floating rates) are determined by supply and demand, and that capital flows rather than trade flows comprise most of the foreign exchange transactions. Analysis of the exchange rate, moreover, is complicated by the fact that the U.S. dollar is a key international currency. Other nations use it as a unit of account, a store of value, and medium of exchange. They often acquire dollars for purposes other than to purchase U.S. exports or invest in the U.S. market.

There is little evidence that macroeconomic variables have consistent strong effects on exchange rates (except during extraordinary circumstances such as hyperinflations). Without this link between a nation's macroeconomy and its exchange rate, part of the adjustment mechanism by which a nation's saving and investment affects the trade deficit disappears. We are left with the demand effects – an increase in exports stimulates the domestic economy which then draws in more imports and offsets some of the original increase in exports. Demand effects alone, however, cannot account for all movements in trade balances.[22]

The inability of macroeconomic theory to explain even simple exchange rate movements also raises questions about the standard interpretation of international trade

---

[19] Frankel, Jeffrey A. and Andrew K. Rose. Empirical Research on Nominal Exchange Rates. In *Handbook of International Economic.* Vol. III, Edited by G. Grossman and K. Rogoff. New York, Elsevier Science, 1995. p. 1705.

[20] *Ibid.* p. 1707. This observation was based on: Flood, Robert P. and Andrew K. Rose. Fixing Exchange Rates: A Virtual Quest for Fundamentals. National Bureau of Economic Research Working Paper No. 4503, October 1993.

[21] Frankel, Jeffrey A. and Andrew K. Rose. Empirical Research on Nominal Exchange Rates. In *Handbook of International Economics,* 1995. p. 1709-1710.

[22] In order for all increases in U.S. exports to be offset by greater imports caused by increased demand, the U.S. import share would have to exceed the inverse of the demand multiplier. For example, if a $1 billion increase in exports raises a nation's gross domestic product (GDP) by $2.5 billion (multiplier of 2.5), then for imports to rise by $1 billion, imports as a share of GDP must equal at least 40% or 1/2.5 and must respond proportionately. In the United States, imports of goods and services account for about 13% of GDP.

policies. If exchange rates do not reflect either underlying trade flows or macroeconomic variables (such as interest rates), then the standard macroeconomic conclusion that all export promotion or import protection is negated completely by market forces is subject to challenge. A country might be able to erect trade barriers or promote exports without eliciting a major response from exchange markets. The current state of macroeconomics allows one to state that reducing U.S. imports will tend to raise the value of the dollar on exchange markets, but whether a combination of the effects on the exchange rate and domestic demand are sufficient to offset the reduced imports to keep the balance of trade the same does not seem to have been established empirically.

In terms of actual trade policymaking, however, U.S. commitments under the World Trade Organization and other trade agreements preclude unilateral protectionist measures or excessive export promotion activity. Economic studies also have shown that import protection does cause higher prices and a narrower choice of products. This benefits domestic companies manufacturing those products but harms consumers who might buy them.

The lack of an empirically established link between the exchange rate and macroeconomic variables also implies that little can be said about whether an exchange rate is at the "right": level or not. Although observers agree that as exchange rates rise and fall they tend to overshoot, there is no agreed-upon formula to determine what the appropriate level should be and when an exchange rate had dropped too low or risen too high.

Some countries maintain a fixed exchange rate that they determine primarily in response to forces of demand and supply. Hong Kong, China, and Chile, for example, intervene aggressively in foreign exchange markets to maintain their fixed rates. They have doggedly fended off speculators who have bet on a depreciation. They also may be willing to sacrifice some amount of domestic economic growth to maintain what they consider their "right" exchange rates. The United States, however, has adhered to the policy that it intervenes in currency markets only in exceptional cases and will not sacrifice the domestic economy to protect the exchange rate.[23]

In June 1998, however, as the yen dropped to 146 yen per dollar, the United States and Japan did intervene in currency markets to bolster the yen's value and weaken the dollar. The weakening yen not only was causing Japan's trade surplus to rise but it was imposing greater difficulty on exporters from the Asian economies in financial crisis, particularly South Korea, whose exports compete with those from Japan. The weak yen also was putting pressure on China to devalue its currency[24] and was hurting U.S. exports to Japan.

In terms of U.S. policy, one may ask just what are the limits to exchange rate changes that will trigger intervention? Are they established in some rational manner or

---

[23] A major defense of a weakening exchange rate usually requires raising interest rates to attract capital inflows or stop capital out flows. Higher interest rates, however, cause economic growth to slow.

[24] U.S. Department of the Treasury. Statement by Treasury Secretary Robert E. Rubin on Japan. Press Release RR-2522, June 17, 1998. On Internet at http://www.treas.gov/press/releases/pr2522.htm. Snager, David. U.S. Intervenes in Currency Markets to Support the Yen. *The New York Times on the Web,* June 18, 1998. On Internet at ,http://www.nytimes.com/library/financial/061898dollar-yen.html>.

are they primarily determined by the "squeal factor"-allowing the dollar to appreciate or depreciate until businesses that are hurt complain loudly enough to compel intervention by the U.S. Federal Reserve or Treasury? Should the United States have an exchange rate policy much like it has a monetary policy?

If other countries regularly intervene in exchange markets, moreover, then the resulting exchange rates can be partly the result of government policy, although with floating exchange rates most intervention appears to have only temporary and psychological effects. One way that governments intervene in foreign exchange markets is to accumulate foreign exchange reserves. Japan's foreign exchange reserves, for example, soared from $98.5 billion in 1993 to $83.3 billion in 1995, and to $223.7 billion in May 1999.[25] This still is small relative to world capital flows, but the increase from 1993 is more than double the size of Japan's trade surplus with the United States.

Countries also may regulate capital flows. Some countries restrict outflows of capital or may cause a surge of foreign borrowing by local institutions (e. g. Thailand in the mid-1990s) by liberalizing their nation's capital flows or may induce a surge in capital outflows by increasing the share of pension funds or other assets that can be invested in foreign securities (e. g Japan in 1998).

Figure 4, shows monthly percentage changes in Japan's official foreign exchange reserves (including holdings of gold) along with changes in Japan's yen-dollar exchange rate from January 1996 to June 1998. The accumulation or disposal of foreign exchange reserves is functionally equivalent to intervention in foreign exchange markets. When Japan's central bank accumulates foreign exchange, it refrains from converting dollars, marks, pounds, and other foreign currencies into yen. This weakens the value of the yen and strengthens the value of foreign currencies, particularly the dollar. (As the volume of Japan's foreign trade increases, its need for foreign currency reserves also may rise, but the level of Japan's currency reserves seems out of line with those of other major trading nations. Germany's reserves [including gold] are about $80 billion, the United Kingdom's about $40 billion, and the U.S. government's about $70 billion.)

---

[25] International Monetary Fund. *International Financial Statistics*. Japan. Ministry of Finance. On Internet at http://www.mof.go.jp.

Figure 4. Monthly Changes in Japan's Yen-Dollar Exchange Rate and Foreign Exchange Reserves (Percent)
(X=Intervention to weaken a weakening yen,
O=Intervention to weaken a strengthening yen,
*=Intervention to strengthen a weakening yen.)

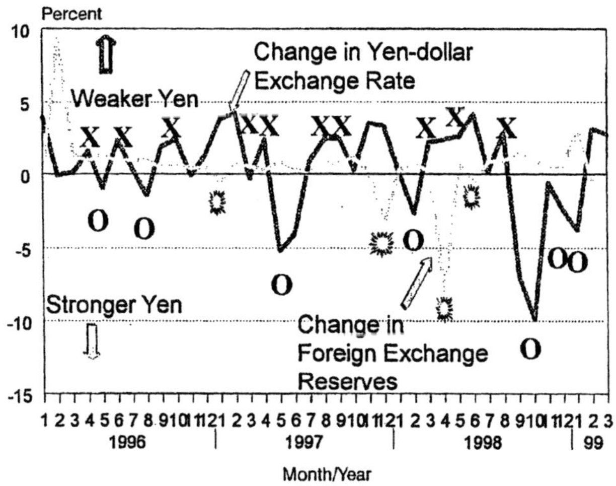

Source: Data from International Monetary Fund, Japan Ministry of Finance

If Japan's policy is to stabilize its exchange rate, changes in its holdings of foreign exchange and in the level of its exchange rate should move in opposite directions. When the yen is weakening, Japan should be selling foreign exchange (buying yen), and vice versa. IF, however, Japan is accumulating foreign exchange at the same time that its currency is weakening, it is pursuing a "cheap yen" policy. It is intervening in the market to further weaken the yen. In Figure 4, such policy episodes predominated during 1996 and into mid-1998. They are indicated by an X along the line showing changes in exchange rates. When Japan is accumulating foreign exchange at a time the yen is strengthening, it also is pursing a policy of weakening the yen. These episodes are indicated with an O and add to the episodes in which Japan pursued a "cheap yen" policy. The times are indicated by a * when Japan was selling dollars to strengthen its yen-which is the policy the United States was encouraging Japan to take during much of this period. These episodes occurred primarily after the onset of the Asian financial crisis (from mid-1997) and primarily after the value of the yen and dropped to levels that threatened to further destabilize world markets. Even during the Asian crisis, however, Japan has, at times, reported net increases in foreign exchange reserves. After intervening in foreign exchange markets to strengthen the yen by selling $17.8 billion in foreign exchange in April 19987, the Bank of Japan added foreign exchange reserves in ten of the next twelve months to bring its total holding of foreign exchange back to the level of $223 billion in April 1999-the amount Japan held before the April 1998 sales.[26]

From the standpoint of economic efficiency, excessive volatility in the exchange rate adds risk, makes investment analysis more difficult, and may reduce economic growth.

---

[26] Data on Japan's Foreign Exchange Reserves are available from Japan's Ministry of Finance on the Internet at <http://www.mof.go.jp/English/gaijun>.

For U.S. exporters to Japan, for example, the depreciation of the yen from 80 yen per dollar in 1995 to 146 yen per dollar in June 1998, was equivalent to Japan's imposing an 82% tariff on imports from the United States.

Twin Deficits. A focus on the savings and investment identity also may produce policy prescriptions that can be incomplete. For example, in the 1970s and the 1980s, the United States experienced so-called twin deficits. A sizable volume of economic and popular literature pointed out that the dissavings of the federal government in the form of its budget deficit was generating a twin in the form of a rising U.S. trade deficit. In order to reduce the trade deficit, the policy prescription was that the Untied States should look beyond trade policy and put its resources instead into increasing its savings rate. (This led to a 1989 policy proposal by Japan in trade negotiations with the Untied States, for example, that in order to reduce the U.S. trade deficit, Americans should curtail their reliance on credit cards.[27])

How valid is the twin deficit connection?[28] An econometric analysis indicates that for industrial countries, budget deficits indeed were positively correlated with current-account deficits over the 1976-1985 period. Over the 1986-1990 period, however, that correlation evaporated.[29] In the mid-1990s for the United States and Japan, the two deficits are negatively correlated and moving in opposite directions. The U.S. budget deficit has shrunk and its turning into a surplus, while the U.S. trade deficit has been rising. Japan's budget deficit is rising, while the country runs a ballooning trade surplus.

Although U.S. government budget deficits do reduce national savings and may induce U.S. borrowing from abroad, a lower budget deficit does not imply a lower trade deficit. In addition to federal government dissavings (deficits), private, business, and local government savings also come into play. The conclusion now seems to be that the twin deficits certainly are not Siamese, identical, or even fraternal and are useful for policy purposes only as a generality.

Intertemporal Savings and Investment. Another area in which the traditional macroeconomic approach to the trade deficit is being extended is to consider the effects of international borrowing on variables such as productivity and consumption at different time periods. If American citizens, for example, a re borrowing from abroad to finance current purchases, they must be doing so according to some valuation of future versus current consumption.

According to a review of economic literature on the intertemporal approach to the current account, economic models that fail to integrate investment, saving, and growth make it virtually impossible to understand persistent current account imbalances. Why, for example, are the current accounts of Canada and Australia perennially in deficit while that of Japan is in surplus despite wide swings in their real exchange rates? The standard macroeconomic approach to trade deficits, moreover, offers no valid benchmark for reevaluating the size of external imbalances. The International Monetary Fund in its

---

27 Frankel, Jeffrey A. The SII Outcome: In Whose Best Interest? *The International Economy*, October/November 1990. p. 70.

28 For a discussion of this issue, see: CRS Report 97-985, *Why the Budget Deficit and the Trade Deficit Haven't Been Moving Together*, by Gail E. Makinen.

29 Obstfeld, Maurice and Kenneth Rogoff. The Intertemporal Approach to the Current Account. *In Handbook of International Economics*, Vol. III, Edited by G. Grossman and K. Rogoff. New York, Elsevier Science, 1995. p. 1763.

dealing with currency crises considers a current account deficit that exceeds 5% of gross domestic product to be a warning signal that the deficit may be unsustainable.[30] But that observation is based more on experience than on theory. In practice, policymakers usually just strive to avoid a negative current account. In considering trade across time periods, however, efficiency often calls for an unbalanced current account (as explained below).[31]

One recent approach to this problem is to treat the international borrowing to fund a current account deficit in terms of standard investment analysis. A current account deficit represents the borrowing against future output in order to purchase more goods and services today (which generates a trade deficit). This potentially could burden future generations with lower consumption in order to repay the debts being incurred today. In standard cost-benefit analysis, this borrowing would be justified if it results in enough consumption being made available in the future to offset borrowing costs (interest rates).

For a nation, rigorous cost-benefit analysis of all international borrowing is not feasible. Capital flows occur because of both pull and push factors. Although inflows of capital may be conceptually equivalent to international borrowing, foreign investors may have their capital "pushed" into the U.S. market for a variety of reasons, including considerations of political risk, which may be unrelated to differences in interest rates or other borrowing criteria.

A stylized approach to assessing whether trade deficits are "good" or "bad," however, is to examine how a deficit in trade and corresponding imports of capital (borrowing) are used. If the capital imports are employed to increase productivity (e. g. used to buy capital equipment) that will bolster economic growth, the capital imports and corresponding trade deficit may be considered to be "good."[32] If the international borrowing is used to finance current consumption, it is considered to be "bad" (in the sense that future consumption will be lower that it other wise would be). The logic of this analysis is similar to that for an individual. If the individual is borrowing to finance investments in productive assets (e. g. an education, automobile for commuting to work, or preventive medical care) that tend to increase productivity and earned income, it may be considered to be "good." However, if the individual is borrowing merely to increase current consumption (e. g. vacation travel, clothes, or entertainment), it may be considered to be "bad."[33]

---

30 Sugisaki, Shigemitsu. The Global Financial System: Status Report. Address at the 11th Conference of the International Federation of Business Economists, Vancouver, Canada, November 18, 1977

31 Obstfeld, Maurice and Kenneth Rogoff. The Intemporal Approach to the Current Account. In *Handbook of International Economics*, Vol. III, Edited by G. Grossman and K. Rogoff. New York, Elseiver Science, 1995. p. 1793-94.

32 In a strict sense, the rate of return on the investment should exceed the interest paid on capital borrowed from abroad.

33 Lippens, Robert E. Are Trade Deficits That Bad? *Business Economics*, April 1977, vol. 32. p. 14-19. See also: CRS Report 98-508 E, *U.S. Trade Balance: AN Analysis of Recent Trends and Policy Options*, by Craig K. Elwell.

Figure 5. U. S. Imports of Merchandise by Major End-use Category, 1990-97

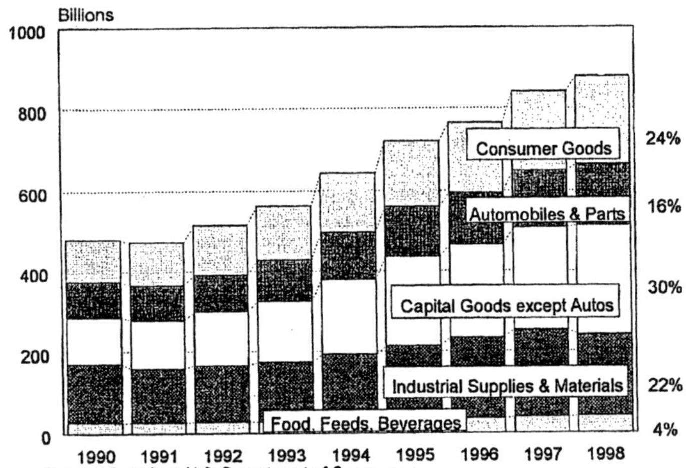

Source: Data from U.S. Department of Commerce

Note: The category of "Other Goods" is not shown (4% in 1998).

As shown in Figure 5., U.S. imports of capital goods (excluding automobiles) have been rising. In 1998, they accounted for 30% of total merchandise imports, up from 23% in 1990. Imports of automobiles, some of which are capital goods, but most of which are consumer durables, eased somewhat from 18% to 16%, while consumer goods grew form 19% to 24%. In dollar amounts, imports of capital goods (excluding automobiles) rose by $154 billion (from $116 billion in 1990 to $270 billion in 1998), while the U.S. current account deficit rose by $141 billion (from $92 billion in 1990 to $233 billion in 1998). IN the 1990s, therefore, imports of capital goods have increased by more that the current account deficit, and capital goods imports have been growing both absolutely and as a percent of total merchandise imports. In this sense, the capital borrowing from abroad seems to have been used to finance productivity-enhancing investments. Consumption imports, however, still are quite large.

The intertemporal approach to the current account deficit does provide one policy implication that most developing nations have implemented. That is, if tariffs are imposed they should fall on consumption and not capital goods.

This approach may indicate to policymakers whether a country is "squandering" the capital being imported to purchase current consumption goods, but it does not provide policy tools to determine the optimal size of a nation's current account deficit. The United States may be borrowing to enhance future economic growth, but are we becoming too reliant on foreign capital? The intertemporal approach has not yet developed to the point that it can indicate to policymakers whether or not a chronic current account deficit can be sustained.

SUSTAINABILITY OF THE TRADE DEFICIT

In the U.S. current account deficit sustainable? Is the United States likely to encounter a situation in which investors lose confidence in dollar-denominated assets and dump them thereby causing a rapid depreciation in the value of the dollar and a currency crisis similar to that experienced by Mexico in 1995 and countries of Asia in 1997 and 1998? This depends on whether the U.S. economy will be able to generate the resources necessary to repay the funds borrowed from abroad.

First, it should be noted that even though the U.S. trade deficit has reached the $200 –billion level, the current account deficit is less at $155 billion primarily because of the U.S. surplus in services trade. As a percent of total U.S. consumption, moreover, the trade deficit at about 3% is down from the 5% in the mid-1980s. The current accounts a percent of gross domestic product also is comparably lower. The U.S. current account deficit is not currently at the 5%-of-GDP level considered to be a danger sign in international financial markets.

Second, it should also be noted that the foreign investments in the Untied States have grown to the point that in 1997 foreign investors in the U.S. market earned $5.3 billion more than Americans earned on their investments abroad.

Concern over the sustainability of the U.S. current account deficit was recently stated by Alan Greenspan, the Chairman of the Federal Reserve:

> A more distant concern, but one that cannot be readily dismissed, is the very condition that has enabled the surge in American household and business demands to help sustain global stability: our rising trade and current account deficits. There is a limit to how long and how far deficits can be sustained, since current account deficits add to net foreign claims on the Untied States. It is very difficult to judge at what point debt service costs become unduly burdensome and can no longer be sustained. There is no evidence at this point that markets are disinclined to readily finance our foreign net imbalance. But the arithmetic of foreign debt accumulation and compounding interest costs does indicate somewhere in the future that, unless reversed, our growing international imbalances are apt to create significant problems for our economy.[34]

In essence, whether the United States can sustain its current account deficit over the foreseeable future depends on whether foreigners are willing to increase their investments in U.S. assets. In short, the current account deficit puts the economic fortunes of the country partially in the hands of foreign investors. Foreign investment in the United States takes two primary forms: direct investment necessary to do business in the U.S. market and portfolio investment to take advantage of higher rates of return in the United States. The latter includes short-term speculative funds that are seeking higher quality markets because of instability abroad and bank deposits.

[3ca4] Greenspan, Alan. *The American economy in a World Context.* Remarks at the 35th Annual Conference on Bank Structure and Competition of the Federal Reserve Bank of Chicago, Chicago, Illinois. May 6, 1999. On the Internet at http://www.bog.frb.fed.us/boarddocs/speeches/1999/19990506.htm.

As shown in Figure 6., net inflows of capital into the United States have more than offset the recent U.S. current account deficit. Net capital flows and the current account tend to mirror each other. (In 1997, net capital inflows were $225 billion while the current account was only --$155 billion because of a -$100 billion statistical discrepancy. This discrepancy has trended toward larger negative numbers. It went from $25 billion in 1989 to $1 billion in 1994, to -$60 billion in 1996, and -$100 billion in 1997.)

Capital inflows include official reserve assets, other government assets, and private assets. Private assets dominate the capital flows. In 1997, of the total $733.4 billion in capital inflows, $717.6 billion was in private assets (of which $93.4 billion was in direct investments, $171.5 billion in Treasury securities and currency, $196.8 billion in U.S. private sector securities, $107.8 billion in nonbanking assets, and $148.1 billion in banking assets). For capital outflows the story is similar. Of the total $478.5 billion in capital outflows, private assets accounted for $477.7 billion (of which $121.8 billion was indirect investments, $88.0 billion in foreign securities, $120.4 billion in other nonbanking assets, and $147.4 billion in banking assets).[35]

Figure 6. Net Capital Flows (Government and Private) and Current Account Balances for the United States, 1965-97

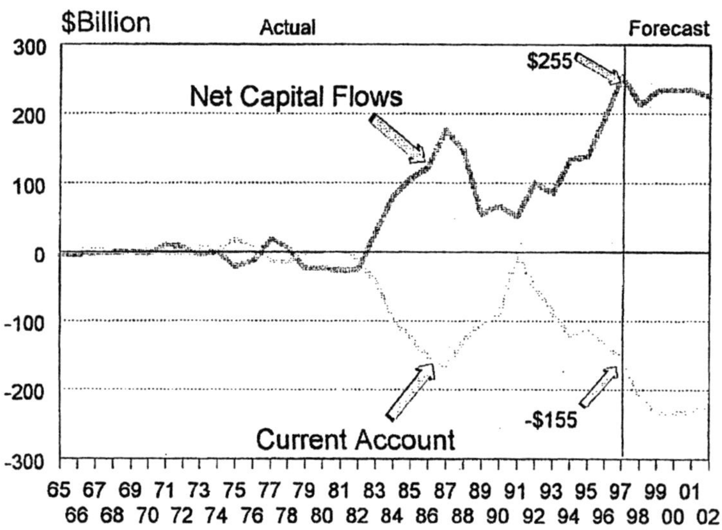

Source: U.S. Bureau of Economic Analysis. Forecast by Standard and Poor's DRI

In terms of private assets, foreign direct investment inflows and outflows tend to offset each other. In 1997, the inflow of foreign direct investment of $93.4 billion was more than offset by .S. direct investment abroad of $121,8 billion. In terms of financing the U.S. trade deficit, direct investment is attractive because it is more stable than portfolio investment. Foreign companies and actual plant and equipment in the United

---

[35] U.S. Bureau of Economic Analysis. *Survey of Current Business*, July 1998. p. 68-69.

States are here somewhat permanently. Foreign owners cannot easily move them out of the U.S. market.

Portfolio investment in securities and equities is much more volatile and depends on relative rates of return, behavior of stock markets, relative interest rates, economic stability, and other variables. In the mid-1990s, the booming U.S. stock market combined with relatively high interest rates and currency instability in Asia to attract considerable capital to the United States. (In mid-June 1998, the U.S. three-month money market rate was 5.6% as compared with 0.4% in Japan, 1.9% in Switzerland, 3.6% in Germany, 3.8% in France, and 5.1% in Italy.) For now, U.S. capital markets are appealing, but as Asian countries discovered during their financial crises, capital can be fickle. It can flow out as fast as it flows in.

How much longer the United States can attract $150 to $250 billion per year in net capital inflows in order to finance its trade deficit is an important question. Net foreign purchases of U.S. Treasury securities have been running at an annual rate of about $150 billion in 1996 and 1997. This almost equals the U.S. current account deficit. According to one analyst, the continuation of the current account deficit and strong dollar-and, hence, of the sequence of happy non-inflationary years with domestic demand growing faster than the trend rate of GDP growth-depends on foreigners' willingness to purchase U.S. Treasuries at a rate equal to about 2 percent of the American gross domestic product. The author concludes that recent trends in the American balance of payments, and-more specifically – in the financing of the current account deficit, are "clearly unsustainable." He reasons that foreign and international investors already own such as high percentage of the U.S. national debt that they will not continue purchasing it at current levels. He warns that in a decade foreign investors could end up owning all the U.S. national debt.[36]

One factor working in the favor of the United States in terms of capital flows is that the dollar has become a key world currency. It is used abroad for the same reasons that it is used at home: as a unit of account, a medium of exchange, and a store of value. Foreigners are willing to purchase U.S. paper currency (which pays no interest) for use in international transactions. As of 1996, the U.S. Treasury estimated that $209.6 billion in U.S. currency (primarily $100 notes) was circulating abroad.

The use of dollars as a key currency, moreover, means that American foreign borrowing can be denominated in dollars rather than in a foreign currency. Even if the value of the dollar falls on exchange markets, the dollar amount of U.S. borrowing does not change. This is quite a different situation from that of Indonesia, South Korea, or Mexico. As the value of their currencies fell, the amount of their foreign debt, which was denominated in dollars and other foreign currencies, rose.

Foreign and international investors also invest their capital in U.S. equity and property markets. Over 1996-97, U.S. equity markets attracted between $100 billion and $200 billion per year from abroad. In the future, whether these markets can keep pulling in such amounts, plus absorb, more of the funds that have been flowing into Treasury securities, is an open question. Much of the recent influx of foreign capital into Treasury securities, U.S. equity markets, or even U.S. bank accounts has been induced by the

---

36 Congdon, Tim. Treasury Warning. *The International Economy*, July/August 1998. p. 34-35. (Actually , foreign purchases of U.S. Treasury securities plus currency amounted to about 2% of U.S. gross domestic product in 1996 and 1997.)

Asian financial crisis and threat of contagion in Eastern Europe and Latin America. Finance capital has been leaving other countries because of instability there. There has been a "flight to quality" despite countermeasures by countries, such as South Korea, that have raised domestic interest rates to levels as high as 20 to 40%.. Once the Asian financial crisis eases, however, some of this capital likely will flow back to these Asian and other nations.

Figure 7. U.S. Foreign and Federal Debt and Foreign Assets in the United States, 1991-2002 (forecast)

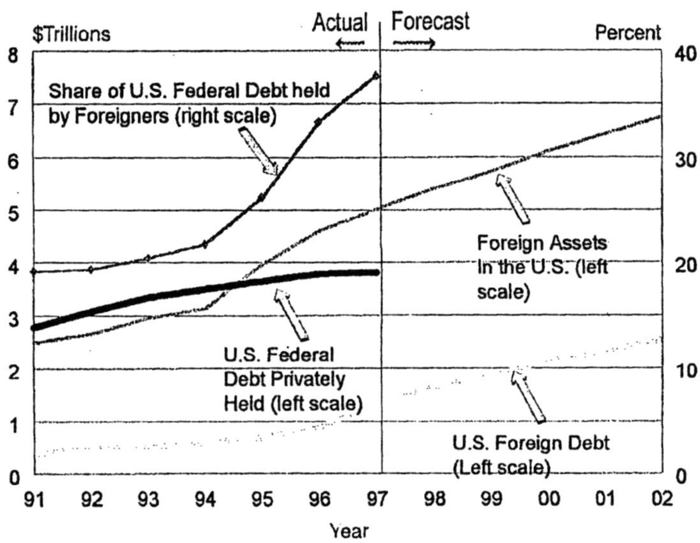

Sources: U.S. Federal Reserve. U.S. Department of Commerce. Forecast from Standard and Poor's DRI

The Standard and Poor's DRI projection of the U.S. current account deficit and net inflows of capital are both at about $230 billion from 1999 to the year 2002. As shown in Figure 7, this implies an increase in the foreign indebtedness of the Untied States of about a trillion dollars every four or five years. The foreign debt (net international investment position of the United States with the sign reversed) has already risen from $355 in 1991 to $1,328 billion in 1997. Following the Standard and Poor's DRI forecast, this position would deteriorate to $2,131 billion in the year 2000 and to $2,543 billion in the year 2002. This implies that U.S. foreign debts as a percent of U.S. gross domestic product would have risen from 16.4% in 1997 to about 25% in 2002. Foreign assets in the United States likewise have already surged about 25% in 2002. Foreign assets in the United States likewise have already surged from $2,487 billion in 1991 to $4,993 billion in 1997. IF current trends continue, they are forecast to reach $6,745 billion by 2002 (or about 67% of the $10,076 billion forecast for U.S. GDP).

One question is where this inflow of foreign investment would be directed. The total U.S. privately held federal debt rose to $3,393 billion in 1997, but its level has stabilized as the federal budget is beginning to generate a surplus. Purchases of federal securities by foreigners, however, have continued. As a percent of total federal debt privately held, the share held by foreigners rose from 19% in 1991 to 38% in 1997. If foreign holdings of U.S. federal debt continue to rise at $100 to $200 billion per year, by the year 2002, between 47% and 67% could be held by foreigners. The question is whether this level would be acceptable to the American people or to foreign investors and lenders. For Americans, this is primarily a political question. For foreign investors, this is primarily an economic question.

Looking forward into the next century, it is unlikely that net capital inflows into the United States will continue at their unusually high rates of 1996-98. The Standard and Poor's DRI forecast merely extrapolates current rends. If the high rates of capital inflows do not continue, the U.S. current account deficit also will have to decline. Put another way, if the United States is able to reduce its trade deficit, its borrowing needs also would decline.

TRADE AND JOBS

Considerable controversy exists as to the effects of imports and exports on American jobs and wages. Most mainstream economists assert that international trade results primarily in reallocation of jobs from less efficient to more efficient industries rather than particular job gains or losses for the economy as a whole. This argument was recently stated by Alan Greenspan as follows:

It is difficult to find credible evidence that trade has impacted the level of total employment in this country over the long run. Indeed, we are currently experiencing the widest trade deficit in history with a level of unemployment close to record lows.

Certainly, the distribution of jobs by industry is affected by international trade, but is also affected by domestic trade. It is the relative balance of supply and demand in a competitive market economy that determines the mix of employment. When exports fall or imports rise, domestic demand and relative prices have invariably adjusted in the long run to leave total employment relatively unaffected. As economists like to say, all imports are eventually paid for with exports.[37]

Other studies, however, indicate that the trade deficit may have an impact on U.S. potential employment. One study, for example, concluded that because of the Asian financial crisis, many of the Asia countries affected are attempting to export their way out of their problems. The resulting $100 billion increase in the U.S. trade deficit could destroy 1.1 million U.S. jobs. The losses would occur in every state, mostly in the manufacturing sector, where, even if interest rates are lowered enough to stave off a

---

[37] Greenspan, Alan. *Trade and Technology.* Remarks before the Alliance for the Commonwealth, Conference on International Business, Boston, Massachusetts. June 2, 19999. On internet at http://www.bog.frb.fed.us/boarddocs/speeches/1999/199990602.htm.

jump in unemployment, 600,000 jobs would be shifted from the high-wage manufacturing to the lower-paying service sector.[38]

As for the North America Free-Trade Agreement, a 1998 study of its effect on employment over the four-and-one-half years if had been implemented concluded that NAFTA had primarily served to accelerate trade, plant relocation, and sectoral job gains and losses that were already ongoing. Approximately 191, 000 primary jobs had been certified by the U.S. Department of Labor in 1,638 plants as potentially threatened by increased imports or plant relocations to Mexico or Canada. Apparel and electronics accounted for 40% of the NAFTA certifications. These potential job losses, however, were balanced by an estimated 680,000 net job gains in the U.S. economy from increased exports to Mexico and Canada since NAFTA took effect. This study did not, however, attempt to estimate net job gains foregone arising from increased imports from Canada and Mexico because there can be no net job losses as long as U.S. output and employment continue to rise.[39] Another study, however, estimated that over the first three years of NAFTA, the reduction in net exports to Canada and Mexico had eliminated 167, 172 American job opportunities, and in total, NAFTA had resulted in a net loss of 394,835 jobs.[40] This area of job losses and gains from trade agreements seems to be one in which data and methods of analysis are still being developed.

CONCLUSION

This brief survey of the U.S. trade deficit and the theory and policies surrounding it indicates that this field of economics is evolving. Recently, some basis economic theory has been called into question as empirical studies fail to validate long accepted theoretical linkages. The policy implications with respect to trade have developed from the prescription that free trade is optimal to one that allows, for example, for strategic trade policy aimed at assisting certain industries-particularly those in high-technology. A strategic trade policy, however, comes with a new set of pitfalls.

The macroeconomic approach to explaining the trade deficit is encountering some obstacles. Many seemingly straightforward theoretical linkages, for example, have not been empirically established. In particular, studies have not been able to link macroeconomic conditions to short- and medium-term changes in a nation's exchange rate. Also, studies have found that changes in exchange rates do not translate completely into price changes for imports and exports. This implies that in order for exchange depreciation to eliminate a trade deficit, it must overshoot the equilibrium rate by quite a margin. This brings other inefficiencies into an economy.

Many nations regularly intervene in foreign exchange markets and influence the values of their currencies. Recent weakness in the Japanese yen, for example, has been

---

[38] Scott, Robert E. and Jesse Rothstein. *American Jobs and the Asian Crisis: The Employment Impact of the Coming Rise in the U.S. Trade Deficit.* Washington, Economic Policy Institute, 1998. 13 p.

[39] CRS Report 98-783 E. *NAFTA: Estimates of Job Effects ad Industry Trade Trends After 4 _ Years,* by Mary Jane Bolle.

[40] Rothstein, Jesse and Robert Scott. NAFTA's Casualties, Employment Effects on Men, Women, and Minorities. Economic Policy Institute Issue Brief No. 120. September 19, 1997.

exacerbated by the Japanese government's intervention into exchange markets. The Untie States, however, has no announced exchange rate policy nor does it have a transparent method of determining when it should intervene in currency markets.

The inability of macroeconomic theory to explain even simple exchange rate movements raises questions about the standard interpretation of international trade policies. If exchange rates do not reflect either underlying trade flows or macroeconomic variables (such as interest rates), then the standard macroeconomic conclusion that export promotion or import protection is negated completely by market forces is subject to challenge. A country might be able to erect trade barriers or promote exports without eliciting a major response from exchange markets. U.S. commitments under the World Trade Organization and other trade agreements, however, preclude unilateral protectionist measures or excessive export promotion activity.

The demand effects of import protection or export promotion, however, are well established in empirical studies of the economy. Trade policies that reduce imports or increase exports provide a stimulus to the domestic economy that usually causes domestic production to rise. This, in turn, brings in more imports which offset, to some extent, the reduction in imports or increase in exports resulting from the trade policies. Also well established in economic studies are the benefits to competing U.S. producers and harm done to the American consumer from higher prices and narrower choice resulting form import protection policies.

The macroeconomic approach also is being extended to account for why the Untied States may be borrowing from abroad and how those funds are being used. Trade data indicate that a rising share of U.S. imports has been of capital goods that should increase U.S. productivity and growth in the future. Treating foreign borrowing with the same methods used to evaluate domestic borrowing might determine an optimal level for the U.S. current account deficit. This has not yet been done, however.

In terms of sustainability, it is difficult to see that the historically large capital inflows of 1996-1998 will continue into the next century. As the Asian financial crisis ebbs and world economies recover, some of the capital that has sought safety in U.S. markets likely will return abroad. If so, the U.S. trade and current account deficits of today will have to diminish. Put in opposite terms, if the U.S. trade deficit is reduced, the need for foreign borrowing also will decline.

The ability of the United States to continue to incur trade and current account deficits at the $200 billion level depends on the willingness of foreigners to lend and invest funds in the American market. The deficit, currently at roughly 3% of gross domestic product, is not at the danger-signal level of 5% of GDP used by the International Monetary Fund. But whether foreigners will continue to move capital to the American market, even if the foreign share of the U.S. federal debt rises to exceed 50% or if the level of foreign assets in the U.S. market increases to the equivalent of two-thirds of U.S. GDP, is both a political question for U.S. policymakers and an economic question for foreign investors. A further issue is whether net U.S. payments to foreign investors will continue to rise enough above their $22.5 billion in 1998 and whether they will offset capital inflows or become a burden to the U.S. economy.

Considerable controversy exists as to the effect of imports and exports on American jobs and wages. Mainstream economists assert that international trade results primarily in reallocation of jobs from less efficient to more efficient industries rather than particular job gains or losses for the economy as a whole. Other studies, however, document potential job losses in specific industries and point out that a rising trade deficit induces a shift of jobs from relatively high-wage manufacturing industries to the relatively lower-paying service sector.

TRADE WITH DEVELOPING COUNTRIES: TRENDS AND PROSPECTS

J. F. Hornbeck

ABSTRACT

This report focuses on changing U.S. trade relationships over the past decade, concentrating on the growing importance of developing country trade. It documents trends in developing country trade by region, country, and product, highlighting some economic implications of these changing trade patterns.

SUMMARY

Increased trade with developing countries has raised a number of policy issues for Congress. Foundational to the debate is understanding a recent trend in this trade growth. Although developed countries dominated the world trade scene for many years, this began to change as the developing world opted for more open economic policies. East Asia aggressively pushed export-oriented growth strategies (with active government support) in the 1960s, followed by Southeast Asia in the 1970s. By contrast, Latin America lagged, opting for closed economic policies until after the 1982 debt crisis, at which point the region began to liberalize trade policies on a broader and deeper scale.

Over the past decade, U.S. trade with developing countries has expanded markedly. From 1987 to 1997, developing country trade rose 195% (compared to 104% for trade with developed countries), increasing its share from 36% to 45% of total U.S. merchandise trade, yet remaining relatively small compared to U.S. gross domestic product (GDP).

Regionally, trade growth with the United States varies among Africa, Latin America, the Middle East, and Asia. Trade with Africa and the Middle East, for example, is very small, representing only 2.0% and 2.6% respectively of total U.S. trade in 1997 and declining slightly over the past decade as a portion of total U.S. trade. By comparison, trade growth with Latin America and the Caribbean (LAC), and Asia has been brisk, rising 149% and 197% respectively, higher than the average growth of U.S. trade with the world of 136%.

U.S. merchandise trade with developing countries ranges from agricultural and other natural resource-based products to manufactured goods of varying sophistication. Much developing country trade involves highly specialized manufacturing that results in production sharing, where U. S. firms send components and materials abroad for partial manufacture or assembly. The resulting product is then re-exported back to the United States for final sale or further production.

Increasingly, trade growth between the United States and developing countries reflects this greater specialization, which allows developing countries to assume the relatively low-skill labor-intensive aspects of the production, process, with the relatively high-skill and capital-intensive aspects of the production process done in the United States. These changing economic relationships are at the heart of the trade policy debate because they raise questions over the broader economic implications of the United States having to adjust to these changing production patterns. Given that trade with developing countries is expected to continue to grow, within limits, these questions are likely to drive much of the trade debate in the future.

*****

By any measure, world trade has expanded dramatically over the past half century. In fact, growth in world trade has eclipsed production, pointing to the increasing importance of trade in the global economy.[1] An important aspect of this growth is that although developed countries are still the dominant world traders, the developing world appears to be catching up.[2] This trend is evident with U.S. trade patterns as well, which reveal closer economic ties with the developing world.

Trade with developing countries is one of many issues subsumed under the catchall phrase "globalization." Uncertainties over the significance of changing U.S. trade patterns in manifested in the ongoing, and frequently stalemated, debate over U.S. trade policy. Labor and environmental issues specific to developing countries, for example, have hindered passage of fast-track trade negotiation authority, extension of the North American Free Trade Agreement (NAFTA) to Chile, and most recently, the Africa trade bill. This report focuses on changing U.S. trade relationships over the past decade, concentrating on the growing importance of developing country trade and some related economic implications.

---

[1] This is not an altogether new trend, but reflect a return to pre-World War I trade levels following the high tariff inter-war period. See: Krugman, Paul. Growing World Trade: Causes and Consequences. *Brookings Papers on Economic Activity*. No. 1. 1995, p. 330.

[2] The U.S. Department of Commerce, *Foreign Trade Highlights,* defines U.S. developed country trading partners as Canada, Japan, Australia, New Zealand, the Republic of South Africa, and all Western European countries. All others are developing countries.

GROWTH IN WORLD TRADE

Two pivotal factors fostered the growth in world trade following World War II: 1) recovery and expansion of the industrial economies and; 2) liberalization of trade rules under the General Agreement on Tariffs and Trade (GATT)[3] and other arrangements. Developed countries dominated the trade scene for many years, but this began to change when the developing world opted for more open trade and investment policies. East Asia aggressively pushed export-oriented growth strategies (with active government support) in the 1960s, followed by Southeast Asia in the 1970s. Latin America lagged, opting for closed economic policies until after the 1982 debt crisis, at which point the region began to liberalize trade policies on a broader and deeper scale.

The expansion of global trade may be seen in **table 1,** which tracks average annual growth in gross domestic product (GDP) and merchandise trade since 1960. For this table, developing countries are split between middle- and low-income countries as defined by the World Bank. High income countries refer mostly to the developed world, but also include some industrialized developing countries such as Singapore, Hong Kong, and Korea. For high-income countries, trade growth exceeded output in each of the four decades, as countries in this group traded mostly among themselves in an increasingly liberalized trade environment. Data for low-and middle-income countries tell a different story. Trade and production growth were nearly even during the 1960s, with a large disparity in trade performance between middle-income and the poorest countries during the 1970s.

Table 1. Average Annual Growth in World Production and Trade, 1960-1995. (in percent – countries grouped by income level)

GDP Growth	1961-70	1970-80	1980-90	1990-95
High Income	5.1	3.0	3.2	2.0
Middle Income	6.0	5.6	1.9	0.1
Low Income	4.6	4.5	6.0*	6.8*
Trade Growth	1960-70 (EX/IM)	1970-80 (EX/IM)	1980-90 (EX/IM)	1990-95 EX/IM)
High Income	8.5/9.5	5.4/4.4	5.2/6.2	5.4/4.6
Middle Income	5.4/6.4	4.1/4.8	2.6/-0.2	6.9/11.0
Low Income	4.9/5.3	-07/2.4	5.3/1.6*	8.3/13.0*

EX=exports, IM=imports

*China skews these data upward significantly.

Source: Table prepared by CRS, data from the World Bank, *World Development Report*, 1983 and 1997.

These data also reflect the poor economic performance by middle-income countries during the 1980s. Note that imports fell dramatically, as did output, reflective in part of

[3] Now the World Trade Organization (WTO).

the 1982 Latin American debt crisis. Low-income countries appeared to do much better, but their relatively poor economic and trade performance during the 1980s is masked in the aggregate data by the highly robust performance of China. Many of these countries are still struggling in the 1990s, as are other "transitional" countries in Central and Eastern Europe. Nonetheless, the effect of the most recent push toward trade liberalization can be seen in the growth of both exports and imports in the 1990s for all countries.

Changes in the trade policies of developing countries should be reflected in their rising share of global trade. Indeed, developed countries dominated global trade in the years following World War II, peaking around 1970 when they captured some 75% of world trade. Their share fell to a low of 66% by 1980, but rose again to 73% in the late 1980s as many developing countries struggled with economic problems. The latest round of economic opening in Eastern Europe and Latin America, and strong economic growth by some large traders such as China, fueled expansion of developing countries as seen by developed country trade falling to only 67% of world trade in 1997.[4] This most recent trend toward the growing importance of developing country trade appears in U.S. trade statistics as well.

PATTERNS OF U.S. TRADE WITH DEVELOPING COUNTRIES

U.S. merchandise trade with developing countries has become a hot policy issue largely because of its dramatic growth in recent years, both in absolute terms and relative to trade with developed countries (see **table 2**). Data for the most recent decade (1987 to 1997) indicated that total U.S. trade with developing countries rose from $237 billion to $698 billion, or 195% compared to 104% for trade with developed countries. U.S. exports to developing countries increased by 243% compared to 135% for developed countries. Import growth was some 167% for developing countries and 84% for developed countries.

[4] International Monetary Fund, *International Financial Statistics Yearbook,* various issues.

Table 2. U.S. Merchandise Trade, 1987 and 1997
($ billions)

	1987				1997			
Region	U.S. Export $	U.S. Imports	Trade Balance	Total Trade	U.S. Exports	U.S. Imports	Trade Balance	Total Trade
Developing Countries	87.4	149.3	-61.9	236.7	299.4	398.8	-99.4	698.2
Developed Countries	165.4	256.6	-91.2	422.0	388.2	471.1	-82.9	859.3
World Total	252.8	405.9	-153.1	658.7	687.6	869.9	-182.3	1,557.5
Developing Countries as % of Total	34.6	36.8	40.4	35.9	43.5	45.8	54.5	44.8

Source: Table prepared by CRS with the data from the U.S. Department of Commerce
*Totals vary slightly from figure 1.

Such growth suggests that U.S. trade patterns are shifting. Indeed, in 1987, developing country trade amounted to 36% of total U.S. merchandise trade; by 1997 this had grown to 45%. Throughout this period, the United States ran a trade deficit. Developing country trade represented about 40 of the U.S. trade deficit in 1987, but 55% by 1997. Although this growth points to dramatic shifts in trade, importantly, total imports from developing countries still amount to only 5% of U.S. gross domestic product (GDP).

Regional Patterns

Regionally, trade growth with the United States varies among Africa, Latin America, the Middle East, and Asia. Trade with Africa and the Middle East, for example, is very small, representing only 2.9% and 2.6% respectively of total U.S. trade in 1997 (data appear in appendix 1). In fact, these two areas have actually seen their portion of trade with the United States fall slightly over the past decade. It follows that the economic effects of trade with these regions is very small.

Figure 1. U. S. Direction of Total Trade, 1987 & 1997

(LAC = Latin America & Caribbean, not Mexico)

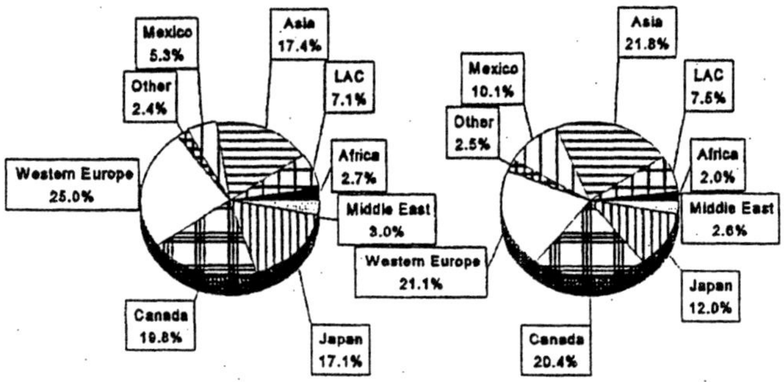

U.S. Trade 1987 (Total = $660 billion) U.S. Trade 1997 (Total = $1,558 billion)

By comparison, trade growth with Latin America and the Caribbean (LAC) and Asia has been quite significant. From 1987 to 1997, total U.S. trade with these regions grew by 149% and 197%, respectively, higher than the average growth of U.S. trade with the world of 136%. Note that for the purpose of comparing developing countries on a regional level, Japan is excluded from the Asian data, and LAC excludes Mexico, which as our third largest trading partner, skews the trade data for the region and so deserves separate attention. U.S. export growth to both regions has exceeded import growth over this time. U.S. exports to LAC grew by 209% and to Asia by 258%, whereas U.S. imports expanded by 103% and 169%, respectively. As shown in appendix 1, in 1997 the United States had a trade surplus of $9 billion with LAC and a trade deficit of $86 billion with Asia.

In addition to growth in trade, **figure 1** presents another way to look at the relative importance of U.S. trading partners. Asia and LAC again emerge as the dominate developing country trading regions. In 1997, Asia (less Japan) represented 22% of total U.S. trade, slightly more than Canada (the largest U.S. trading partner) or Western Europe. LAC trade was much smaller at 7.5% of the total, less in fact than Mexico as a single country, but more than triple the amount of trade with either the Middle East or Africa. Interestingly, Japan and Western Europe constituted a smaller percentage of total global trade with the United States in 1997 than a decade earlier, Canada remained about the same, and Mexico, LAC, and Asia showed the largest growth in relation to total U.S. trade with the world.

Table 3. Top Ten U.S. Developing Country Trading Partners, 1997 ($millions)

Developing Country	U.S. Exports	U.S. Imports	Trade Balance	Total Trade	1987 Total Trade	% Change 1987-97
Mexico	71,378	85,830	(14,452)	157,208	34,853	351.1%
China	12,805	62,552	(49,747)	73,357	9,790	669.7%
Taiwan	20,388	32,624	(12,236)	53,012	32,035	65.5%
South Korea	25,067	23,159	1,908	48,226	25,086	92.2%
Singapore	17,727	20,067	(2,340)	37,794	10,254	268.6%
Malaysia	10,828	18,017	(7,189)	28,845	4,818	498.7%
Brazil	15,912	9,630	6,282	25,542	11,905	114.5%
Hong Kong	15,115	10,297	4,818	25,412	13,837	83.7%
Venezuela	6,608	13,449	(6,841)	20,057	9,165	118.8%
Thailand	7,357	12,595	(5,238)	19,952	3,7644	430.1%
Subtotal	203,185	288,220	(85,035)	491,405	157,494	212.0%
All Other	484,413	581,654	(97,241)	1,066,067	502,869	112.0%
World Total	687,598	869,874	(182,276)	1,557,472	660,363	135.8%

Source: Table prepared by CRS from data provided by the U.S. Department of Commerce.

Country Patterns

Table 3 lists the top ten developing country trading partners of the United States, ranked in descending order by total trade. All ten countries are either in Asia or Latin America, with Asia accounting for seven countries and 59% of the total trade in this group. In 1997, these were clearly the fastest growing and most important developing country trade partners of the United States; collectively they accounted for 32% of total U.S. trade and 70% of trade with the developing world.

Within regions, certain countries tend to dominate trade. Mexico stands alone with fully 10% of total U.S. trade and over twice the trade volume of the number two country, China. In 1997, China, however, accounted for 27% of the U.S. trade deficit. The United States exports relatively little to China so the bilateral trade deficit equaled 66% of total U.S. –China trade. The U.S. trade deficit wit Mexico, buy contrast, was relatively small and amounted to only 9% of the bilateral trade, which historically is actually quite high and a lingering result of Mexico's struggle to recover from the economic downturn following the 1994 peso devaluation.[5]

After China, the next three largest developing country trading partners in 1997 were three of the four East Asian Newly Industrialized Countries (NICs): Taiwan, South Korea, and Singapore (the fourth is Hong Kong). Together the three accounted for approximately 9% of total U.S. trade. The U.S. had trade deficits with Taiwan and

[5] For more detail on Mexico, see: CRS Report 97-811 E, *NAFTA, Mexican Trade Policy, and U.S. –Mexico Trade: A Longer Term Perspective*, by J. F. Hornbeck.

Singapore and a trade surplus with South Korea. Brazil and Venezuela are the only LAC countries in the top ten list, accounting for 3% of U.S. trade. As a whole for 1997, the top three developing country trading partners (Mexico, China, and Taiwan) constituted 18% of total U.S. trade (41% of developing country trade), but accounted for 43% of the U.S. trade deficit, or most of the trade deficit (78%) with the developing world. The current financial crises that beset many of the East Asian countries is only expected to increase these bilateral trade deficits for some time.

To summarize, Asia and Latin America are the most important areas on which to focus any analysis on developing country trade. Within these regions, Mexico, China, Taiwan, Sough Korea, and Singapore dominate the trade trends. Significantly, most trade specialists agree that the trend toward growing U.S. trade with the developing world is expected to continue, if not accelerate.

Product Patterns

U.S. merchandise trade with developing economies varies. Given that the top five developing countries dominate the trade data, it is instructive to separate their product trade into different groups based on the amount and type of trade. Except for China, the top five developing country trading partners have trade patterns with the United States that appear to be similar in some ways with developed countries. Products include sophisticated manufactures in addition to natural-resource based goods. Trade data at this point need to be disaggregated further because the economic implications of this distinction are important.[6]

U.S. Exports. As a simple typology of U.S. exports to developing countries, consider two distinct groups of products and a third group based on production sharing. In each case, the specific product may vary with each country based on the country's demand, level of development, and degree of integration with the United States and the world trading system.

First, there are relatively sophisticated manufactured products. These include primarily integrated circuits, computers, aircraft, office-machines, and parts to all the above. Data for 1997 show that the dollar value of U.S. exports to the five largest developing country markets were mostly from three Harmonized System (HS) categories: 85-electrical machinery; 84-machinery; and 88-aircraft and parts. They accounted for some 50% of U.S. exports to the four Asian countries and 37% of exports to Mexico. Machinery and electrical machinery were the top two export categories for the Asian markets and Mexico. Aircraft and parts were in the top three for all countries except Mexico, where automobiles ranked third.

Second, the United States exports agricultural commodities such as seeds, grains, and cereals for consumption. For example, the large export to Egypt is cereals, a commodity that also ranks fourth for Venezuela and the Dominican Republic. These product categories are not mutually exclusive. The less industrial developing countries also import sophisticated U.S. manufactured products.

---

[6] For product detail, see: CRS Report 97-183 E, *The U.S. Trade Deficit in Manufactures: The Rise of China and NAFTA*, by Dick K. Nanto.

A third category includes production sharing trade where U.S. firms send components and materials abroad for partial manufacture or assembly, with the resulting product re-exported back to the United States for final sale or further production. This group shares many products with the first category such as semiconductors and automobiles. Southeast Asia (particularly Malaysia) accounts for most for the production-shared trade in electronics, and Mexico for this type of trade in automobiles. Production sharing also extends to more simple assembly work such as textiles (clothing, shoes, other apparel) and medical supplies, where U.S. firms use labor in Mexico, the Caribbean (particularly the Dominican Republic), and many of the less industrialized developing countries.[7]

U.S. Imports. The import picture is more complicated, involving a greater number and diversity of products to the Untied States. Nonetheless, it is useful to consider U.S. imports from developing countries in the same basic categories as U.S. exports. As with exports, the specific product imported from abroad, varies depending on the natural resources and abilities of the exporting country, its level of development, and degree of openness and integration with the world economy.

U.S. merchandise imports from the more industrialized developing economies tend to be manufactured goods. Machinery and electrical machinery are the top two product groups imported from the top five developing country trading partners. They account for 44% of U.S. imports from these countries and 51% if China is excluded. The most sophisticated products (integrated circuits and motor vehicles) come from the East Asian NICs-Taiwan, Singapore, Hong Kong, and South Korea. U.S. imports of electrical machinery from Mexico and China, by contrast, consist of radio and television equipment, although the United States also imports motor vehicles and parts form Mexico. All countries send computers or computer components.

Developing countries also export to the United States textile and natural resource-based products such as: oil; seafood; coffee; spices; fruit; apparel; metals; and footwear. These products make up the remainder of U.S. imports from the more industrialized developing economies, but constitute the majority of merchandise imported from the less industrialized countries. For example, 15% of U.S. imports from China are toys and 12% are various types of footwear. Taiwan sends iron and steel products; Mexico, Colombia, and Venezuela export crude oil; and China, Malaysia, Thailand, Hong Kong, Brazil, Indonesia, Colombia, Costa Rica, and Honduras, along with many others, export textile apparel in various forms. Fruit, metals, and other natural resource products round out the list.

In many cases, manufacturing trade again reflects production sharing arrangements that although in place for some time, are expanding with greater specialization of global production. In 1996, U.S. production-shared goods were 13% of total imports from developing countries.[8] This number understates the total because many production-shared imports from Mexico enter the United States under provisions set out in the North

[7] For more on U.S. production sharing arrangements, see: United States International Trade Commission. *Production Sharing: Use of U.S. Components and Materials in Foreign Assembly Operations, 1993-1996.* USITC Publication 3077, December 1997.

[8] Ibid., pp. 2-5 and B-6.

American Free Trade Agreement (NAFTA) and are not counted under production sharing rules.[9]

Summary and Conclusions

U.S. trade with developing countries has grown. On one level, this represents changes in the trading environment (GATT and other trade liberalization efforts) that simply encourage greater exchange among countries. On another level, there is more to this trade growth than trade itself, such as changing investment and production patterns, which suggests that it is not only the size of trade with developing countries that raises policy issues, but also the effects of changing U.S. economic relationships related to this trade.

For example, the benefits of trade come largely through specialization of production. Increasingly, trade between developed and developing countries involves specialization below the final product level, where different stages of production may be done in different countries. This important form of specialization allows developing countries to assume the relatively low-skill labor-intensive aspects of the production process, such as computer wiring or semiconductor assembly, with the relatively high-skill and capital-intensive aspects of the production process, such as microprocessor design, done in the United States.

One economist aptly describes this process as "slicing up the value chain" in which a good is manufactured in various stages and locales, with an incremental portion of value added at each state. This process has contributed significantly to increased trade volume worldwide because a good's final value may be the product of efforts by many countries and show up in the trade data multiple times as intermediate goods are shipped among countries.[10] It is not surprising then, as seen in **table 3,** that with the exception of China, the developing countries with the highest growth in total trade with the United States (Malaysia, Thailand, Mexico, Singapore) have significant production sharing arrangements with U.S. firms.

These changing economic relationships imply that as firms adjust to take advantage of specialization driven by lower costs, the U.S. economy undergoes change. Such change is at the heart of the trade policy debate because it raises questions over the implications of the Untied States having to make the necessary adjustments, for example, workers and industries producing goods that compete with low-wage imports. Although not limitless, trade with developing countries will probably continue to grow, including greater use of production sharing, suggesting that these questions are likely to drive much of the trade debate in the future.[11]

---

[9] See: CRS Report 98-66 E, *Maquiladoras and NAFTA: The Economics of U.S.-Mexico Production Sharing and Trade*, by J. F. Hornbeck.

[10] Krugman, op. cit., pp. 333-36.

[11] See CRS Report 98-742 E, *Trade with Developing Countries: Effects on U.S. Workers*, by J.F. Hornbeck.

Appendix 1. U.S. Directions of Trade, 1987 and 1997
($ billions)

U.S. Exports	1987	1997	% Change 87-97
Western Europe	69.8	155.4	122.6%
Canada	59.8	150.1	151.0%
Mexico	14.6	71.4	389.0%
Japan	28.3	65.7	132.2%
LAC (not Mexico)	20.4	63.0	208.8%
Asia (not Japan)	35.5	127.1	258.0%
Middle East	9.5	20.9	120.2%
Africa	6.3	11.2	77.8%
Other	9.9	22.8	130.3%
World Total	254.1	687.6	170.6%
U.S. Imports	1987	1997	% change 87-97
Western Europe	95.6	172.9	80.9%
Canada	71.1	168.1	136.4%
Mexico	20.3	85.8	322.7%
Japan	84.6	121.4	43.5%
LAC (not Mexico)	26.5	53.7	102.6%
Asia (not Japan)	79.1	212.8	169.1%
Middle East	10.8	20.4	88.4%
Africa	11.9	10.8	66.4%
Other	6.4	15.0	134.4%
World Total	406.3	869.90	114.1%
Total Trade	1987	1997	% Change 87-97
Western Europe	165.4	328.3	98.5%
Canada	130.9	318.2	143.1%
Mexico	34.9	157.2	350.4%
Japan	112.9	187.1	65.7%
LAC (not Mexico)	46.9	116.7	148.8%
Asia (not Japan)	114.6	339.9	196.6%
Middle East	20.3	41.3	103.3%
Africa	18.2	31.0	70.3%
Other	16.3	37.8	131.0%
World Total	660.4	1,557.5	135.8%
U.S. Trade Balance	1987	1997	
Western Europe	-25.8	-17.5	
Canada	-11.3	-18.0	
Mexico	-5.7	-14.4	
Japan	-56.3	-55.7	
LAC (not Mexico)	-6.1	9.3	
Asia (not Japan)	-43.6	-85.8	
Middle East	-1.3	0.6	
Africa	-5.6	-8.6	
Other	3.5	7.8	
World Total	-152.2	-182.3	

Data Source: U.S. Department of Commerce

AGRICULTURAL EXPORTS: TECHNICAL BARRIERS TO TRADE

Geoffrey S. Becker

SUMMARY

Technical barriers to trade (TBTs) are widely divergent measures that countries use to regulate markets, protect their consumers, and preserve natural resources, but which can also discriminate against imports in favor of domestic products. Most TBTs in agriculture are sanitary and phytosanitary (SPS) measures designed to protect humans;, animals, and plants from contaminants, diseases, and pests. Since implementation of trade agreements aimed at reducing tariffs, import quotas, and other trade barriers, TBTs have become more prominent concerns for agricultural exporters and policymakers.

WHAT ARE TECHNICAL BARRIERS?

Key trade agreements-notably the 1993 North American Free Trade Agreement (NAFTA) with Canada and Mexico, and the 1994 World Trade Organization-Uruguay Round (WTO-UR) multilateral agreements-include commitments by member countries to eliminate or reduce their barriers to trade in agricultural and other goods. Trade barriers included tariffs (taxes on imported products), as well as many nontariff measures that can restrict trade, including import quotas, restrictive licensing systems, export and domestic production subsidies. Prior to the NAFTA and WTO-UR agreements, these types of tariff and nontariff barriers (NTBs) were at the center of major disputes between countries regarding access to each other's markets.

The agreements subject these barriers to rules and disciplines aimed at reducing their trade-distorting impacts. Also, the agreements attempt to establish stronger disciplines for yet another type of NTB that countries now use frequently: so-called technical barriers to trade (TBTs). These are various measures that countries use to regulate markets, and to protect their consumers and natural resources (among other goals), but which can also discriminate against imports to protect domestic industries, including agriculture.

TBTs with the greatest impact on agriculture are the various sanitary and phytosanitary (SPS) measures designed to protect humans, animals, and plants from diseases, pests, and other contaminants. Examples are residue limits for pesticides in foods, processing standards for meat products to reduce pathogens, and fumigation requirements on grain or produce imports to kill unwanted pests. Besides SPS measures, TBTs include rules for product weight, size, or packaging; ingredient or identity standards; mandatory nutrition labeling; and shelf-life restrictions.

The broad term "technical *barriers* to trade" is frequently applied to all of these measures, even where they may be consistent with NAFTA and WTO rules (i. e., legitimate efforts by a country to protect its consumers and agricultural resources). "Still, it is widely recognized that there is enormous potential for, and perhaps widespread misuse of, technical measures as nontransparent [disguised or unclear] obstacles to trade, even when the broad desirability of lowering risks to health and safety is acknowledged, and despite ...international rules."[1]

Impacts on U.S. Agricultural Exports and Trade Policy

Simply identifying and keeping track of the many technical measures countries are using has become a major challenge for trade officials. Negotiating the removal of those designed primarily to protect a country's domestic products from foreign competition can be even more difficult-but it is a high priority for U.S. agricultural interests. Following are examples of technical barriers that U.S. interests believe are unjustified-but that the implementing countries contend are both consistent with international trade obligations and necessary to protect their consumers and/or agricultural resources:

- A European Union (EU) ban, in place since 1989, on imports of meat products from animals treated with growth-promoting hormones, which has effectively blocked most U.S. mean (mainly beef) exports there. Although the WTO in 1999 agreed with U.S. (and Canadian) arguments that the ban lacks scientific justification and must be removed, the EU has maintained it;

- Lengthy approval procedures in the EU for genetically modified organisms (GMOs) and mandatory labeling of products containing GMOs that the United States considers cumbersome and not scientifically justified-effectively hampering U.S. exports there of such crops as corn and soybeans;

---

[1] Orden, David, and Donna Roberts. Foreword to *Understanding Technical Barriers to Agricultural Trade,* proceedings of a conference of the International Agricultural Trade Research Consortium, January 1997. Other sources of information include the following USDA/ERS publications: Roberts and Kate DeRemer, *Overview of Technical Barriers to U.S. Agricultural Exports* (Staff Paper AGES-9705), March 1997; Roberts, Timothy E. Josling, and David Orden, *A Framework for Analyzing Technical Trade Barriers in Agricultural Markets* (Technical Bulletin 1876), March 199, and *Agriculture in the WTO* (WRS-98-4), December 1998.

- Korean border procedures that can delay imported food and agricultural products for 2 weeks to 2 months, compared with several days elsewhere in Asia. Among numerous procedural problems is Korea's required incubation testing of Florida fruit even if accompanied by a USDA certificate that it is from a pest-free area;

- Australian phytosanitary regulations restricting imports of U.S. fruits including Florida citrus, grapes, blueberries, stone fruit, apples, and pears.

USDA's Economic Research Service (ERS) and Foreign Agricultural Service (FAS) attempted to inventory, summarize, and quantify the overall cost impacts of foreign TBTs on U.S. agricultural exports for 1996, using information gathered from, among other sources, USDA's foreign agricultural attaches and industry groups.[2] Working form that database, FAS found in 1997 more than 350 measures negatively affecting an estimated $5.8 billion in potential U.S. agricultural exports. East Asia had the most technical barriers, with an estimated impact on U.S. exports of nearly $2.9 billion. The Americas accounted for nearly $1.3 billion, and Europe for more than $900 million. Processed products accounted for about $1.3 billion of the $5.8 billion total. Others were grains and oilseeds, about $1.3 billion; animal products, nearly $900 million; fruits and vegetables, over $600 million ; and "other products" including cotton, seeds, nuts, fish and forestry products, about $1 billion in all.

Other nations argue that the Untied States maintains its own SPS measures and other TBTs, many of which they view as unjustifiable. Examples include a prohibition against shrimp imports from Southeast Asian countries because their trawlers do not use the type of nets used by U.S. shrimpers to protect sea turtles (the WTO has since ruled the ban was applied in a discriminatory manner); and U.S. import restrictions against more than 100 products because foreign pest risk analyses have not been completed. Because free trade is a two-way street, and if the U.S. challenges are to have credibility, U.S. interests must be prepared to acknowledge these barriers and to negotiate their removal, it is argued.

PROVISIONS OF KEY TRADE AGREEMENTS

Negotiators had anticipated that the inclusion of stronger agricultural disciplines in the WTO and NAFTA agreements might provide more incentive for countries to replace expiring NTBs with new technical barriers in order to continue to protect their domestic

---

[2] *Overview of Technical Barriers to U.S. Agricultural Exports.* This report has not been updated by USDA. Another source is the Office of the U.S. Trade Representative, which is required to file an annual report on foreign trade barriers faced by all U.S. exporters, including agriculture. The report categorizes, describes, and in some cases, quantifies, these barriers on a country-by-country basis. The 1999 *National Trade Estimates Report on Foreign Trade Barriers* can be accessed on the Internet at [http://www.ustr.gov/reports/nte/1999/contents.html}.

producers. To address this potential problem the WTO and NAFTA agreements include extensive language governing the circumstances under which countries may impose both TBTs in general, and SPS measures in particular. This language is intended to commit each country to imposing only SPS and other technical measures that are legitimate (e.g., to protect human, animal or plant health), not merely disguised barriers to trade.

SPS Provisions

In NAFTA, SPS measures are in the chapter on agriculture. The UY-WTO is written as a series of agreements, including separate ones on agriculture and on SPS-the Agreement on the Application of Sanitary and Phytosanitary Measures. Despite these differences in format, the SPS provisions in both the UR accords and NAFTA are similar.

Basic Rights and Obligations. Each country may decide its own "appropriate level of protection" of human, animal, or plant life or health. Such measures-which can be more stringent than other countries' and differ from international benchmarks-are acceptable as long as they are based on scientific principles and risk assessment, applied consistently to all countries, and not used as disguised trade barriers.

Harmonization and Equivalence. To facilitate trade, countries are encouraged to use relevant international standards and work toward harmonization-that is, the adoption of common SPS measures. TO promote harmonization, the agreements cite, as sources of scientific expertise and globally recognized standards, international bodies such as the Codex Alimentarius Commission, which deals with food safety issues; the International Office of Alimentarius Commission, which deals with food safety issues; the International Office of Epizootics (IOE), for animal health and diseases; and the International Plant Protection Convention (IPPC), for plant health. Equivalence means that each importing country must accept the SPS measures of another country as equivalent to its own (even if they are not exactly the same), as long as the exporting country objectively demonstrates to the importing country that its measures achieve the same level of protection.

Transparency. In recognition that SPS regulations can be unclear or even capricious, countries must have a mechanism for notifying others in advance about measures that could affect trade, and providing a means to ask questions about, and comment on, them.

Regionalization. Countries have banned imports of a product if it has been associated with an unwanted pest or disease in the exporting country. Until recently, these countries would not permit any of that product from the exporting country, even if it came from a region without the disease or pest. Regionalization provides for acceptance of such imports if the exporting country can prove that they are from a disease-free or pest-free area.

TBT Provisions

The WTO's Agreement on Technical Barriers to Trade "protects the right of Members to adopt measures which ensure the quality of exports; protect human, animal, or plant life; protect the environment; or prevent deceptive practices, as long as these measures do not breach the disciplines set forth in the Agreement. Many of the disciplines in the TBT Agreement are essentially identical to those in the SPS agreement [including the obligation to notify and allow for comments on proposed standards affecting trade], but the TBT Agreement explicitly states that SPS measures are bound only by the terms of the SPS agreement."[3] NAFTA's TBT provisions, which are part of the chapter on Standards-Related Measures, take a generally similar approach.

Dispute Settlement

The UR accords also include an "Understanding on Rules and Procedures Governing the Settlement of Disputes" to provide a mechanism for resolving, in a timely and objective manner, trade disputes between countries, including those involving SPS measures and other TBTs. Under pre-UR dispute settlement procedures, a country involved in the dispute effectively could block a decision against it, which cannot occur under the newer system. If a WTO dispute settlement panel ultimately determines that a country's SPS or TBT measure is inconsistent with WTO obligations and WTO members adopt the panel report, the "guilty" country (which can appeal the decision on matters of law and legal interpretation) could still maintain the measure, but only if it also provides compensation to the complaining country. If compensation is not provided and the two countries still fail to reach a mutually acceptable solution, the WTO panel can authorize trade retaliation against the country. NAFTA also contains a dispute resolution mechanism that can be used to challenge SPS measures and others TBTs. Both the WTO and NAFTA procedures allow for scientific advice to the panels.

U. S. Procedures for Identifying and Addressing TBTs

With SPS and TBT disciplines now in place, the U.S. process for identifying and dealing with them is an important consideration. For agriculture, most of this effort is coordinated, at least in the initial stages, by the Food Safety and Technical Service Division (FSTSD) of FAS, the lead USDA trade agency. The division maintains a database on foreign TBT measures with a potential impact on trade, which are listed even though they may comply with WTO or other international trade agreement provisions.

FSTSD continually collects information on these measures from the WTO, which countries are obligated to notify whenever they propose a new TBT measure; industry groups attempting to export products; the U.S. Trade Representative (USTR); FAS's overseas posts; and various regulatory agencies such as USDA's Animal and Plant Health Inspection Service (APHIS) and Food Safety and Inspection Service (FSIS), the Environmental Protection Agency (EPA), and HHS Department's Food and Drug Administration (FDA). In 1996, for example, 52 new TBT issues were identified.

---

[3] *Overview of Foreign Technical Barriers to U.S. Agricultural Exports.*

FAS chairs a weekly meeting of USDA technical staff of various USDA agencies to discuss the status of emerging and ongoing TBT issues, including options for resolving a potential dispute. Monthly meetings are co-chaired by FAS and APHIS to discuss general SPS issues which are attended by State Department, USTR, FDA, and EPA representatives. USTR also chairs an interagency group that meets regularly on WTO SPS issues. Meanwhile, technical and other government officials are likely to have initiated at least informal dialogue with countries concerning the measure in question, and they also are communicating with affected industries in the private sector, both to keep them informed and to gather additional information. Eventually, bilateral consultations with the foreign country over an outstanding SPS or TBT issue might be pursued by USTR, with USDA's assistance. USTR also can decide at any point to elevate the issue via a formal complaint with the WTO or NAFTA, triggering formal dispute resolution procedures.[4]

Critics had maintained that the U.S. structure for coordinating, prioritizing, and deciding on how to address these issues was ambiguous and unclear. In response, USDA

Created a formal TBT policy group headed by the Secretary's special trade advisor and composed of senior officials of relevant agencies, who meet at least monthly.

RELATED ISSUES

Despite the steps so far to address problems related to TBTs, numerous issues remain. For example, food safety and environmental advocates have long expressed concerns that the ongoing efforts to harmonize international standards (such as under Codex, IOE, and IPC) might encourage the Untied States to weaken its own food safety and environmental protections. Relatedly, U.S. health and safety standards could be undermined if WTO dispute settlement panels question their scientific basis and/or attempt to compare them to weaker international standards, some advocates argue.

Others counter that the current trade agreements explicitly recognize the right of individual nations (as well as states and localities) to enact stronger protections if they belief the are appropriate. If a WTO or NAFTA dispute panel is convened to determine whether an SPS measure has a scientific basis, it is only tasked with determining whether the SPS measure at issue is based on scientific principles (and is being applied consistently)-not whether the measure necessarily use the "best science."

Another issue is the effectiveness of the WTO dispute settlement mechanisms to resolve trade issues including those relating to technical barriers. On the one hand, critics point to examples such as the continued failure to open the EU to U.S. beef exports despite WTO ruling in favor of the U.S. position. On the other hand, a March 1999 report by a WTO committee concluded that, despite a few such high-profile

[4] Sections 301 *et seq.* of the Trade Act of 1974 delineate the domestic legal authority and procedures for U.S. officials in investigating and challenging unfair trade practices, and enforcing U.S. rights under international trade agreements. Interested parties, including agricultural groups, can-and do-petition USTR to initiate such procedures under Section 301 if they believe that a challenge is warranted and that the Administration is not addressing the issue. For an explanation of Section 301, see House Committee on Ways and Means, *Overview and Compilation of U.S. Trade Statues* (WMCP 105-4), June 25, 1997.

disputes, the SPS agreement has helped to defuse potential disputes before they occur, bring transparency to countries' application of SPS and related measures, and improve trading relations.[5]

One challenge for U.S. and foreign negotiators is the recent proliferation of agricultural products containing GMOs. Biotechnology was not at issue when the TBT and SPS agreements were finalized in 1994, and one question is whether the agreements contain an effective framework for resolving disputes in this area. While some argue that future WTI negotiations should re-examine these agreements to clarify how biotechnology concerns should be addressed, others believe they are adequate-and that some countries might attempt to use such an examination to introduce new considerations (i.e. consumer preferences, etc.) that could undermine their scientific basis.[6]

Because the SPS and TBT provisions, and dispute settlement procedures, are relatively new, analysts are still seeking the most appropriate methods for measuring their economic and other impacts; even their definition and relative importance are still being debated.[7]

---

[5] The report can be viewed on the Internet at [http://www.econ.ag.gov/epubs/pdf/tb1876/].

[6] See: "Biotechnology in Agriculture Confronts Agreements in the WTO," *Agriculture in the WTO.*

[7] ERS's *A Framework for Analyzing Technical Trade Barriers in Agricultural Markets* can be viewed on the Internet at [http://www.econ.ag.gov/epubs/pdf/tb1876/].

NAFTA, MEXICAN TRADE POLICY, AND U.S.-MEXICO TRADE: A LONGER TERM PERSPECTIVE

J.F. Hornbeck

SUMMARY

The North American Free Trade Agreement (NAFTA) has been in place for over three years, and Congress continues to evaluate it as part of the trade policy process. "Free trade" is a contentious debate and has become even more complicated in the NAFTA context because of Mexico's 1995 economic crisis. Many critics consider the sudden shift from surplus to deficit in the U.S. trade balance with Mexico a clear indication of NAFTA's failure. Others see NAFTA as a positive force supporting U.S. exports. To sort out the effects of trade agreements, this report evaluated the U.S.-Mexico trade relationship over the past two decades to place recent events and NAFTA in a broader economic context.

Over time, U.S.-Mexico trade has grown and diversified as the two economies have become increasingly integrated. Yet, trade patterns have been volatile at times for many reasons, including economic downturns in Mexico. To understand the role of trade policy and agreements on trade flows, it is instructive to compare Mexico's 1982 and 1995 economic crises because in the first Mexico operated under a closed trade policy and in the second it had recently acceded to NAFTA as part of a long-term transition to an open trade policy. Both downturns had similar antecedents: an overvalued peso, a balance of payments crisis, large capital outflows, and a currency devaluation. Both were also severe, but the trade effects on the United States proved much worse in the first instance.

With Mexico's 1995 balance of payments crisis, the United States saw its bilateral trade balance fall into a large deficit position, as it did in 1982. However, U.S. exports to Mexico declined by only 11%, compared to 34% in 1982 and 23% in 1983. Yet, in 1995, Mexico's economy had contracted more severely than earlier, with GDP falling 6.2% compared to 0.6% and 4.3% in 1982 and 1983. A critical difference in the trade effects between the two periods was Mexico's change in trade policy, particularly adopting NAFTA, which kept Mexico from raising barriers to U.S. trade in response to the crisis.

The 1995 decline in U.S. exports to Mexico was due to the recession-induced fall in demand and the price effects of the peso devaluation. *What the decline does not reflect is a trade policy bent to restricting the flow of imports from the United States, which was in place in 1982, but absent in 1995.* NAFTA solidified Mexican commitments to an open trade policy and actually cushioned U.S. exports from a more serious fall. Further, the trade deficit with Mexico has not been a major economic problem for the Untied States as a whole given its global trading position. Finally, under freer trade conditions, economists generally have expected U.S. exports to Mexico to recover more quickly form the 1995 decline than they did from the 1982 crisis under a closed Mexican trade policy, which so far seems to be the case.

*****

The North American Free Trade Agreement (NAFTA) has been operating for over three years and Congress continues to evaluate its effect as part of the trade policy process. Many hold NAFTA responsible for the dramatic events that unfolded in 1994-95: the peso devaluation, Mexico's economic collapse, and shift from surplus to deficit in the U.S. balance of trade with Mexico. On the other hand, others cite NAFTA as a major factor in opening Mexican markets to U.S. goods, thereby contributing significantly to continued growth and prosperity of the U.S. economy. As is frequently the case in polarized debates, neither extreme is fully vindicated by economic theory or evidence.

In evaluating extreme changes in trade balances between two countries, it is important to understand the fundamental economic forces at work. In the case of the most recent U.S. trade deficit with Mexico, two major economic questions are frequently posed. First, what role did trade policy and particularly NAFTA play in causing the sudden shift in the U.S. trade balance with Mexico? Second, does a bilateral trade deficit with Mexico present a major economic problem for the Untied States?

This report considers trends in U.S.-Mexico merchandise trade over two decades to evaluate how NAFTA may have affected the economic situation in Mexico and U.S. trade. To gauge the effects of the agreement, it is instructive to revisit the "debt crisis" period of 1982-83, when Mexico had a closed trade policy, and contrast it with the repercussions of the 1994 peso devaluation, when Mexico operated under a more open trade policy. What shall be seen is that trade agreements can affect the long term *level* of trade, but do not cause sharp fluctuations in the *balance* of trade, which are largely defined by domestic economic conditions and policies.[1] Finally, it is worth repeating

[1] This report does not delve into employment issues. See: U.S. Library of Congress. Congressional Research Service. *NAFTA: Economic Effects on the Untied States After Three Years.* Report No. 97-612 E, by Arlene Wilson. June 13, 1997, *NAFTA: Estimated U.S. Job "Gains" and "Losses" by State.* Report No. 96-788 E, by Mary Jane Bolle. September 25, 1996, and Weintraub, Sidney. *NAFTA at Three: A Progress Report.* Washington, D. C., Center for Strategic and International Studies, pp. 5 and 11-15.

that the benefits of freer trade are not measured in terms of annual trade balances, but by broader economic changes that unfold over longer periods of time.[2]

UNITED STATES-MEXICO TRADE: 1977-1996

The United States and Mexico have had a long and sometimes stormy economic relationship, and so the movement toward freer trade with Mexico continues to raise concerns in the United States. Mexicans also have expressed reservations about being overwhelmed by the "economic colossus" to their north. Because trade occurs between a comparatively large and small economy, there is a disproportional aspect to the relationship that should be recognized.

The United States is by far Mexico's most important trading partner, accounting for approximately 83 percent of Mexico's exports and 77 percent of its imports in 1996. By contrast, Mexico is the United States' third largest trading partner, but accounted for only 9 percent of U.S. exports and imports in 1996.[3] This is an important distinction because despite ongoing interest in the level of U.S. exports to Mexico, the U.S. economy is not greatly affected overall by the economic fortunes of Mexico. To the contrary, because Mexico is dependent on the large U.S. economy as its primary export market, it is far more vulnerable to changes in U.S. economic trends.

Figure 1. U.S.-Mexico Merchandise Trade (1977-1996)

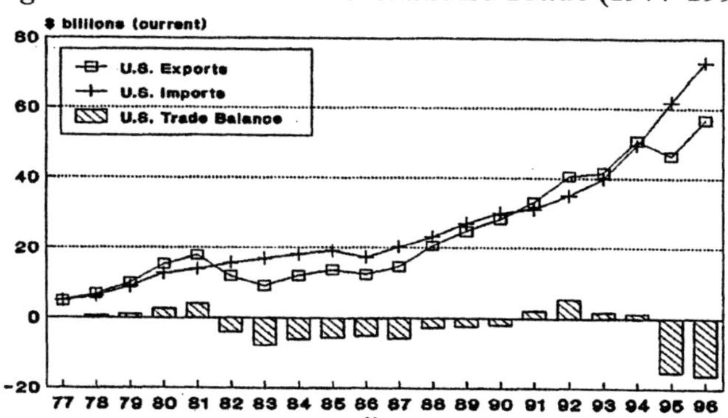

Despite this discrepancy in relative trade importance, bilateral trade for the most part expanded evenly, if not briskly at times, over the past two decades. Between 1977 and 1996, trade turnover (exports plus imports) between the United States and Mexico grew from $9.5 billion to $130 billion (see figure 1 and appendix 1.) The U.S. balance of trade shifted back and forth from surplus to deficit, reflecting changing economic fundamentals in both countries.

---

[2] For an economic discussion of the "gains from trade" see: U.S. Library of Congress. Congressional Research Service. *Trade Policy in an Economic Perspective.* Report No. 95-529 E, by Craig K. Elwell. March 9, 1995.

[3] International Monetary Fund, *Direction of Trade Statistics*, June 1997. p. 135 and U.S. Department of Commerce trade data.

At least four distinct periods can be seen in figure 1. First, the late seventies show a pattern of balanced trade growth, supported in Mexico by the oil boom. A second period followed in the 1980s characterized by a decline and stagnation of trade following the global recession, collapse of world oil prices, and increase in world interest rates that triggered Mexico's 1982 debt crisis. U.S. exports fell substantially after 1981, requiring seven years to recover. Beginning in 1986, a third period of nearly balanced trade growth resumed largely, as shall be seen, because of Mexico's trade reforms. Finally, 1995-96 reflect Mexico's most recent recession and incipient recovery. Although U.S. exports to Mexico plunged in 1995, they actually grew faster than U.S. imports from Mexico in 1996 and the first half of 1997.

In addition to the shifting fortunes in U.S.-Mexico trade over the past two decades, the composition of trade between the two countries has changed rather dramatically, particularly for Mexican exports. In the early 1980s, Mexico was, above all else, an oil exporter, with oil accounting for nearly 60 percent of total export revenue (see table 1). Half of all oil exports went to the United States at that time. A major goal of Mexico's trade liberalization was to diversify production and exports away from such heavy dependence on oil. By 1996, although still an important sector, oil production had not increased much from 1984 levels and accounted for only 12 percent of total Mexican exports and 9 percent of exports to the United States (see appendix 2.)[4]

Table 1. Structural Changes in Mexican Merchandise Exports (in percent)

Export type	1984	1987	1990	1993	1996
Agriculture, Livestock, and Fishing	5.0	5.5	5.3	4.8	3.8
Oil and Minerals	58.9	33.4	26.3	14.8	12.6
Manufactures	36.1	61.1	68.4	80.4	83.6

Source: Banco de Mexico. *The Mexican Economy 1997.* Table 47.

Interestingly, despite Mexico's once heavy dependence on oil exports to the United States, as it diversified its export base away form petroleum toward manufacturing, the United States became an even more important trading partner. In the early 1980s, the United States accounted for 55 percent of Mexico's exports. This ratio rose to 65 percent in 1987 and 83 percent by 1996. Some 84 percent of Mexico's exports are not manufactured goods, 70 percent of which end up in the United States.[5]

Maquiladoras, through a joint production operations, play an important role in this trade, with half of all Mexican manufacturing exports coming from these firms. Maquiladoras are domestic- or foreign-owned assembly plants in Mexico, which produce

[4] Weintraub, Sidney. *A Marriage of Convenience: Relations Between Mexico and the Untied States*. New York, Oxford University Press, 1990. pp. 86 and 119, and Banco de Mexico, *The Mexican Economy 1997,* tables 13 and 47.

[5] Weibtraub, ibid, pp. 73-75, Banco de Mexico, *The Mexican Economy 1997,* table 47, and Vargas, Lucinda. The Maquiladora Industry: Still Going Strong (part 2). *Business Frontier,* Issue 4, 1996. Federal Reserve Bank of Dallas, El Paso Branch.

for export (mostly to the United States). U.S. and Mexican trade laws provided preferential treatment for imported inputs and capital goods related to maquiladora production even prior to NAFTA. The three largest maquiladora industry sectors are electric and electronics equipment, transportation equipment, and textiles/apparel.[6]

On Mexico's import side, between 70 and 80 percent tend to be intermediate goods, or goods that are further processed. Capital goods, used to manufacture other goods, account for approximately 15-25 percent of Mexico's imports, with consumer goods ranging from 5 percent during recessions to 15-20 percent during periods of economic growth.[7] The dominance of intermediate goods again points to the importance of the intra-industry maquiladora relationship as partially manufactured goods are sent across the border for further assembly and then returned to the United States. Intermediate gods support non-maquiladora manufacturing as well. The largest categories of imports from the maquiladora manufacturing as well. The largest categories of imports from the United States are various types of tractor/automotive and electrical parts. Imports from the United States are highly diversified with the top 25 import commodity groups accounting for only one-third of the total (see appendix 3).

Economic Factors Affecting Trade

As seen above, U.S.-Mexico trade changed considerably over the past two decades. The long-term trend has been one of growth and diversification as the two economies have become increasingly integrated. Yet, trade has not always expanded in a smooth upward direction, and to discern NAFTA's possible role in Mexico's recent economic problems, it is essential to understand some of the factors that affect short-term fluctuations in trade including economic growth, exchange rate policy, and capital flows. Because events causing the collapse of the 1994 peso are reminiscent of those in 1982, and because Mexico was operating under different trade policies, the two periods are contrasted.

Macroeconomic Performance

Trade between two countries can fluctuate over the short-term as their economies move through their respective business cycles, which is particularly evident among major trading partners where economies are more highly integrated, such as the United States and Mexico. When economies enter recessions, demand falls, often abruptly, which also diminishes demand for imports. These short-term swings can affect trade balances irrespective of trade policy or agreements.

---

[6] Ibid.

[7] Banco de Mexico, *The Mexican Economy 1997*, table 47.

Figure 2. Real Growth in Mexican GDP and U.S. Exports to Mexico (1978-1996)

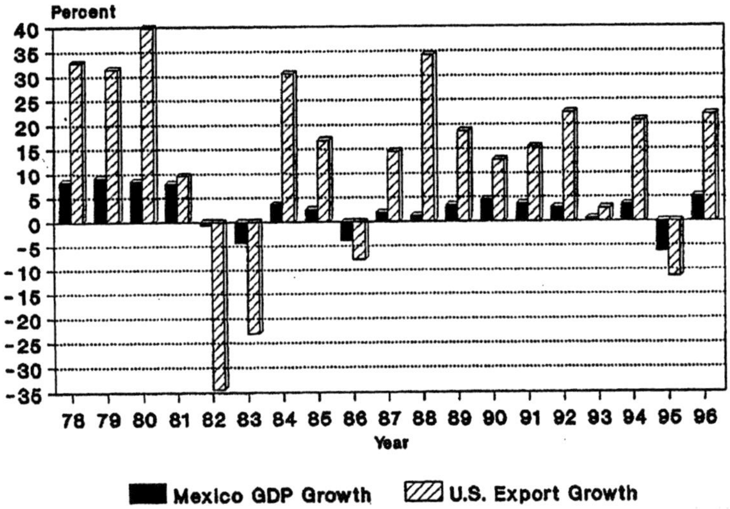

To highlight the relationship between trade and short-term economic performance, figure 2 contrasts real annual growth of Mexico's gross domestic product (GDP) with real annual growth of U.S. exports to Mexico from 1978 to 1996. Figure 2 shows the potential for volatility in annual bilateral trade balances on the vagaries of the Mexican business cycle. In particular, growth in U.S. exports to Mexico was highest in the late 1970s during a period of strong economic growth (8-9 percent annually) and decidedly negative when the economy fell on hard times in 1982-83, 1986, and 1995. The 1996 recovery shows expected return to growth of U.S. exports to Mexico.

Sudden declines in U.S. Exports to Mexico are clearly evident for the 1982-83 and 1995 recessions. In 1982 and 1983, Mexico's GDP dipped by 0.6% and 4.2 percent, respectively, for a total fall in GDP of nearly 5 percent over the two years. At the same time, U.S. exports to Mexico fell by 34 and 23 percent for a total decline of approximately 50 percent. In the wake of the 1994 peso devaluation, Mexican GDP fell 6.2 percent in 1995 alone, the largest single year decline since the Great Depression and 50 percent more than in 1983. Yet, U.S. exports to Mexico fell only 11 percent in 1995 or about half of the decline witnessed in 1983. This suggests that in both cases the recession was an important factor affecting U.S.-Mexico trade, but raises an interesting question (to be explored in the next section) of why U.S. exports to Mexico declined much less in 1995 than might have been expected given such a sharp contraction in the Mexican economy and the previous experience of 1982-83?

Exchange Rate Policy and Capital Flows

Exchange rate policy and capital flows can exert a major influence on trade balances. Over the long run, stable and predictable exchange rates promote confidence in the future value of a country's currency, which in turn encourages trade and investment and discourages speculation and the potential for sudden large shifts in the flow of capital. Exchange rate stability, however, is not always easy to achieve. In a floating exchange rate system, market forces determine the exchange rate. In a fixed exchange rate system, policy sets the value of a country's currency in keeping with broader economic goals.

Both can generate stability, but in Mexico's case, its fixed exchange rate policy became suspect in 1994 when very large inflows of foreign capital caused the peso to become overvalued and Mexican economic policy did not make the necessary adjustments.[8]

In 1987, as part of a long-term anti-inflation policy, Mexico pegged the "nominal" or current market value of the peso to the dollar and then in 1989 adopted a "crawling peg" exchange rate. The "crawling" aspect of this concept refers to what amounts to a constant nominal mini-devaluation of the currency, ideally at a rate that would be equal to the inflation differential with the country to which the peso is pegged (the United States.) In 1991, Mexico employed a band or defined trading-range within which the peso could be traded, while continuing the regular mini-devaluation by widening the band.

When a country pegs its currency, exchange rate credibility rests on adopting macroeconomic policies similar to those of the country to which the currency is pegged (the United States) to avoid currency misalignments. Policy coordination is all the more critical in Mexico's case because the United States is both its primary trading partner and a much larger economy. Two problems often merge when a country adopts a fixed exchange rate, both of which can raise the specter of devaluation. First, when the difference in inflation rates is not fully closed, the "real value" (adjusted for inflation) of the pegged currency tends to appreciate. As the real value of the peso appreciates, the "nominal value" becomes increasingly less credible, raising concerns about a possible devaluation.[9]

The second and related problem arises when domestic economic policy diverges from that of the country to which the peso is pegged, which, as mentioned above, raises questions about the credibility of maintaining the fixed nominal exchange rate. In 1982, Mexico's economic policies were overtly expansionary, contributing to inflation, the peso appreciation, and impending crisis. Similarly, in mid-1994 the Mexican government adopted looser fiscal and monetary policies, albeit rather subtly, as a matter of presidential politics. If macroeconomic policy becomes expansionary and relatively more expansionary than the United States, which was actually moving in the opposite direction with the Federal Reserve raising interest rates throughout 1994, then the inflationary gap between the United States and Mexico discussed above grows and the nominal fixed exchange rate becomes suspect.[10]

---

[8] Because of the similarities between 1982 and 1994, emphasis is placed on the latter period. Prior t 1982, Mexico had a fixed exchange rate by 1994 (if not earlier) so these technical differences did not affect the final outcome, which was devaluation in both cases.

[9] Not adjusting fully for the inflation difference was a matter of broader and deliberate Mexican policy involving wage and price controls. On the pitfalls see: Dornbusch, Rudiger and Alejandro Werner. Stabilization Reform and No Growth. *Brookings Papers on Economic Activity.* No. 1, 1994. p. 271-76 and Dornbusch, Rudiger, Ilan Goldfajn, and Rodrigo I. Valdes. Currency Crises and Collapses. *Brookings Papers on Economic Activity.* No. 2, 1995. p. 250-53.

[10] Dornbusch, Goldfajn, and Vlades, ibid, p. 240. It has been argued that had Mexico been able to retain international credibility in its anti-inflationary policy, it might have avoided this latest crisis. See: Obstfeld, Maurice and Kenneth Rogoff. The Mirage of Fixed Exchange Rates. *Journal of Economic Perspectives*, v. 9, Fall 1995. p. 84.

Capital flows into Mexico were also a driving force that led to the overvalued currency, rising current account deficit, and Mexico's financial problems within the context of a pegged exchange rate system. As Mexico recovered from the debt crisis of the 1980s and adopted market-based economic reforms, investors came to believe that long-term stable growth might once again be possible. With rising interest in the potential for large returns in so-called "emerging markets," investors committed capital generously. Capital investment began to trickle into Mexico in 1989, and as documented in table 2, rushed in thereafter until 1994.[11]

Table 2. Net Capital Flows into Mexico 1989-95 ($billions)

Invest Type	1989	1990	1991	1992	1993	1994	1995
Direct	2.8	2.6	4.7	4.4	4.4	11.0	7.0
Portfolio	0.3	-4.0	12.1	19.2	28.4	7.6	-10.8
Other	-2.0	9.9	8.3	3.4	1.0	-2.8	-7.9
Total	1.1	8.5	25.2	27.0	33.8	15.8	-11.7

Source: IMF, *International Financial Statistics*, August 1997, p. 474.
Other = currency and deposits, loans, and trade credits.

When capital moves into a country that maintains fixed exchange rates, the domestic money supply increases, prices tend to rise, and the exchange rate tends to appreciate. The real appreciation of the peso lowered the price of imports and raised the price of exports, so Mexico began to run large trade and current account deficits that matched the capital inflows. When circumstances change, capital flows can suddenly slow or reverse themselves, particularly portfolio capital (stocks and bonds), which is highly liquid compared to direct foreign investment (plant and equipment). The sudden reversal of capital flows in 1994 presented serious problems for Mexico because it then had a large current account deficit, an overvalued exchange rate, and insufficient foreign exchange reserves to defend the exchange rate, which was under downward pressure from the massive capital outflows.[12]

In addition to exchange rate policy and capital flows, noneconomic factors sparked capital flight from Mexico. Concern over political stability was a key issue leading to investor uneasiness. In January 1994, a peasant revolt occurred in the state of Chiapas. March proved to be an even more unsteady month with the assassination of a presidential candidate. These events triggered a major speculative attack on the peso in late March, which Mexico defended by selling its foreign exchange reserves. Further political

[11] 1994 was the turnaround year. The $7.6 billion in portfolio capital is deceptive because it reflects an inflow of capital at the beginning of the year followed by a large capital outflow the rest of the year.

[12] One view argues that an extremely high level of capital inflows, particularly in a small economy, is simply not a realistic equilibrium level over the long un and should be treated as a short-term phenomenon at the outset. See: Edwards, Sebastian. Comments and Discussion. *Brookings Papers on Economic Activity*. No. 2, 1995. p. 277.

turmoil led to a final run on the peso in November 1994 as the fear of devaluation spread.[13]

Economic Policy

Although changing economic and political events (shocks) encouraged capital flight, it was Mexico's economic policy that doomed the peso to devaluation. Rising U.S. interest rates were responsible, in part, for the initial decline in capital inflows. Mexico would have had to tighten its monetary policy in like manner to continue to attract capital, but during an election year Mexico found it difficult to raise interest rates to maintain its relative competitiveness in the international capital market. In effect, it no longer subordinated domestic monetary and fiscal policy to the maintenance of a fixed exchange rate with the United States.[14] This decision was tantamount to allowing higher inflation relative to the United States, which, with a pegged exchange rate, meant that the real appreciation of the peso would accelerate to potentially untenable levels, further exacerbating the current account deficit.

At this point, Mexico faced three unattractive options: (1) raise interest rates to match U.S. policy and continue to attract (or slow the retreat of foreign capital; (2) devalue the peso; or (3) do nothing to buy time, but risk more severe financial difficulty in the future. Option one proved unacceptable because it risked almost a sure recession prior to a presidential election. Option two was apparently debated, but discarded because Mexico staked its economic reputation on defending the peso.[15] Option three unfolded by default.

Investors, both foreign and domestic, actually realized the tenuous nature of the peso in 1994 and began abandoning it when given the opportunity to move toward a short-term, dollar-indexed investment instrument known as the *tesobono*.[16] This amounted to "currency flight" prior to the final capital flight that occurred in November and December. When investor finally fled in late 1994, Mexico defended its currency with foreign reserves as long as it could before devaluing and eventually floating the peso. Mexico's refusal to face the inconsistency of its macroeconomic and exchange rate policies helped cause the peso's undoing. Under adverse conditions, Mexico could not continue to peg the peso's undoing. Under adverse conditions, Mexico could not continue to peg the peso to the dollar and follow a divergent macroeconomic policy from the United States. When an adjustment did not occur, it was only time before markets forced the peso's devaluation.

The unresolved debate over the proper Mexican response continues and the two main camps are: Mexico should have tightened fiscal and monetary policies to avoid

---

[13] For a summary of events see: U.S. Library of Congress. Congressional Research Service. *Mexico: Chronology of a Financial Crisis.* Report No. 95-1007 E, by Patricia A. Wertman. September 27, 1995.

[14] Dornbusch, Goldfajn, and Valdes, *Current Crises and Collapses*, p. 240-41.

[15] Ibid, p. 241.

[16] Tesobonos grew from 6 percent of total public sector internal debt in April 1994 to 55 percent by the time the peso was devalued in December. They proved to be only a stopgap measure in the attempt to halt capital flight.

devaluation, or it should have devalued the peso much earlier and accepted the consequences before they became so severe. In any event, as Mexico was forced to adjust to dwindling capital, its trade deficit had to correct, so exports rose and imports fell. Accordingly, the balance of trade with the Untied States went forma surplus to a deficit. The key points are that the seeds of this broad problem were planted years before NAFTA was contemplated and that the final collapse of the peso resulted more from domestic economic rather than trade policy reasons.[17] In fact, Mexico faced this problem in 1982 under a closed trade policy and again in 1994 under a more open trade policy.

Mexican Trade Policy

The preceding discussion points to many interconnected economic factors that can disrupt long-term trade patterns. The effect of Mexican trade reform, by contrast, should be evident over longer periods of time and promote stability in trade relations. To recap, in 1982-83 and 1995, Mexico experienced severe recessions (see figure 2.) Both were similar in that they were preceded by an overvalued peso, balance of payments crisis, capital outflows, and a major devaluation, causing U.S. exports to fall.[18] One of the critical variables that differed between the two setbacks was trade policy. As will be shown, a more open policy in 1995, solidified by NAFTA (and GATT), had no significant effect on the macroeconomic situation given other factors, but had a noticeable trade effect by keeping Mexico from imposing import restrictions on the United States as it did in 1982.

Closed Trade Policy and the 1982 Crisis

Prior to the 1982 crisis, the Mexican economy was considerably more closed to trade than it was in 1995. Mexico had long followed an import substitution approach to development, which by maintaining high tariffs and other barriers to imports, protected domestic industry from foreign competition. In 1981, the average tariff rate was 27 percent, 83 percent of imports required licenses, and domestic content requirements covered key industries such as automobile and computer manufacturing. The sole purpose of these policies was to restrict imports in order to facilitate domestic industrial development in Mexico. Given the wealth effect of new found oil reserves in the late 1970s, there was little financial or political pressure to change policies.[19]

A the 1980s approached, Mexico's economy continued to grow based on heavy external borrowing backed by seemingly unlimited oil revenues, resulting in large current account deficits. The 1982 balance of payments crisis occurred because Mexico

---

[17] Anticipation of NAFTA, however, may have contributed to the high expectations that drove large capital flows into Mexico after 1989.

[18] U.S. Library of Congress. Congressional Research Service. *Mexican Financial Crises, 1982 and 1995: Similarities and Differences.* Report No. 95-239 E, by Patricia A. Wertman. 6 p.

[19] Lustig, Nora. *Mexico: The Remaking of an Economy.* Washington, D.C., The Brookings Institution, 1992. pp. 114-15.

over borrowed and could not meet growing international debt service payments when world interest rates rose and oil prices plummeted. Mexico devalued the peso twice in 1982 and immediately faced economic decline: inflation climbed to nearly 100 percent and economic growth fell by nearly 5 percent over two years.[20]

To resume meeting its debt obligations, Mexico raised barriers to imports in order to earn foreign exchange. The primary tool was the import license (*permiso previo),* which in 1982 was extended to 100 percent of imports. Exchange rate controls wee also introduced and tariffs raised, but as one experienced observer has pointed out, "Under this import structure, it was fatuous to speak of average tariffs levels in Mexico. Denial of a *permiso previo* was the equivalent of an infinite tariff."[21] The result for the United States was a huge fall in exports to Mexico, as seen in figure 2.

Trade Reform in the 1980s

Despite the initial strengthening of import barriers, one outcome of the debt crisis was reform in Mexican trade policy. Mexico began gradual unilateral reductions in trade barriers after 1982. These accelerated after 1985 when Mexico made overt moves to integrate itself more completely with the world economic system by becoming a member of the General Agreement on Tariffs and Trade (GATT) in 1986 and the Organization for Economic Cooperation and Development in 1994. Becoming a party to NAFTA was also a logical step in this progression.[22]

Mexico's specific trade reform policies included reducing licenses from 100 percent of imports in 1982 to 36 percent in 1985, 27 percent in 1986, and 22 percent by the end of 1988. Mexico also simplified its tariff schedules, with maximum tariffs falling from 100 percent in 1982 to 20 percent in 1988. The trade-weighted average tariff rate continued downward and today stands at approximately 10 percent (5 percent under NAFTA). By 1987, these and other policy changes "transformed Mexico from an extremely closed economy into one of the most open ones in the world.[23] All this transpired seven years before NAFTA took effect.

Because Mexico instituted major trade policy reform before entry into NAFTA, the trade agreement may be seen as the continuation of a long-term process, at least as it effects the United States and Canada. Under NAFTA, Mexico's few remaining import license requirements ere converted to a system of tariff-rate quotas that will be phased

[20] The details can be found in chapter 1 of Lustig, ibid.

[21] Weintraub, Sidney. The Promise of United States –Mexican Free Trade. *Texas International Law Journal*, v. 27, Summer 1992. p. 555.

[22] Lustig, *Mexico: The Remaking of an Economy*, p. 39. It should be noted that trade liberalization affected primarily manufactured goods; agriculture, services, and other important areas are still protected and will be opened up under NAFTA.

[23] Tornell, Asron. Are Economic Crises Necessary for Trade Liberalization and Fiscal Reform? The Mexican Experience. In Dornbusch, Rudiger and Sebastian Edwards, eds. *Reform, Recovery, and Growth: Latin American and the Middle East.* Chicago, University of Chicago Press, 1995. p. 53. See also: U.S. International Trade Commission. *Review of Trade and Investment Liberalization Measures by Mexico and Prospects for Future United States-Mexican Relations.* Publication 2275. April 1990. pp. 4-1 to 4-5 and USITC. *1995 National Trade Estimate Report on Foreign Trade Barriers. Pp. 229-236.*

out. Tariff rates remain low and will also disappear as the free trade agreement is fully implemented. Importantly, as shall be seen, NAFTA consolidated Mexico's position on free trade with the United States.

The effect of Mexico's trade liberalization on its trade volume with the world is easily documented. From 1982 to 1996, Mexican exports grew from $24.1 to $96.0 billion or nearly 300 percent. Perhaps most telling is that oil, as a percent of total exports, fell from 77.6 to 12.6 percent. Over the same time period, Mexican imports rose over 400 percent from $17.0 to $89.5 billion.[24]

Because the United States is Mexico's most important trading partner, shifts in trade policy are particularly noticeable in the bilateral trade data. As seen in figure 1, the level of trade between the United States and Mexico experienced steady growth between 1983 (the beginning of Mexican trade policy reform) and 1994 (NAFTA); both imports and exports rose dramatically, at a time when the Mexican economy grew at an average annual rate f only 2 percent. In fact, real GDP per capita had not grown at all.[25]

Table 3. US.-Mexico Trade Turnover and U.S. Exports to Mexico as a Percent of Mexican GDP, 1982-1996 (Selected Years)

	1982	1987	1992	1994	1996
Trade Turnover/ Mexican GDP	15.7	25.3	22.7	26.8	44.7
U.S. Exports/ Mexican GDP	6.7	10.6	12.2	13.6	19.6

Source: IMF, *International Financial Statistics Yearbook*, 1996 and U.S. Department of Commerce. TPIS.

Data in table 3 also show the growing importance of U.S. trade to Mexico's economy. In 1982, total trade between the United States and Mexico, or trade turnover (imports plus exports), equaled 15.7 percent of Mexico's GDP and U.S. exports to Mexico alone amounted to 6.7 percent of its GDP. By 11994, these ratios rose to 26.8 and 13.6 percent, respectively. Clearly, trade with the United States has become a more important part of Mexico's economy. This growth in the level and importance of trade is what would be expected of freer trade policies and it is no coincidence that this growth occurred precisely at the same time that Mexican trade policy reforms were implemented.[26] (The large jump in these ratios for 1996 reflect these same trends, but also the effect of the 1995 recession on GDP, which served to lower the ratio's denominator.)

---

[24] International Monetary Fund. *International Financial Statistics Yearbook 1996,* p. 543 and Banco de Mexico, *The Mexican Economy 1997,* table 47.

[25] In 1990 dollars, Mexico's per capita GDP was $3,090 in 1985 and only $3,041 in 1994. Inter-American Development Bank. *Economic and Social Progress in Latin America: 1995 Report.* Washington, D.C., the Johns Hopkins University Press, October 1995. p. 263.

[26] Exchange rate policy and capital flows, as discussed earlier, were contributing factors.

Open Trade Policy and the 1995 Crisis

The details of the economic crisis in 1995 differed from 1982 in some respects, but Mexico faced the same fundamental problem: the inability to cover its international obligations. By 1995 the large trade and current account deficits had to be corrected and as Mexico's largest trading partner, the United States saw its bilateral trade balance reverse to a large deficit position. Mexican imports to the United States continued to climb as U.S. exports to Mexico fell. However, U.S. exports declined by only about 11 percent in 1995. As mentioned above this was a much smaller decrease than experienced in 1982 (34 percent) and 1983 (23 percent) despite a much larger contraction in Mexico's economy.

The difference points to Mexico's more open trade policy, including acceding to NAFTA, which kept Mexico from raising barriers to U.S. trade in response to the crisis. Hence, the decline in exports represents the fall in demand that accompanied the deep recession and the effects of the peso devaluation, as would be expected. *What the decline does not reflect is a formal policy to restrict the flow of imports from the United States which was in place in 1982, but absent in 1995.* NAFTA, for its part, helped solidify Mexican commitments to an open trade policy and actually cushion United States exports from tariff increases ranging from 20 to 35 percent that Mexico imposed on many goods from countries with which it had no equivalent agreement. The U.S. trade deficit therefore, was smaller than it might have been under a less open trade regime.[27]

In fact, it has been argued that this is one of the more important achievements of NAFTA. Not only could Mexico not fallback on a protectionist trade regime, but it is committed to continuing liberalization of trade policies in agriculture, services, and other areas.[28] Although this is scant comfort to those who are concerned with a trade deficit with Mexico, a bilateral deficit is not a major economic problem for the United States given its broad global trade relationships.[29]

Additionally, under freer trade conditions economists generally expected U.S. exports to Mexico to recover more quickly than they did from the 1982 crisis under a closed Mexican trade policy, which figure 1 and appendix 1 suggests has so far been the case.

Conclusions and Outlook

Mexico remains a natural, and over the long run, growing market for U.S. goods, which will become more evident as the Mexican economy recovers and the long-term trend of trade and investment growth reemerges, as it appears to be doing. This is a trend

---

[27] United States Trade Representative. *1996 Foreign Trade Barriers.* Washington, D. C. p. 239.

[28] Tornell, Asron and Gerardo Esquivel. *The Political Economy of Mexico's Entry to NAFTA.* Working Paper 5322. Cambridge, National Bureau of Economic Research, October 1995. p.27.

[29] For a discussion of the significance of the entire U.S. trade deficit, see: U.S. Library of Congress. Congressional Research Service. *U.S. Trade Performance: Recent Trends and Policy Options.* Report No. 97-487 E, by Craig K. Elwell. April 24, 1997.

that has been evident for decades and one that is dependent on Mexico's economic stability and its willingness to maintain an open trade policy, an option for which NAFTA may serve as an insurance policy. The Mexican case supports the contention that trade liberalization, relative to a closed trade policy, supports growth in trade and provides greater stability during times of economic setbacks, other things being equal.

One problem is that other things are not always equal and it is these other things (economic and political shocks) that often cause short-term disruptions to long-term trade trends. Mexico periodically experiences macroeconomic problems that are common among developing economies, and in 1994 Mexico repeated many mistakes made in 1982, except for trade policy. Its primary economic policies focus on resolving such basic problems as tempering runaway inflation, maintaining a stable exchange rate, managing current account balances, and attempting to achieve long-term savings rates necessary for development. Mexico, like most developing countries, looks abroad for resources to take up any slack in domestic savings. Given Mexico's tendencies toward exchange rate and indebtedness problems, often exacerbated by policy decisions, balance of payment or liquidity problems can arise periodically that eventually disrupt trade and investment flows. Importantly, these problems can arise under either an open or closed trade regime.

Although trade policy can encourage trade growth over the long run, it is only one economic policy tool and not the most influential in managing macroeconomic problems. In this case, a trade agreement such as NAFTA was not the cause of Mexico's 1995 recession, but it was able to reduce, although not eliminate, the recession's negative trade effects on the United States. Only with Mexico's recovery, which depends more on Mexico than a trade agreement, will U.S. export growth continue its upward climb.

Finally, it is worth reiterating the limitations of trade agreements. They are intended to reduce barriers to trade and encourage growth in trade between countries. This has occurred with Mexico and the United States. Trade agreements, however, cannot guarantee any particular balance of trade between countries, nor can they guarantee that all businesses will prosper. They do hold out the promise that business and trade success or failure will be less affected by deliberate policies to block imports, as was evident in Mexico in 1982, but not 1995. Despite the doubts voiced by many over NAFTA, moving back to a more closed trade posture with Mexico not only would risk losing broader gains from freer trade, but also would not guarantee the United States of being insulated from Mexican economic problems, as a comparison of the 1982 and 1994 crises demonstrates.

Appendix 1. U.S. Merchandise Trade With Mexico, 1977-97 ($ millions)

Year	U.S. Exports	U.S. Imports	Trade Balance	Trade Turnover	% Growth in U.S. Exports	% Growth in U.S. Imports
1977	4,733	4,769	-36	9,502	---	---
1978	6,678	6,100	578	12,778	41.1	27.9
1979	9,843	8,829	1,1014	18,672	47.4	44.7
1980	15,141	12,573	2,568	27,714	53.8	42.4
1981	17,780	13,799	3,981	31,579	17.4	9.8
1982	11,739	15,566	-3,827	27,305	-34.0	12.8
1983	9,079	16,776	-7,697	25,855	-22.7	7.8
1984	11,978	18,020	-6,042	29,998	31.9	7.4
1985	13,628	19,132	-5,504	32,760	13.8	6.2
1986	12,379	17,302	-4,923	29,681	-9.2	-9.6
1987	14,570	20,271	-5,701	34,841	17.7	17.2
1988	20,633	23,277	-2,644	43,910	41.6	14.8
1989	24,969	27,186	-2,217	52,155	21.0	16.8
1990	28,375	30,172	-1,797	58,547	13.6	11.0
1991	33,276	31,194	2,082	64,470	17.3	3.4
1992	40,597	35,184	5,413	75,781	22.0	12.8
1993	41,635	39,930	1,705	81,565	2.6	13.5
1994	50,840	49,493	1,347	100,333	22.1	23.9
1995	46,401	61,705	-15,304	108,106	-8.7	24.7
1996	56,761	72,963	-16,202	129,724	22.3	18.2
1997(P)	65,430	81,846	-16,416	147,276	15.3	12.2

P = preliminary numbers annualized from 1997 mid-year (six month) trade data.
Note: Figures are in current dollars so growth rate calculations vary some form those adjusted for inflation in figure 2.
Source: U.S. Department of Commerce. TPIS. Exports measured F.a.s.; Imports measured on customs basis.

Appendix 2. Top 25 U.S. Imports From Mexico ($millions)

	1984	1987	1990	1993	1996
Total all commodities	18,020	20,271	30,172	39,930	72,963
78120-Motor vehicles/transport of persons, nes	34	1,176	2,164	3,084	7,902
33300-Crude oil petroleum/bituminous minerals	6,700	3,520	4,822	4,245	6,356
78219-Motor vehicles/transport of goods, n.e.s.	59	90	229	543	3,052
77313-Ignition wiring sts, etc, used in vehicles	312	731	1,216	1,878	3,014
76110-Television receivers, color	179	338	916	1,589	2,749
93100-Special transactions & command not classif by kind	326	622	1,008	1,335	2,241
71322-Reciprocating pist engs, cul cap exceeding 1000 cc	533	823	543	749	1,625
75230-Digital processing units	0	68	151	54	1,263
78439-Pts & access of tractor, mtr veh, spec purpose, nes	212	317	582	957	1,187
78432-Oth pts & access of motor veh bodies (include cabs)	93	226	507	1,155	1,143
76431-Transmission apparatus, tv, radio, etc.	117	152	199	183	1,095
76211-Radiobroadcast receivers com sound, extern power	137	437	520	601	1,079
82119-Parts of seats nes	70	137	115	532	938
75997-Parts of auto data proc mach & optical readers etc.	93	86	265	485	924
76493-Pts of tv rec, radiobroad rec, sound record	486	487	672	806	844
84140-Trousers, overalls, shorts etc, men/boys, not knit	45	120	154	335	833
71631-Electric motors exceeding 37.5 w, ac	73	131	209	355	612
75260-Input or output units for data processing systems	39	99	120	209	604
05440-Tomatoes, fresh or chilled	169	159	371	304	580
84260-Trousers etc, women/girls, textile fab, not knit	41	35	88	162	507
98400-Estimate of low valued import transactions	139	127	292	359	498
84540-T-shirts, singlets & oth vests, knit or crochet	3	7	6	65	495
77121-Static converters (e.g., rectifiers)	116	177	130	160	480
74159-Parts for air conditioning machines of hd 741.5	14	55	60	133	479
77315-Elec conductrs, exc 80 v nt exc 1000 v	15	187	325	269	476
Total of Items Shown	10,005	10,307	15,664		40,977
Total Other	8,015	9,964	14,508		31,986

Source: U.S. Department of Commerce. TPIS. Imports reported customs value SITC 5 digit level.

Appendix 3. Top 25 U.S. Exports to Mexico ($ millions)

	1984	1987	1990	1993	1996
Total all commodities	11,978	14,570	28,375	41,635	56,761
78439-Pts & access of tractor, mtr veh, spec purpse	356	511	1,812	1,779	2,343
99400-Est. low val shp; can low value & n.i.k (exports)	97	339	1,110	1,412	1,952
78432-Oth pts & access of motor veh bodies (include cabs)	152	231	807	1,574	1,188
04490-Maize (not including sweet corn) unmilled, no seed	402	275	402	43	1,014
75997-Parts of auto data proc mach & optical readers etc	255	340	403	656	933
77611-Television picture tubes, color	0	16	142	360	927
89399-Articles of plastic nes	27	38	214	399	891
78120-Motor vehicles for the transport of persons	5	11	183	122	865
22220-Soybeans	485	220	211	121	859
77282-Pts of elec app for switching, protecting elec circt	59	66	349	372	703
77313-Ignition wiring sts, etc, kind used in vehicles	179	401	374	815	701
75230-Digital processing units	21	24	99	189	628
77643-Nondigital monolithic integrated units	17	20	12	17	576
77259-Electrcl app for switch/protect nes nt ex 1000	41	43	83	182	545
77220-Printed circuits	66	84	103	102	541
69969-Articles of iron or steel, n.e.s.	5	13	88	132	539
33411-Gasoline including aviation (except jet) fuel	2	33	197	457	530
77645-Hybrid integrated circuits	13	20	117	167	503
69421-Screws, bolts, nuts, threaded, iron or steel	13	23	63	130	476
64211-Cartons, boxes, cases, corrugated paper/board	44	60	170	271	476
77129-Pts of elec pwn machry (oth rotating ele plnt)	37	69	305	437	445
82119-Parts of seats nes	13	6	181	458	443
77641-Digital monolithic integrated units	81	103	123	212	419
71391-Parts, n.e.s. suitbl for spk-ig int com eng	207	151	199	242	405
76493-Parts of tv rec, radiobroad rec, sound record	133	170	623	750	401
Total of Items Shown	2,710	3,266	8,370	11,699	19,304
Total Other	9,268	11,304	20,005	29,936	37,457

Source: U.S. Department of Commerce. TPIS. Exports reported F.a.s. SITC 5 digit level

NAFTA: ESTIMATED U.S. JOB "GAINS" AND "LOSSES" BY STATE OVER 5 – YEARS

Mary Jane Bolle

ABSTRACT

U.S. "gains" and "losses" from trade with Mexico and Canada seem from changes in trade. Job "gain" data cover the North American Free Trade Agreement (NAFTA)'s first *five* years and job "loss" data cover a little more than NAFTA's *first five and one-half* years. Between January 1, 1994 and September 28, 1999, approximately 259,618 workers were certified as potentially suffering NAFTA-related job "losses." These data are sorted by state. Earlier versions of this report also included a table which sorted these data within states b business, indicating for each business, its products, reason for certification, and industry. Because of its increasingly unwieldy size, this table has been dropped from this report. However, these data for any state are available from CRS by calling the author at 7-7753. In addition, between January 1994 and the end of December 1998, nearly 710,000 net jobs were "created" from new exports to Mexico and Canada. These figures are sorted by state. In all, six tables present the data from varying perspectives, including major industries of job certifications and major industries of increased exports to Mexico and Canada. This report is generally updated once or twice a year.

SUMMARY

What has been the effect of the North American Free Trade Agreement (NAFTA) on jobs in individual states? NAFTA-the trade agreement between the United States, Mexico, and Canada-appears to have served primarily to accelerate trade-related job trends that were already ongoing. Thus, any reference in this report to effects "*of* NAFTA" is really a reference to effects "*since* NAFTA." Since NAFTA went into effect January 1, 1994, both imports from and exports to Mexico and Canada have increased-boosted by reductions in tariff, nontariff, and investment barriers, particularly in Mexico.

U.S. job "gains" and "losses" from trade with Mexico and Canada stem from changes in trade. In 1998 the value of trade with Mexico was slightly more than half the value of trade flows with Canada. Since NAFTA went into effect through the end of 1998, exports to Mexico and Canada combined have increased 64%, while imports have increased by 78%. Between 1993 and 1998, the annual merchandise trade deficit with

Canada increased from $13 billion to $24 billion, while a $1 billion surplus with Mexico evolved into a $17 billion deficit. (The U.S. trade positions with both Mexico and Canada worsened in 1998 over 1997.)

"Job gain" data cover NAFTA's first *five* years, and "job loss" data cover NAFTA's first *five-and-a-half* years. Measuring "job gains" and "losses" from trade with NAFTA partners is an inexact process. "Job loss" and "job gain" data were derived from different methods and databases and, therefore, are not comparable. In addition, job loss figures represent the outside limit of, rather than actual job losses. That is, they represent total employment at plants where workers have been certified to receive NAFTA-Transitional Adjustment Assistance (NAFTA-TAA) benefits. Only 20-30% of these workers actually collect benefits. Trying to further apportion these job gains and losses by state compounds the problems. Thus, the figures come with strong caveats. Nevertheless, they provide some useful information.

Moreover, estimates of NAFTA-related job "gains" and "losses" are small relative to total U.S. employment. Approximately 259,618 workers were certified between January 1, 1994, and September 28, 1999, as potentially suffering NAFTA-related job *losses*. This represents less that the number of jobs *created* in a single month in 1998. On the other hand, an estimated 1,212,357 gross jobs and 709,989 *net* jobs were created from new exports to Mexico and Canada between 1994 and 1998. (The net figure factors in job losses from countervailing productivity growth and inflation.)

States suffering the greatest potential total job *losses* from trade with Mexico and Canada since NAFTA went into effect are North Carolina (27,725), Texas (23,386), Pennsylvania (18,663), New York (17,487), California (14,825), Georgia (12,457), and Tennessee (12,191). States estimated to have experienced the greatest *gross* job *gains* (not reduced by productivity and inflation growth) from trade with Mexico and Canada since NAFTA went into effect are Texas(175,407), Michigan (149,382), California (147,284), Illinois (60,181), New York (56,256), Ohio (53,895), and Indiana (43,192).

*****

What has been the effect of the North American Free Trade Agreement NAFTA on jobs in individual states? NAFTA-the trade agreement between the United States, Mexico, and Canada-appears to have served primarily to accelerate trade-related job trends that were ongoing before NAFTA. Thus, any reference in this report to effects "*of* NAFTA" is really a reference to effects "*since* NAFTA." One broad observation that can be made is that since NAFTA went into effect in January 1994, both imports from and exports to Mexico and Canada have increased-boosted by reductions in tariff nontariff, and investment barriers, particularly in Mexico.[1]

---

[1] For details on exports and imports traded with NAFTA partners, by industry, see NAFTA-Estimates of Job Effects and Industry Trade Trends After Five and One-Half Years, by Mary Jane Bolle. CRS Report 98-783E.

U.S. job "gains" and "losses" from trade with Mexico and Canada (the U.S.'s first and third largest trading partners) stem from changes in trade flows, but are also affected by domestic increases in productivity. Since NAFTA, exports to and imports from Canada have each increased by about 55-60%. This has resulted in relatively suggests few net job effects from trade with Canada. Exports to and imports from Mexico, however, have more or less doubled (exports less and imports more than doubled). This suggests some sectoral job "losses" from production shifts to Mexico. However, since about two-thirds of the increase in imports is covered by an increase in exports, net job effects are estimated to be relatively small in relation to overall U.S. employment.[2]

Figure 1. Quick NAFTA State Data *Finder

Job Losses from New Imports	Page
Potential Job Losses	4
Gross and Net Job Gains from New Exports	
Total, 1993-98	7
By Year	12
Exports	
Total Exports to Mexico and Canada	11

*State data may include data on the District of Columbia and U.S. territories

In fact, NAFTA's overall effect on the U.S. economy has been relatively small. Foreign trade itself accounts for about 14% of U.S. gross domestic product (GDP); and trade with Mexico and Canada represents roughly one-fifth of all U.S. trade. Larger effects on the overall U.S. economy result from structural changes taking place as companies shed employment due to trade and other economic factors. At the same time, however, the U.S. economy is both dynamic and robust. As jobs are eliminated in one industry, they are added in another. The United States, as a job-creating nation, is the envy of many developed countries, particularly Canada and many European nations, where employment is in some cases one-and-a-half to two times the U.S. rate.

This report provides estimates on NAFTA-related job effects. Indeed, by state, are estimates of job gains covering NAFTA's first *five* years and potentially job-losses covering roughly NAFTA's first *five-and-a-half* years. (State export data, from which job gains by state are derived, are available only annually.) Measuring job gains and losses form trade with NAFTA partner is an inexact process. Trying to further apportion these job gains and losses by state compounds the difficulties. Thus, these figures come with strong caveats:

---

[2] See also, U.S. Library of Congress. Congressional Research Service. NAFTA, Mexican Trade Policy, and U.S.-Mexico Trade: A Longer-Term Perspective, by J.F. Hornbeck. CRS Report 97-811 E.

First, the terms "job gains" and "losses" are, to a certain extent, misnomers. In an economy operating *at full employment, trade results in neither net job gains nor net job losses, only in relocations* from less efficient to more efficient industries. Economy-wide, job gains balance out job losses. However, at the industry and firm level, *job "gains" from trade* will not likely equal *job "losses" from trade."*[3]

Second, it should be emphasized that job-effect, estimates included in this report were developed by different methods and are arguably incomplete and incompatible. In particular, job "losses" captured by Department of Labor (DOL) certifications arguably both underestimate and overestimate the actual number of job losses from NAFTA, for reasons mentioned below. Job "gains," while perhaps reasonably reflective of actual job gains from exports at the national level, are not as accurate at the state level, for reasons discussed below.

ESTIMATED JOB "LOSSES"[4]

The DOL certifies the eligibility of workers to apply at the state level for benefits under the NAFTA-Transitional Adjustment Assistance (NAFTA-TAA) Program. The certification identifies potential dislocated workers who, if separated from their jobs, would be eligible for training and income replacement benefits because, either imports from Mexico and Canada "contributed importantly" to their job loss, or their plant relocated to Mexico or Canada. Hence, the certified NAFTA job losses are but a subset of total job losses from NAFTA; they include only those job losses for which a displaced worker applied for benefits and a direct linkage to trade with Mexico or Canada, or a shift in production to either of these countries, can be verified.

However, NAFTA-TAA certification figures may overestimate job losses among certified workers. This is because not all workers certified actually lose their jobs. In fact, recent data from the Department of Labor suggests that as few as 20-30% of the certified workers actually collect NAFTA-TAA benefits. (The others who were pre-certified may either not have actually lost their jobs, may have found another job in lieu of needing benefits, or for other reasons may not have collected their benefits.)

---

[3] Economists continue to debate what level the full-employment rate of unemployment should be. Many believe unemployment rates below 5.5% suggest an excess demand for labor. During the past several years, unemployment rates have dipped to under 4.5% - the lowest they have been since the late 1960s.

[4] The lengthy table included in previous versions of this report that listed each certified business in each state, together with reasons for certification, has been omitted because of size. However, these data for any state are available from CRS by calling the author at 7-7753.

Table 1. NAFTA-TAA Certification by Reason, January 1, 1994-September 28, 1999

Reason for Certification		Cases	Workers
% of all certified workers			
C-1 Production shift to Mexico	948	120,888	47
C-2 Production shift to Canada	233	23,010	9
C-3 Increased customer imports from Mexico	196	22,852	9
C-4 Increased customer imports from Canada	168	14,995	6
C-5 Increased customer imports not identified by source country	214	27,487	11
C-6 Increased company imports from Mexico	194	26,352	9
C-7 Increased company imports from Canada	66	8,802	3
C-8 Increased company imports not identified by source country	19	3,419	1
C-9 High and Rising aggregate imports from Mexico and/or Canada[1]	141	11,843	5
Total Certified	**2,179**	**259,618**	**100**

Source of data: U.S. DOL Office of Trade Adjustment Assistance. Compiled by CRS
[1] C-9 represents a new category in 1997.

Table 1 sorts certified workers by reason for certification. The growth in the number of workers certified under the NAFTA-TAA program has leveled of in the past year. The single most important reason for certification, and with it eligibility to receive income and job training under NAFTA-TAA, continues to be production shifts to Mexico. This accounts for the largest and the largest growing part of all worker certifications-47%. Numbers of workers potentially dislocated are sorted by state in table 2.[5]

[5] The DOL Office of Trade Adjustment Assistance keeps several different lists of numbers reflecting workers certified under the NAFTA-TAA program. Thus, totals in table 1 do not agree precisely with totals in table 2 because of errors in the data base. (Entries for which certain data are missing are not picked up by various "sorts" of the data.)

Table 2. Potential Job Loss by State: Number of Cases and Workers Certified by the NAFTA-TAA Program, January 1, 1994-September 28, 1999

	Total Jan. 1, 1994-Sept, 28, 1999 NAFTA-TAA Certified			Total Jan 1, 1994-Sept 28, 1999 NAFTA-TAA Certified	
STATE	Cases	Workers	STATE	Cases	Workers
North Carolina	171	27,725	Arizona	30	2,054
Texas	252	23,386	Minnesota	20	1,921
Pennsylvania	193	18,663	New Mexico	12	1,771
New York	126	17,487	Maine	18	1,702
California	124	14,825	Kansas	13	1,364
Georgia	110	12,457	West Virginia	18	1,343
Tennessee	109	12,191	Connecticut	11	1,291
Indiana	59	9,406	Mississippi	4	1,144
Arkansas	48	8,993	Puerto Rico	2	1,090
Michigan	74	8,334	Utah	13	1,047
Wisconsin	52	7,776	Montana	24	790
Washington	85	7,351	Alaska	5	780
New Jersey	69	7,064	Wyoming	19	620
Alabama	40	6,627	South Dakota	5	566
South Carolina	46	6,551	Iowa	9	454
Virginia	64	6,513	Vermont	4	429
Ohio	53	6,074	North Dakota	4	393
Missouri	67	5,984	Maryland	3	390
Florida	72	5,756	Oklahoma	12	331
Illinois	50	5,718	Nebraska	4	283
Oregon	90	4,907	Nevada	10	257
Louisiana	18	4,688	New Hampshire	7	224
Idaho	38	3,073	Delaware	0	0
Kentucky	30	2,904	Rhode Island	0	0
Massachusetts	31	2,562	Hawaii	0	0
Colorado	28	2,359	Dist of Columbia	0	0
			Total	**2,346**	**259,618**

Source: U.S. Department of Labor, Office of Trade Adjustment Assistance. Database sorted by CRS.

While certification figures may overestimate some potential NAFTA job loses, they may miss others. Other workers whose job losses may be related to NAFTA, but who are not counted in the NAFTA-TAA figures, include the following major groups: (1) primary job losers who for some reason either: (a) did not apply for NAFTA-TAA benefits; or (b) applied and were rejected because they did not meet the criterion for certification (e.g., trade with Mexico or Canada contributed "Somewhat" rather than "importantly" to their job loss); (2) some secondary job losers (who typically account for more than half the total number of job losers) in supplier or distributor industries, who for reasons similar to (1) above were not certified to receive NAFTA-TAA benefits; and (3) other job losers whose job loss is less directly related to NAFTA.[6]

Some workers maybe able to claim loss of jobs due to NAFTA even though other factors may be involved. For example, some argue that labor-intensive jobs are shifted out of the United States to Mexico because the U.S. job market is tight and Mexico has a ready supply of workers willing to work for lower wages.

ESTIMATED JOB "GAINS"

NAFTA-related job-gain estimates are based on Department of Commerce (DOC) data. The DOC publishes data on the number of total jobs in the economy supported by exports. This figure is derived through an input-output model which incorporates output-per-worker ratios for each sub-industry. Thus, the model estimates jobs added to the economy when output for any given sector increases. DOC data on *all* jobs supported by *total* merchandise exports can be used to derive the *average* number of jobs supported by 1 billion in merchandise exports each year. The number of jobs supported by $1 billion in exports declines each year because of productivity gains and inflation.[7]

Table 2 includes two measures of job gains from exports. One is a gross number. If focuses only on jobs created by new exports each year. The other is a net number. It takes into consideration jobs created by new exports and jobs lost by productivity gains among workers producing for export both before and since NAFTA went into effect. Thus, the net figure measures the difference between all workers needed to produce exports to Mexico and Canada in 1998 and all workers needed to produce exports in 1993. Gross and net numbers would be identical if productivity gains and inflation did not reduce the number of workers required to produce a given dollar value of exports each year. (More details on the mathematics of this is included in the appendix, p. 14.)

Results of the gross and net measures of NAFTA-related job growth are shown in table 3. Figures in table 3 are derived using data from two sources: 1)DOC state export data (included in appendix table 6, p. 11); and 2) DOC averages of jobs supported by exports (listed in footnote 6). From these numbers it can be estimated that increased

---

6 U.S. Department of Commerce, Economics and Statistics Administration. U.S. Jobs Supported by Goods and Services Exports, 1983-94, p. 27 suggests that approximately two additional jobs support each manufacturing job by producing intermediate inputs, capital goods, and transportation and other services to the goods going to market. The NAFTA-TAA program coves some workers whose job loss is indirectly linked to trade with Mexico or Canada-for example, workers in a business which supplies a company directly affected by trade with Mexico or Canada.. Others, however, whose supplier relationship is less direct, may "slip between the cracks."

7 Data published by the Department of Commerce Economics and Statistics Administration included in a November 1996 report: U.S. Jobs supported by Goods and Services Exports, 1983-1994 and updated by a separate data release, show that the number of jobs supported by $1 billion in merchandise exports was 15,123 in 1993, 14, 361 in 1994, 13,774 in 1995, 13,258 in 1986 and 12,755 in 1997. The average annual decline in the number of jobs supported by a billion dollars worth of exports is about 4%; thus, the estimated figure for 1998 is 12.245.

merchandise exports to Mexico and Canada combined during NAFTA's first five years (1994 through 1998) have *created* approximately 1,212,357 *gross* export-related jobs in the United States (table 3, TOTAL). It can also be estimated that when job losses from productivity gains among those producing for export before and since NAFTA have *added* to the total number of workers producing for export to Mexico and Canada combined, only about 709,988 in *net* jobs.

Estimated numbers of net jobs in each state which support *total* exports to Mexico and Canada for 1993, and 1998 are included in columns (5) and (6) of table 7.

For the country as a whole, the net jobs-from-new-NAFTA-exports figure covering the period 1994-1998, is less than two-thirds the gross figure(59%). However, *net* job gains may be a much higher percent of *gross* job gains in specific states whose export levels started out small and increased since NAFTA went into effect. See. For example, in table 3, Alaska, (right hand column) where the net figure is 76% of the gross figure. For Alaska, exports, initially at a low level, grew by 172% between 1993 and 1997 (as can be seen in appendix table 6).

It should be emphasized that estimated of jobs supporting exports in each state (in table 3) are only very rough estimates, and not an accurate reflection of actual jobs supporting exports, for two reasons. First, state export data on which these figures are based reflect *total sales,* not *value added* by each state. Second, the jobs-supporting-each-billion-dollars-worth-of-exports figure includes jobs both *directly* and *indirectly* involved in manufacturing the merchandise. Since more than half the jobs are indirect-either "upstream" (primarily supplier) or "downstream" (primarily distribution)-and indirect jobs can be carried out anywhere in the country, they are not necessarily attached to the state which the export figures represent.

Table 3. Job Gain by State: Estimated Number of Gross and Net Jobs Supporting New Merchandise Exports to Canada and Mexico Combined, 1993-98

Jobs added in export industries 1993-98				Jobs added in export industries 1993-98			
		(3) Net jobs added				(3) Net jobs added	
(1) STATE	(2) GROSS jobs added	adjusted for productivity changes*	as a % of gross jobs	1) STATE	(2) GROSS jobs added	adjusted for productivity changes*	as a % of gross jobs
Texas	175,407	116,816	67	Connecticut	8,990	3,237	36
Michigan	149,382	79,304	53	Colorado	8,402	4,312	51
California	147,284	101,406	69	Louisiana	6,594	4,858	74
Unallocated[1]	79,859	27,713	53	Delaware	5,802	3,124	54
Illinois	60,181	37,389	62	Vermont	5,501	(996)	(18)
New York	56,256	28,387	50	Mississippi	5,262	3,991	76
Ohio	53,895	24,583	46	Arkansas	5,123	3,207	63
Indiana	43,192	24,591	57	Oklahoma	4,784	2,812	59
Pennsylvania	38,565	23,261	60	Puerto Rico	4,296	2,186	51
N. Carolina	35,298	24,559	70	N. Hamp.	4,229	2,623	62
Minnesota	27,773	19,206	69	Nebraska	4,163	2,775	67
Wisconsin	23,119	14,798	64	Maryland	4,115	2,019	49
Kentucky	20,636	15,112	73	W. Virginia	3,297	2,217	67
Tennessee	20,056	12,212	60	Utah	2,947	1,598	54
New Jersey	20,049	8,775	44	Nevada	2,526	1,903	75
S. Carolina	19,652	14,157	72	N. Dakota	2,387	1,479	62
Arizona	19,128	12,861	67	Maine	2,126	763	36
Georgia	19,036	12,701	67	Alaska	2,075	1,584	76
Missouri	14,860	8,791	59	Idaho	1,973	1,195	61
Mass.	14,474	4,304	30	D of Col	1,799	1,481	82
Washington	13,672	6,833	50	Rhode Island	1,392	428	31
Virginia	13,437	8,692	65	Montana	1,387	877	63
Florida	12,525	5,365	43	S. Dakota	1,005	576	57
Louisiana	11,938	8,190	69	Wyoming	544	366	67
Alabama	11,760	8,132	69	Hawaii	128	23	18
Oregon	10,084	6,991	69	New Mexico	(7)	(407)	5,758
Kansas	9,664	6,719	70	V. Islands	(67)	(106)	158
				Total	**1,212,357**	**709,988**	**59**

[1]Unall: unallocated among states.

***Net jobs added** takes into account estimates of people already working to produce exports who would have lost their jobs to productivity improvements between 1994 and 1998, and subtracts this from the number of jobs added from new exports. Thus, a negative net jobs added number generally means either very slowly growing exports, or an actual decline in exports to Mexico and Canada combined.

Source of data: calculated by CRS from DOC data. This table is a condensation of appendix table 7, p. 12. See footnotes to that table. For explanation of difference between gross and net jobs, see discussion on p. 5, and discussion of the algebraic formula beginning on p. 14.

PERSPECTIVE ON NAFTA-RELATED JOB EFFECTS

As mentioned, data on job losses and of gains due to trade are derived from different methods and databases. They are therefore incompatible and comparisons between the two could be inaccurate.

Estimates presented above on NAFTA-related job losses are relatively small. The more than 259,618 workers certified as of September 28, 1999 as potentially suffering NAFTA-related job *losses* represent less than the number of U.S. jobs *created* in a single month in 1998.

According to the Department of Commerce,[8] roughly half of all jobs supporting exports are included in the manufacturing sector. This suggests that of the approximately 710,000 estimated *net jobs gained* from trade with Mexico and Canada between 1993 and 1998, about 355,000 would be in manufacturing. After four straight years of decline just prior to NAFTA, during NAFTA's first four years, manufacturing jobs increased from about 18 to almost 18.7 million. The NAFTA-related estimated job gain in manufacturing represents about 50% of all manufacturing jobs gained between 1993 and 1998. Therefore, it can be argued that NAFTA may have made a significant contribution to the manufacturing employment turnaround.

To complete the larger picture, tables 4 and 5 identify major industries of potential *job loss* and *export gains* since NAFTA. (*Job gains* from increased exports have not been estimated for specific industries because the number of jobs supported by each billion dollars worth of exports varies by industry.) Several industries [identified by boldface type and by an asterisk (*)] are included on both lists. These are: electronics, transportation equipment, nonelectrical machinery, apparel, paper products, and scientific instruments. This suggests that certain less efficient parts of these industries are being shifted to Mexico and Canada while more efficient parts are expanding domestically. The apparel industry is the biggest potential job lose, with 28% of all NAFTA-related potential job losses. Electronics is second, with 13%.

As mentioned at the beginning of this report, in an economy operating at full employment, trade results in neither net job gains nor net job losses, only in relocations from less efficient to more efficient industries. Job *gains* from trade with Mexico and Canada under NAFTA. Even before NAFTA went into effect there were some estimated that job losses would be concentrated in early years after NAFTA was adopted. Tables 4 and 5 document mid-term industry relocations.

---

[8] U.S. Jobs Supported by Goods and Services Exports, 1983-94, op. cit., p. 27.

Table 4. Mahor Industries of NAFTA-TAA Job Certification, Jan. 1, 1994-Sept 28, 1999

SIC	Industry	No. of jobs certified	% of all NAFTA-TAA certified jobs
23	*Apparel	73,568	28
36	*Electronics	33,684	13
37	*Transportation equip.	17,090	7
34	Fabricated	15,372	6
22	Textiles	14,150	5
35	*Nonelec. Machinery	11,747	5
24	Lumber	9,826	4
38	*Scientif. instruments	9,433	4
26	*Paper products	8,982	3
30	Rubber	7,722	3
31	Leather	7,521	3
	Subtotal	209,095	81
	Other Manufacturing	35,171	14
	All Manufacturing	244,266	95
	Non-Manufacturing	15,352	6
	Total	259,618	101

SIC: Standard Industrial Classification codes. Manufacturing includes 20 2-digit codes which span numbers 20-39.

Source: NAFTA-TAA database, sorted by CRS. See also text footnote 5.

*indicates industries listed in both tables 4 and 5.

Table 5. Major Industries of Increased Exports to Mexico and Canada, 1993-1998

		Growth in Industry_Export Value 1993-98		
SIC	Industry	in $billions	% change 93-98	% of total NAFTA commodity export gain
37	*Transportation Equip	16	56	18
36	*Electronics	16	81	18
35	*Nonelectric machinery	16	74	17
28	Chemicals	8	72	9
33	Primary metals	4	76	5
30	Rubber	4	81	5
38	*Scientific instruments	3	48	3
26	*Paper products	2	69	3
23	*Apparel	2	100	2
20	Food	2	45	3
	Subtotal	**74**	--	**82**
	Other Manufacturing	12	--	13
	Total Manufacturing	**87**	**66**	**95**
	Nonmanufacturing	4	44	4
	TOTAL	**91**	**64**	**100**

Source: DOC Office of Trade and Economic Analysis

APPENDIX: DATA AND EXPLANATION OF METHODOLOGY

This appendix includes supplemental data and explanations. Table 6 includes state exports to Canada, Mexico, and two countries combined for 1993, 1997, and 1998, and also shows growth rates for exports for 1993-98.

Table 7 included calculations supporting job gain figures in table 3. In table 7, column (4) lists *gross* job gains, by state during NAFTA's first five years. The same figures also appear in table 3, p. 7, column (2). In table 7, column (7), lists *net* job gains. The same figures also appear in table 3, p. 7. column (3). Net job gains are gross job gains from new exports minus job losses from productivity growth and inflation in manufacturing and services. Actual calculations are explained in the table 7 footnotes. In table 7, estimates of the total number of workers supporting all exports to Mexico and Canada combined for 1993 and 1998, are included in columns (5) and (6), respectively.

Pages 14 and 15 include an algebraic formula showing how the numbers were calculated.

Table 6. Merchandise Exports to Canada, Mexico, and Combined, 1993-1998

State	U.S. Exports to Canada (in $millions)			U.S. Exports to Mexico (in $millions)			U.S. Exports to Mexico and Canada Combined (in $millions)			%
	1993	1997	1998	1993	1887	1998	1993	1997	1998	93-98
U.S. TOTAL	100,190	150,124	154,151	41,635	71,378		79,010	221,503	233,161	62%
Ala.	622	1,251	1,281	185	814	380	807	2,065	1,661	106%
Ak.	84	305	229	1	2	5	85	307	234	175%
Ariz.	533	1,072	1,059	1,097	1,963	1,993	1,621	3,035	3,052	88%
Ark.	421	820	688	69	141	179	490	961	867	77%
Calif.	7,158	11,492	12,644	5,117	9,942	10,798	12,274	21,434	23,442	91%
Colo.	595	672	729	604	1,418	1,105	1,200	2,090	1,834	53%
Conn	1,407	1,848	1,872	336	530	544	1,743	2,377	2,417	39%
Del.	628	788	938	159	308	290	788	1,097	1,228	56%
D.C.	36	142	158	17	17	29	53	159	187	253%
Fla	1,572	1,928	2,058	770	1,221	1,272	2,341	3,149	3,330	42%
Ga.	1,469	2,000	2,116	324	686	1,136	1,793	2,685	3,252	81%
Hi.	14	33	17	0	1	2	14	34	19	36%
Idaho	157	278	280	36	44	56	193	322	336	74%
Ill.	4,860	8,044	7,943	1,364	2,190	2,798	6,224	10,234	10,741	73%
Ind.	4,265	5,060	5,672	1,168	2,573	3,046	5,432	7,634	8,718	60%
Iowa	919	1,569	1,742	78	168	158	997	1,737	1,900	91%
Ka.	473	834	879	187	449	485	660	1,284	1,364	107%
Ky.	1,058	2,369	2,325	190	345	451	1,248	2,714	2,776	122%
La.	372	663	736	61	133	196	433	796	932	115%
Maine	362	557	528	29	18	17	391	576	545	39%
Md.	601	653	690	96	199	337	698	752	1,027	46%
Mass.	2,541	3,677	3,388	374	468	564	2,915	4,145	3,952	36%
Mich.	11,434	19,760	19,666	5,630	6,459	7,888	17,065	26,218	27,554	61%
Miss.	306	430	493	25	127	242	331	558	735	122%
Mo.	1,113	1,490	1,570	540	1,042	1,190	1,653	2,532	2,760	67%
Mont.	145	236	193	1	21	59	146	257	242	73%
Neb.	296	529	524	61	142	143	357	671	667	87%
Nev.	123	272	301	13	60	23	137	332	324	136%
N.H.	377	672	643	40	74	86	417	746	729	75%
N.J.	2,539	3,837	3,873	789	884	954	3,328	4,721	4,827	45%
N.M.	47	56	68	106	87	87	152	142	155	3%
N.Y.	6,581	10,616	9,957	1,171	1,805	1,936	7,752	10,421	11,893	53%
N.C.	2,289	3,748	3,719	365	1,321	1,565	2,654	5,069	5,284	99%
N.D.	227	428	387	3	18	18	230	445	405	76%
Ohio	7,672	10,472	10,669	927	1,584	1,959	8,598	12,005	12,628	475
Okla.	426	670	656	158	240	295	584	910	951	63%
Ore.	871	1,082	1,329	109	89	452	980	1,170	1,81	82%
Penn.	3,730	5,616	5,857	627	1,140	1,425	4,358	6,756	7,282	67%
R.I.	286	330	372	42	77	68	328	407	440	34%
S.C.	1,009	1,621	1,711	293	936	1,054	1,303	2,557	2,765	112%
S.D.	108	167	166	4	11	19	112	179	185	65%
Tenn.	1,679	2,389	2,589	650	1,188	1,288	2,329	3,577	3,874	66%
Texas	3,811	8,118	8,506	12,861	18,864	21,627	16,672	26,982	30,133	81%
Utah	343	514	505	30	73	87	374	587	592	58%
Vt.	2,075	2,310	2,486	12	9	11	2,087	2,319	2,497	20%

Va.	1,052	1,536	1,836	302	430	547	1,355	1,966	2,383	76%
Wash.	1,723	2,457	2,360	208	272	583	1,931	2,730	2,943	52%
W. Va.	285	479	503	21	34	56	306	513	559	83%
Wis.	1,947	3,096	3,457	288	427	512	2,235	3,524	3,969	78%
Wyo.	38	88	76	4	5	6	42	93	82	95%
P.R.	387	690	657	129	217	160	517	906	817	58%
V.I.	10	4	3	0	4	1	10	8	4	-60%
Unall.	15,163	17,162	17,658	3,744	9,288	7,958	18,907	26,451	25,616	74%

Source: DOC, Office of Trade and Economic Analysis. Website: http://www.ita.doc.gov. Go to "Trade Statistics" and then to "State Export Data."
%_=%change.

Table 7. Gross and Net Jobs Supported by *New* and *All* Merchandise Exports to Mexico and Canada Combined, by State, 1993-1998 (See column explanations at end of table)

GROSS Jobs Added Each Year by *New* Exports to Mexico and Canada					NET Jobs (after compensating for Productivity Growth and inflation) from *All* Exports to Mexico and Canada:			Net as % of Gross
STATE	(1) 1994	(2) 1997	(3) 1998	(4) TOTAL 1994-1998	(5) 1993	(6) 1998	(7) TOTAL1993-1998	(8) Col.(7) /Col.(4)
All U.S.	334,167	410,175	142,777	1,212,35 7	2,144,83 42,854,8 23709,98 9	59%		
Alabama	2,939	7,175	(4,947)	11,760	12,205	20,337	8,132	69%
Alaska	534	1,589	(894)	2,075	1,281	2,865	1,584	76%
Arizona	3,304	5,651	208	19,128	24,508	37,369	12,861	67%
Arkansas	1,800	3,114	(1,151)	5,123	7,409	10,616	3,207	63%
California	24,953	39,157	24,586	147,284	185,618	287,024	101,406	69%
Colorado	(556)	7,367	(3,134)	8,402	18,143	22,455	4,312	51%
Conn.	2,580	3,211	478	8,990	26,357	29,594	3,237	36%
Delaware	1,686	901	1,616	5,802	11,912	15,036	3,124	54%
D.C.	1,399	615	343	1,799	809	2,290	1,481	82%
Florida	2,256	9,957	2,216	12,525	35,408	40,773	5,365	43%
Georgia	4,635	3,464	6,930	19,036	27,116	39,817	12,701	67%
Hawaii	78	(463)	(184)	128	210	233	23	18%
Idaho	709	106	171	1,973	2,919	4,114	1,195	61%
Illinois	19,598	20,687	6,208	60,181	94,124	131,513	37,389	62%
Indiana	9,392	6,045	13,285	43,192	82,152	106,743	24,591	57%
Iowa	3,665	4,455	1,996	11,938	15,074	23,264	8,190	69%
Kansas	9,392	(707)	992	9,644	9,982	16,701	6,719	70%
Kentucky	7,970	6,741	759	20,636	18,877	33,989	15,112	73%
Louisiana	1,790	1,369	1,665	6,594	6,553	11,411	4,858	74%
Maine	738	951	(367)	2,126	5,910	6,673	763	36%
Maryland	341	1,584	2,143	4,115	10,556	12,575	2,019	49%
Mass.	6,900	3,437	(2,363)	14,474	44,084	48,388	4,304	30%
Michigan	155,574	(5,334)	16,358	149,382	258,067	337,371	79,304	53%

Minnesota	3,724	3,904	3,024	27,733	32,953	52,159	19,206	69%
Miss	1,243	1,004	2,179	5,262	5,008	8,999	3,991	76%
Missouri	6,722	1,981	2,792	14,860	25,002	33,793	8,791	59%
Montana	(11)	642	(61)	1,387	2,208	3,085	877	63%
Nebraska	1,140	1,075	(49)5	4,163	5,392	8,167	2,775	67%
Nevada	386	729	(98)	2,526	2,064	3,967	1,903	75%
N. Hamp.	704	510	(208)	4,229	6,303	8,926	2,623	62%
N. Jersey	9,822	8,446	1,298	20,049	50,327	59,102	8,775	44%
N. Mexico	(157)	(114)	(147)	(7)	2,305	1,898	(407)	(5758 %)
New York	15,213	27,566	(6,456)	56,256	117,231	145,618	28,387	50%
N.C.	8,929	7,986	2,632	35,298	40,138	64,697	24,559	70%
N. Dakota	320	701	(502)	2,387	3,480	4,959	1,479	62%
Ohio	19,045	14,411	7,004	53,895	130,034	154,617	24,583	46%
Oklahoma	753	2,040	502	4,784	8,832	11,644	2,812	59%
Oregon	2,323	2,901	7,469	10,084	14,816	21,807	6,991	69%
Penn.	8,262	14,073	6,440	38,565	65,900	89,161	22,261	60%
R. Island	(452)	778	404	1,392	4,959	5,387	428	31%
S.C.	5,749	5,314	2,547	19,652	19,698	33,855	14,157	72%
S. Dak.	352	87	86	1,005	1,689	2,265	576	57%
Tennessee	5,740	5,918	3,636	20,506	35,221	47,433	12,212	60%
Texas	36,236	60,951	38,581	175,407	252,132	368,948	116,816	67%
Utah	746	865	61	2,947	5,650	7,248	1,598	54%
Vermont	(101)	(857)	2,179	5,501	31,569	30,573	(996)	(18%)
Virginia	3,329	3,409	5,106	13,437	20,485	29,177	8,692	65%
Wash.	4,836	479	2,620	13,672	29,201	36,034	6,883	50%
W. Va.	651	1,480	563	3,297	4,627	6,844	2,217	67%
Wisconsin	8,839	6,218	6,461	23,119	33,798	48,596	14,798	64%
Wyoming	151	260	(135)	544	638	1,004	366	67%
P.R.	4,185	1,321	(1,102)	4,296	7,817	10,003	2,186	61%
V.I.	16	(139)	(49)	(67)	155	49	(106)	158%
Unalloctd	(70,790)	115,159	(10,211)	79,859	285,929	313,642	27,713	35%

For explanation of calculations, see next page. Numbers in parentheses are negative. Numbers may not total exactly because of rounding.

[1]Figures for 1995 and 1996 are not shown (between columns (1) and (2) because of space constraints.

Explanation of columns in table 7: (Export data are taken from table 6).

Columns (1)-(4): GROSS jobs supported by new NAFTA-related exports (i.e., additional exports to Mexico or Canada since NAFTA).

Column (1): Total number of gross jobs supported by new exports to Mexico and Canada in 1994: Value of export growth in 1994 (in $billions) **times 14,361** (the estimated number of workers supported by each $billion in exports in 1994). Not shown are figures for 1995 and 1996; the value of export growth times **13,774** and **13,258** respectively.

Column (2): Same figure for 1997: Value of export growth in growth in 1997 **times 12,755**. (The number representing additional workers supported by each $billion in exports each year it takes into consideration both productivity changes and inflation since the previous year.)

Column (3):Same figure for 1998: Value of export growth in 1998 **times 12,245**.

Column (4): Total number of gross jobs supported by new NAFTA-related exports during NAFTA's first five years (94+95+96+97+98).

Columns 4-(8): Net jobs supported by NAFTA-related exports.

Column (5): Total estimated number of net jobs supported by exports to Mexico and Canada combined n 1993. Value of exports in 1993, in $billions, **times 15,123** (number of workers supported by $1 billion in exports).

Column (6): Total estimated number of net jobs supported by exports to Mexico and Canada combined in 1993: Value of exports in 1993, in $billions, **times 15,123** (number of workers supported by $1 billion in exports).

Column (7): *Net* job growth from new NAFTA-related exports, 1993-1998: Columns (6)-(5):

Column (8): *Net* NAFTA-related job growth as a percent of **gross** NAFTA-related job growth: Column (7)/column(4).

NOTE: See p. 14 for the algebraic formula by which these figures were calculated.

ALGEBRAIC FORMULA: RELATIONSHIP BETWEEN GROSS AND NET JOBS CREATED FROM NEW EXPORTS SINCE NAFTA

This section sets forth the equation that quantifies the relationship between the gross and net methods for calculating job changes from trade with Mexico and Canada since NAFTA went into effect. (Gross and net job changes are included in table 3, p. 7, and table 7, p. 12).

The estimated *gross* number looks only at the *increase in the dollar value of* exports each year, in billion, and *multiplies it by the number of workers required* to produce a billion dollars worth of exports. It ignores any decline in employment of those already working to produce exports, which occurs because productivity growth renders them "redundant" or no longer necessary.

The *net* number looks at the *total value of exports each year*, in billion of dollars, and *multiplies that by the number of workers required* to produce a billion dollars worth of exports.

The estimated number of *net* workers added to the payrolls to produce exports for each state calculated in this way reflects three things:

1. Additions to the number of workers because of an increase in exports;

2. Subtractions to the number of workers from:
   a. Productivity gains that occurred during that year, and
   b. Inflation (meaning that fewer items produced would represent the same value as the previous year.)

For any state, the difference between the two numbers (gross and net) is equal to the *sum, for each of the years (1994, 1995, etc.) of:*

The value of exports (in $billions) to Mexico and Canada combined in that year **times** the number of *jobs* supporting each billion dollars worth of exports which are *lost to productivity* and inflation in that year.

Mathematics of Calculation:

Let symbols represent values as follows:

L_g = gross jobs supporting new exports to NAFTA partners, 1993-1998.

L_n = net number of jobs supporting new exports to NAFTA partners, 1993-1998.

X^I = valuc of cxports in initial year "i" in billions of dollars (numbers listed in table 6 divided by 1,000)

J_I = number of jobs estimated to produce a billion dollars worth of exports in initial year; and

J_f = number of jobs estimated to produce a billion dollars worth of exports in final year ("f")

Where, for both X and J:

I = 1993;
i + 1 = 1994;
i+2 = 1995;
i+3 = 1996;
i+4 = 1997; and
i+5 = f = 1998

And in actual numbers,

$J_i = J_{93} = 15{,}123$;
$J_{i+1} = J_{94} = 14{,}361$;
$J_{i+2} = J_{95} = 13{,}774$;
$Ji_{+3} = J_{96} = 13{,}258$;
$Ji_{+4} = J_{97} = 12{,}775$;
$J_{i+5} = J_f = J_{98} = 12{,}245$[9]

The *gross* number of jobs supporting new exports to NAFTA partners can be represented by multiplying the number of jobs supporting a billion dollars worth of exports in a given year by the growth in exports for that year:

---

[9] The figure for 1998 is a CRS estimate based on Department of Commerce estimates for the previous 5 years.

$$(1)\ L_g = J_{i+1}(X_{i+1} - X_i) + J_{i+2}(X_{i+2} - Xi_{+1}) + J_{i+3}(X_{i+3} - X_{i+2}) \ldots J_f(X_f - X_{f-1}).$$

The *net* number of jobs supporting new exports to NAFTA partners can be represented by the following equation showing the difference between the numbers of jobs supporting a billion dollars worth of exports and the value of exports for the beginning and end years:

$$(2)\ L^n = J_f X_f - J_i X_i$$

To find the difference between the gross and net numbers of new jobs created from trade with Mexico and Canada since NAFTA went into effect equation (2) is subtracted from (1):

Thus, for any state, for any year, the *difference between the gross and net estimates* of jobs created from new exports to Mexico and Canada combined since NAFTA went into effect represents the sum total of the number of jobs held by previously employed workers producing exports which are subsequently lost to productivity growth.

CARIBBEAN BASIN INTERIM TRADE PROGRAM: CBI/NAFTA PARITY

Vladimir N. Pregelj

SUMMARY

The entry into force, on January 1, 1994, of the North American Free Trade agreement (NAFTA) has eliminated the advantage that the beneficiaries of the Caribbean Basin Economic Recovery Act (CBERA) and related provisions of the Caribbean Basin Initiative (CBI) have enjoyed in trade with the United States relative to Mexico, and has since given Mexico an increasingly significant competitive edge over the CEBRA countries. The scheduled further implementation of the NAFTA will result in a substantial advantage to Mexico over the CBREA countries and vitiate in part the purpose of the CBERA.

Since the 103rd Congress, Congress has considered legislation to provide, temporarily, to CBI beneficiary countries tariff and quota treatment equivalent to that accorded to Mexico under the NAFTA. The legislation also would be set up mechanisms for the accession of such countries to NAFTA or equivalent bilateral agreements with the Untied States. Due to its controversial nature, based on the perceived adverse consequences for the U.S. textile industry and substantial estimated negative effect on the U.S. budget, however, the legislative process reached an impasse in mid-1995. Although favorably reported in several instances since then, the parity legislation has not been enacted.

In the 105th Congress, parity provisions were added by the House to its budget reconciliation bill but omitted by the Senate and in conference. Parity provisions in a somewhat different language also were introduced in several other measures, of which a House and two Senate bills were reported favorably, but the House bill was defeated and the Senate measures did not come to vote.

Parity legislation was introduced in both houses of the 106th Congress as freestanding measures or as part of broader legislation providing also assistance to Central America and the Caribbean affected by the Hurricanes Mitch and Georges, and ordered reported in the House; the language of a freestanding reported Senate bill was included in a comprehensive trade legislation, and reconciled with the House version in a conference report, passed by both houses and signed by the President May 18, 2000 (P.L.

106-200). The program has been implemented with respect to 11 countries by Presidential proclamation, and by a determination by the USTR of their compliance with the statutory requirements.

MOST RECENT DEVELOPMENTS

In the 106th Congress, CBI/NAFTA parity measures have been included in two instances in legislation of broader scope, providing enhanced trade preferences and assistance to Central American and Caribbean countries affected by the Hurricanes Mitch and Georges: S. 371 (Central American and Caribbean Relief Act) and H.R. 984 (Caribbean and Central America Relief and Economic Stabilization Act); also introduced as freestanding measures are H. R. 1834 and S. 1389. H.R. 984 has been ordered reported in the House, and S. 1389 has been reported favorably and its language subsequently added (with a restriction) to a greatly expanded H.R. 434, which passed the Senate in November 1999. Agreement on the final language has been reached in informal consultations between the two houses; a conference report was filed on May 4, 2000, and passed on the same day by the House and on May 11 by the Senate; it was signed by the President May 18, 2000 (P.L. 106-200). Twenty-four countries have been designated by the Presidential proclamation as beneficiaries of the program, 11 of which have been determinated by the USTR to be in compliance with the statutory customs requirements for participation in the program.

BACKGROUND AND ANALYSIS

SOME BASICS

In its fundamental elements, the U.S. trade and tariff policy treats both .he Caribbean Basin countries and Mexico, in many respects their competitor and a major U.S. trading partner, in an equal manner. Both are accorded most-favored-nation (nondiscriminatory) treatment, to both apply the general tariff advantages of the "production sharing" (also by U.S. firms), and, prior to the entry into force of the North American Free Trade Agreement (NAFTA), both were designated beneficiary countries (BDCs) of the U.S. generalized system of preferences (GSP). Until NAFTA, however, most Caribbean Basin countries had a significant advantage over Mexico because of their participation in the Caribbean Basin Initiative (CBI).

With the entry into force, on January 1,1994, of the preferential tariff and quota provisions of the NAFTA, however, the earlier advantage of CBI countries over Mexico was totally eroded. Moreover, much of NAFTA's further staged implementation has already put CBI countries at a distinct competitive disadvantage compared to Mexico with respect to a substantial portion of U.S. imports from either area. The gap would be even wider when NAFTA liberalization is fully completed (by January 1, 2008). To mitigate, if not eliminate, the adverse effect of the anticipated advantages that Mexico already has gained and will continue to gain relative to CBI countries, legislation was introduced in the past three Congresses to authorize for imports from CBI countries tariff and quota treatment that is identical with or very similar to that accorded Mexico under NAFTA. This treatment would be of limited duration and, in some instances, with a specific view toward eventual accession of Caribbean Basin countries to the NAFTA or the proposed Free Trade Area of the Americas, or conclusion of an equivalent bilateral agreement with the United States.

To provide an idea of the nature and scope of changes in trade competitiveness between the CBERA countries and Mexico that have resulted or still will result form the implementation of the NAFTA, the relevant preferential or special tariff treatments, applicable, are described below. The aspects of trade policy that apply generally to all (or most) U.S. trading partners (e.g., most-favored –nation status, or production-sharing provisions) are not included in any detail.

Caribbean Basin Preference

The Caribbean Basin trade preference is the centerpiece of the Caribbean Basin Initiative (CBI), proposed in February 1982 by President Reagan as a comprehensive program "to promote economic revitalization and facilitate expansion of economic opportunity in the Caribbean Basin region." The preference and some other less comprehensive benefits wee enacted in 1983 by the Caribbean Basin Economy Recovery Act (CBERA) and put into effect as of January 1, 1984. The CBERA has been amended several times, most substantively by the Caribbean Basin Economic Recovery Expansion Act of 1990 ("CBI II"), which added several improvements and made the program permanent.

In its key provisions, the CBERA authorizes unilateral preferential treatment (either duty-free, or at duty rates lower than those generally applicable) for most articles imported from 24 Caribbean Basin countries designated as its beneficiaries (Antigua and Barbuda, Aruba, Bahamas, Barbados, Belize, British Virgin Islands, Costa Rica, Dominica, Dominican Republic, El Salvador, Grenada, Guatemala, Guyana, Haiti, Honduras, Jamaica, Montserrat, and the Grenadines, and Trinidad and Tobago). Eligible for the duty-free preference under the CBERA are all otherwise dutiable products except import-sensitive articles: textiles and apparel subject to textile agreements, footwear ineligible for the GSP as of January 1, 1984, canned tuna, petroleum and its products, and watches and watch parts containing any material originating in countries denied the most-favored-nation status.

Certain import-sensitive articles originally ineligible for duty-free treatment (handbags, luggage, flat goods, work gloves, and certain leather wearing apparel) have been accorded by the 1990 amendment preferential tariff treatment at reduced but still positive rates. This preference consists of a 20% cut in the regular (MFN) duty rates in effect at the end of 1991, phased-in through five stages beginning on January 1, 1992, and completed on January 1, 1996. The reduction, however, could not exceed 2.5% and valorem or, for general rates reduced in the Uruguay Round, be 1% ad valorem greater than that reduction.

To be accorded the duty-free or reduced-rate preference, an eligible article must be a "product of" (as defined in the U.S. general rules of origin) a CBERA beneficiary country an imported directly from it, and at least 35% of the article's import value must have originated in one or more CBERA beneficiaries. In this context, Puerto Rico and the U.S. Virgin Islands are counted as CBERA beneficiaries, and up to 15% of the 35% of the article's qualifying import value may be accounted for by value originating in the U.S. customs territory (other than Puerto Rico).

Duty-free importation of sugar and beef products is subject to a special eligibility requirement that the beneficiary country submit and carry out a stable food production plan ensuing that increased production of sugar and beef will not adversely affect the overall food production of the country.

CBERA duty-free treatment may be suspended for any otherwise eligible article by Presidential proclamation implementing a remedial measure under the import-relief provision (Section 203) of the Trade Act of 1974 or the national-security provision (Section 232) of the Trade Expansion Act of 1962.

Not part of the CBERA but applicable only to CBERA beneficiaries is a provision under which any articles (other than textiles, apparel, and petroleum and its products) assembled or processed in a CBERA country entirely from components or ingredients made in the Untied States may be imported free of duty or quantitative restrictions.

Although textile apparel is ineligible under the CBERA for any type of tariff preference, a special access program (SAP) is in effect for apparel assembled in a CBERA country and imported under the "production sharing" tariff provision (i.e., with regular duty rates applied to a duty-base excluding the value of U.S. origin components) provided it is assembled from fabric formed as well as cut in the Untied States. Such apparel may be imported from CBERA countries in quantities above the regular import quotas up to the bilaterally agreed "guaranteed access levels" (GALs) (although with no reduction in the duty rate). GAL agreements are in force with Costa Rica, Dominican Republic, El Salvador, Guatemala, and Jamaica.

Most CBERA beneficiaries (except Aruba, Bahamas, Netherlands Antilles, and Nicaragua) are also beneficiaries of the GSP (described below), and may utilize its benefits alternatively to those of the Caribbean preference.

The overall statistical picture of U.S. imports from the 24 CBERA countries in 1999 shows that out of the total value of $19,364.8 million, $13,336 (68.9%) was imported free of duty, of which $2,563.2 million (13.2%) under the CBERA preference and $94.9 million (0.5%) under the GSP; the remaining $10,678.0 million was duty-free under the regular rates or as the duty-free share of the production-sharing provisions. Including the value of imports subject to reduced rates, total U.S. imports under the CBERA program (duty-free and at reduced rates) amounted to $2,673.2 million (13.6% of total U.S. imports from CBERA countries).

PRE-NAFTA SPECIAL TARIFF TREATMENT OF MEXICO

Before the NAFTA entered into force, Mexico was a designated beneficiary developing country (BDC) of the GSP and, as such, enjoyed certain benefits that were similar to, if somewhat less generous than those of the CBERA beneficiaries. While the GSP authorizes duty-free importation (but has no provisions for imports at reduced rates), the range of articles eligible for the preference is narrower than that of the NCBERA. Generally ineligible by law under the GSP are textile and apparel articles subject to textile agreements; watches, except those that the President determines will not cause injury to U.S. domestic watch or watch band, strap, or bracelet manufacturing or assembly industry; import-sensitive semi-manufactured and manufactured glass products; footwear, handbags, luggage, flat goods, work gloves and leather wearing apparel; and any other articles determined by the President as import sensitive in the GTSP context. The GSP also is of temporary duration and must be renewed periodically by enactment. The most recent renewal remains in effect through September 30, 2001.

GSP eligibility can be suspended for individual articles imported from individual countries, usually following a review of the specific situation; it is also suspended when such imports exceed specified statutory levels, a criterion referred to as the "competitive need limit." The latter suspension may be waived under specified conditions. Under these provisions, suspension of GSP eligibility was in effect prior to NAFTA for imports from Mexico falling within some 90 tariff items, mostly fresh vegetables, copper ore and primary copper, and sundry auto parts.

In a rule of origin similar to that of CBERA, an eligible import qualifies for the GSP preference if it is a product of a BDC and imported directly from it, and at least 35% of the article's import value has originated in the country of export in two or more counties that are members of the same association of countries)Andean group, Association of South East Asian nations, Caribbean Common Market, Southern Africa Development Community, and West African Economic and Monetary Union), of none of which, however, Mexico is a member. Unlike the CBERA, the GSP does not allow the value of the components of U.S.-, Puerto Rico-, or U.S. Virgin Islands-origin to count toward the required 35% BDC-origin value requirement.

A "special regime" arrangement for textile apparel, virtually identical to the CBI's special access program, also was in effect with Mexico prior to the entry into force of the NAFTA.

Total U.S. imports from Mexico in 1993, the last year before the implementation of NAFTA, amounted to (in millions) $38, 667.7 of which $19,800.5 (51.2%) was duty free, further broken down into $4,498.1 (11.6%) under regular rates, $9,871.9 (25.5%) under the production sharing provisions and $5,430.5 (14.0%) under the GSP. Dutiable imports totaled (in millions) $18,867.2 (48.8%), of which $9,095.8 (23.5%) represented the dutiable portion of production-sharing products and $9,771.4 (25.3%) imports under regular duty rates.

A summary comparison of special trade benefits available to CBI countries with those available to Mexico before the entry into force of the NAFTA shows that CBI countries enjoyed a distinct advantage over Mexico because:

a) The range of articles accorded preferential treatment under the CBERA is significantly broader than under the GSP because CBERA ineligibility applies only tot hose product categories specifically listed in the statute; under the GSP, however, not only is the range of articles excluded from the preference by statute broader, but additional discretionary and "competitive need" exclusions have been made.

b) Under the "rule of origin" for the eligibility of a Mexican product for the GSP, its value could not include any value of U.S., Puerto Rican, or U.S. Virgin Islands origin.

c) Import-sensitive articles eligible under CBERA for reduced-rate preference are excluded altogether from GSP eligibility.

d) Duty- and quota-free treatment that applies to qualifying articles assembled or processed in a CBERA country entirely from components or ingredients originating on the United States did not apply to articles similarly processed in Mexico.

e) The CBERA is a permanent program, whereas the GSP is authorized for a specific period of time and must be periodically reauthorized by legislation in order to remain in force.

MEXICO'S BENEFITS UNDER THE NAFTA AND THEIR EFFECT ON CBERA BENEFICIARIES

When Mexico acceded tot he NAFTA, its tariff position with the United States changed radically and improved substantially relative tot hat of the CBI countries as well as absolutely.

Although Mexico's GSP eligibility was revoked as of January 1, 1994-the date NAFTA went into effect-the earlier duty-free status of articles imported from Mexico under the GSP was continued in force under NAFTA on a permanent basis (rather than being contingent on extensions of the GSP authority), although under the somewhat less favorable NAFTA rules of origin. Moreover, duty-free status was accorded for the first time to many previously dutiable articles, including handmade or folklore textile and apparel articles. These actions equalized Mexico's duty-free preferential status with that of CBI countries, thus eliminating their earlier advantages over Mexico.

Also on January 1, 1994, the first stage of reductions that eventually (at the latest by January 1, 2008) are to eliminate the pre-NAFTA tariffs in a specified number of annual cuts was implemented. Further staged tariff reductions have taken place on January 1 of every year since. This process has created an initially still marginal but eventually substantial actual advantage to Mexico with respect to articles ineligible for the Caribbean Basin duty-free preference (e.g., textiles and textile apparel) which, under the NAFTA, are in the phase-in process toward eventual duty-free and quota-free status. Similarly, the NAFTA staged reductions have already resulted in reversing CBERA's erstwhile advantage over Mexico with respect to import-sensitive articles eligible for the CBERA 20%-reduced duty rates. The phasing-in of these reductions)to zero) either ahs already been completed or has at least exceeded the CBERA 20%-reduction. Of the two reduction schedules still being phased in, the one with the longer phase-in period) ending in 2008) has already cut the rates by 40% and the shorter one (ending in 2003), by 60%.

Imports of articles ineligible for duty-free treatment under the CBERA (see above) account for over one-half, by value, of all U.S. imports from the group. The most crucial and potentially injurious to CBERA countries is the NAFTA treatment of textiles and apparel article which, in addition to constituting the largest single category of U.S. imports from CBERA countries by far, are subject to relatively high duty rates. Some of the adverse effect of this NAFTA treatment on the CBERA countries has been mitigated by the relatively long (6 or 10 annual stage, some even 15 stages) phasing-in period of the NAFTA duty elimination. Another mitigating factor is the extensive use by American firms in imports of apparel from CBERA countries of the production-sharing provision, where a portion of the value of the import already is duty free, which effectively reduces its duty cost to the U.S. importer. The same tariff treatment, however, is also available generally to similar imports from Mexico and at decreasing duty rates.

Moreover, the NAFTA authorized eventual duty-and quota-free importation from Mexico of textile and apparel goods that had previously fallen under the "special regime" and of those that had not qualified for "special regime" treatment because of additional processing, such as bleaching or dyeing, that was beyond mere assembly. In addition, reduced rates were authorized under NAFTA within an overall quota for imports of textile apparel and other articles assembled in Mexico from components cut in the United States from fabrics imported from any third country. Reduced rates also were authorized, within separate quotas, for textile and apparel article of wool, and cotton and man-made fiber assembled in a NAFTA country from components cut or made from fabric or yarn originating outside the NAFTA area.

Less crucial for the CBERA countries is the NAFTA treatment of petroleum and its products. Its adverse effect on the competitiveness of CBERA-origin petroleum is likely to be limited: petroleum products have accounted for a relatively small share (by value) of total U.S. imports from the group, U.S. duty rates on products in this category are very low (equivalent to a fraction of or slightly over 1%) and will take 10 years to be eliminated under NAFTA. Moreover, this action affects directly only the three CBERA petroleum-exporting countries: Bahamas, Netherlands Antilles, and Trinidad and Tobago.

The adverse effect of NAFTA on U.S. imports of footwear from the CBERA countries also is likely to be less serious: footwear accounts for a relatively small share of imports from either source and much of it is imported into the United States under the production-sharing provision. The NAFTA duty elimination is being phased-in in ten stages, thus mitigating the severity of the change.

The CBERA ineligibility of watches and watch parts containing any material originating in non-MFN countries, is, in practice, irrelevant since no imports of such watches have been taking place.

To recapitulate: the implementation of the NAFTA has not only eliminated all earlier tariff advantages of the CBI countries over Mexico, but has created actual-and increasing-advantages for Mexico over the BCERA countries, specifically with respect to articles ineligible for the CBERA preference. Either the further phasing-in of the NAFTA reductions, the BCERA competitive disadvantage vs. Mexico will be increasing and eventually many become quite serious.

Although not directly related to the NAFTA problem it should also not be overlooked that the overall advantages of the CBERA (as well as of the NAFTA(are being diluted in any event by the phasing-in of the implementation of concessions agreed to by the United States in the Uruguay Round of multilateral negotiations and applied to imports from virtually all countries.

PARITY LEGISLATION AND ACTION

Legislation intended to remedy the perceived most serious aspects of the NAFTA's adverse consequences for the CBERA countries-the actual advantages that Mexico had already gained, would continue to gain, over the CBERA countries-was introduced in the 103rd and the 104th Congress, but saw no action beyond committee hearings.

The legislation was held back primarily because of its in practice inevitable focus on textiles and apparel, and that in two aspects; (1) textiles and apparel, the principle category of articles affected by the proposals, are considered highly import sensitive and there was concern that significant increases in their imports would be disruptive of the domestic textile industry, and (2) because of their relatively high import duty rates, their reduction and eventual elimination would entail a significant loss of customs (hence, budget) revenues.

The most important-and, in terms of affected trade, broadest-feature of CBI/NAFTA parity legislation would be the new preferential treatment of textiles or apparel imported from CBERA countries. These articles are not subject to import quotas and ineligible for the CBERA preference. In its main aspects, such treatment wold consist of quota-free or at least increased-quota imports, subject to an identical progressive elimination of customs duties on imports from CBERA countries as would apply to such imports originating in Mexico; it would, however, also subject them to the somewhat stricter NAFTA-like rules of origin.

Opponents of parity legislation claimed early on that, since NAFTA's entry into force on January 1, 1994, imports from CBI countries of textiles and apparel, a product category that allegedly would be severely adversely affected by the implementation of the NAFTA, not only had not abated but had increased significantly. In view of the pay-as-you-go budget requirements, an additional important adverse consideration has been the projected decrease in customs revenues that gradual freeing of the still dutiable articles (mostly textiles and textile apparel, which are duties at relatively high rates) would bring about. Customs duty losses resulting from the CBI/NAFTA parity legislation were initially (1995) estimated variously at 41.1 billion over 5 years and $1.7 billion over 10 years.

105th Congress

The Congressional Budget Office (CBO), as cited in S. Rept. 105-280, estimated that the CBI/NAFTA parity legislation in the proposed Trade and Tariff Act of 1998 (S. 2400) would result in revenue losses (by fiscal year, in millions of dollars) of $98 in 1999, $138 in 2000, $147 in 2001, and $26 in 2002; and an Administration estimate of the cost of its most recent proposal places it at $326 million in 2000 and $444 million in 2001. The latest projections by the CBO of reductions of federal revenues (S. Rept. 106-160) due to the CBI/NAFTA parity legislation estimate such losses (in millions) in FY2000 at $252, in FY2001 at $260, in FY2002 at $272, in FY2003 at $289, in FY2004 at $309, and in FY2005 at $83. In view of the projected termination of the program at the end of 2005, no losses have been projected for subsequent fiscal years.

Although several versions of CBI/NAFTA parity legislation were considered in the 105th Congress, none was enacted. The United States-Caribbean Trade Partnership Act, a subtitle of H.R. 2014 (Budget Reconciliation Act), was passed by the House, but omitted in its Senate, conference, and enacted versions. A freestanding measure with the same title and virtually identical operative provisions (H.R. 2644), was reported favorably in the House, but defeated in the floor vote. Two measures entitled United States-Caribbean Basin Trade Enhancement Act were reported favorably in the Senate but did not come to a vote: a freestanding bill (S. 1278), and a subtitle in the Trade and Tariff Act of 1998 (S. 2400), incorporating similar provisions.

106th Congress

In the 106th Congress, parity legislation was introduced in four different versions, of which only two received some legislative consideration. No action was taken on the United States-Caribbean Basin Trade Enhancement Act (Title I of the Central American and Caribbean Relief Act (S. 371) or the Administration proposal (H.R. 1834), also named United States-Caribbean Basin Trade Enhancement Act (CBTEA).

The other two bills, the United States-Caribbean Trade Partnership Act (Title I of the Caribbean and Central America Relief and Economic Stabilization Act (H.R. 984) and the United States-Caribbean Basin Trade Enhancement Act (S. 1389), received some legislative action. H.R. 984 was reported favorably (H. Rept. 106-519, pt. 1) March 13, 2000, but not voted on. S. 1389 was reported favorably (S. Rept. 106-160) September 16, 1999, and its language was added to H.R. 434. The language of these two measures was used as the basis for the eventual compromise language agreed to in conference on the final version of H.R. 434.

The language of S. 1389 as reported has been included in its entirety as Title II (Trade Benefits for Caribbean Basin) in S. Amdt. 2325 to an expanded H.R. 434, passed by the Senate (76-19) November 3, 1999. Reconciliation of the parity provisions of the House and Senate versions of H.R. 434, focusing primarily on the preferential treatment of textile products, took place in protracted informal consultations between the two houses.

A formal conference report on H.R. 434 (H. Rept. 106-606) was filed May 4, 2000, passed the House that same day (309-110) and the Senate on May 11, 2000 (77-19). It was signed by the President May 18, 2000 (P.L. 106-200) (Trade and Development Act of 2000), but not yet implemented. Its implementation was authorized by Presidential proclamation 7351 of October 2, 2000 (65 F.R. 59329; October 4, 2000), but the preferential treatment provided by it was to become effective with respect to each of its individual beneficiary countries upon the determination by the U.S. Trade Representative, published in the *Federal Register*, that the country has satisfied the customs requirements for such treatment.

The key provisions of the **enacted version of the United States-Caribbean Basin Trade Partnership Act-CBTPA** (Title II of P.L. 106-200) reflect the policy, stated in the legislation, to offer Caribbean Basin countries willing to prepare to become parities to a free-trade agreement with the United States treatment equivalent to that accorded to

NAFTA countries, and to seek Caribbean Basin countries' participation in a free-trade agreement by 2005. The provisions focus primarily on the preferential treatment of textile products. The conference version has retained many provisions of the initial legislation and added others. It extended the transitional *period of preferential treatment* to run from October 1, 2000, through September 30, 2008, or, if earlier, the date a free-trade agreement between the United States and CBTPA country enters into force.

Several *eligibility criteria* have been added (to those for the basic CBERA preference) specifically for a country's designation as a CBTPA beneficiary country of the transitional program with respect to the country's WTO obligations and accession to the FTAA, intellectual rights protection, worker rights, elimination of worst forms of child labor, counter-narcotics certification, participation in the Inter-American Convention Against Corruption, and government procurement.

With regard to *textile articles*, the conference versions provides duty- and quota-free treatment as follows:

1) Apparel assembled in a CBTPA beneficiary country from fabric made in the United States from U.S..-made yarn, and cut in the United States; or from fabric made in the Unite Stated from U.S.-made yarn, cut in the CBTPA country, and sewn together in a CBTPA country with U.S.-made thread.

2) Apparel articles (except socks) knit-to-shape from U.S.-made yarn in a beneficiary country, or articles (other than non-underwear T-shirts) assembled from fabric knit in the united States or in a beneficiary county from U.S.-made yarn, and cut in a beneficiary country. Duty-free treatment of knit-to-shape articles applies to 250 million square meters equivalent (SME) for the year beginning October 1, 2000, with 16% annual increases through September 30, 2004, and after that, through September 30, 2008, at the level for 2004, or in amounts set by law. The annual limit for non-underwear T-shirts has been set at 4.2 million dozen for the year beginning October 1, 2000 , with 16% annual increases through September 30, 2004, and after that at the latter level, or in amounts set by law.

3) Brassieres cut and assembled in the United States and/or one or more beneficiary countries during the six-year period beginning with October 1, 2001, if the cost of the U.S.-made fabric components used in their manufacture by their individual producer during the preceding year is at least 75% of their customs value; if the U.S.-component requirement is not met in any year, the producer will not be eligible for the preference until the year following the year in which the value of U.S.-made fabric components is at least 85% of the customs value of the brassiere produced by the individual producer.

4) Apparel articles assembled in a beneficiary country from fibers, fabric, or yarn not formed in the Untied States or a beneficiary

country, that are not widely available in commercial quantities (as described in Annex 401 of the NAFTA). The President is authorized to proclaim, upon request and under specified procedure, this preference for other fibers, fabric, or yarn.

5) Certified handloomed, handmade, and folklore articles,

6) Preferential treatment is not denied to articles containing limited quantities of foreign-origin findings or interlinings, or de minimis quantities of fibers or yarns of non-U.S. or non-CBTP origin, or nylon filament yarn made in a country with which the Untied States has a pre-January 1, 1995 free-trade agreement (Canada, Mexico, and Israel).

7) Textile luggage assemble in a CBTPA beneficiary country from fabric made in the United States from U.S.-made yarn, and cut in the United States; or from fabric made in the United States from U.S.-made yarn, and cut in a CBTPA country.

Penalties are provided for exporters transshipping textiles articles ineligible for the preference, and for countries not taking transshipment prevention measures; and NAFTA-like emergency action is provided to remedy or prevent injury to a U.S. industry by surges in imports.

Other *import-sensitive articles* (ineligible for CBERA duty-free treatment, but some of which are dutied at CBERA preferential reduced rates) are to be dutied at NAFTA-Mexico rates (if lower than CBERA rates).

The measure contains definitions of concepts used and a variety of administrative provisions: customs procedures are to be identical to those under NAFTA, and the Customs Service is to study and prepare a report, to be submitted to Congress by the U.S. Trade Representative by October 1, 2001, on cooperation by CBTPA countries in prevention quota circumvention.

The President is authorized to withdraw or suspend the designation of any country as a CBTPA beneficiary or withdraw, suspend, or limit the preferential treatment under the CBTPA of any article of any country, if its performance under the specific eligibility criteria for CBTPA preference is not satisfactory.

The measure changes several reporting requirements: beginning with December 31, 2010, the triennial USTR report on the overall operation of he CBERA is changed, for the duration of the transitional period, to a biennial report with added information on each CBTPA country's performance under the special eligibility criteria; and beginning with September 30, 2001, the annual report by the U.S. International Trade Commission to Congress and the President on the economic impact of the CBERA on U.S. industries and consumers (including those in Puerto Rico) is changed to a biennial report.

The measure provides, under specified conditions, CBERA-like duty-free treatment for spirituous beverages made in Canada with rum produced in the U.S. Virgin Islands or a CBERA beneficiary country.

The President is directed to convene a meeting of the USTR and trade ministers of the CBTPA countries for the purpose of reaching an agreement on initiating negotiations for CBTPA countries' entering into free-trade agreements with the United States.

The *implementation* of the CBTPA was authorized by Presidential proclamation 7351 of October 2, 2000 (65 F.R. 59329; Cot 4, 2000), designating 24 Caribbean Basin countries as beneficiaries of the program, and put into effect as of the same date with respect to 10 countries (Belize, Costa Rica, Dominican Republic, El Salvador, Guatemala, Haiti, Honduras, Jamaica, Nicaragua, and Panama) by USTR determination of their compliance with the statutory customs requirements (65 F.R. 60236; Oct. 1, 2000); Guyana was added to the list effective November 9, 2000 (65 F.R. 69988; Nov. 21, 2000).

LEGISLATION

P.L. 106-200, H.R. 434

Title II (United States-Caribbean Basin Trade Partnership Act-CTPTA). H.R. 434 originally did not contain CBI/NAFTA parity provisions; Title II was proposed on the floor of the Senate October 27, 1999, as amendment (by addition) to H.R. 434. H.R. 434, as amended, passed Senate (76-19) November 3, 1999. The House and Senate versions (essentially, parity language of H. R. 984 and S. 1389) have been reconciled in informal consultations between the two houses; a formal conference report (H.Rept. 106-606) was filed May 4. Conference report passed the House on the same day (309-110); passed the Senate on May 11, 2000 (77-19). H.R. 434 was signed into law (Trade and Development Act of 2000) May 18, 2000. (Its implementation was authorized as of October 2, 2000, by Presidential Proclamation 7351 (65 F.R. 59329), but the preferential treatment provided by it was to become effective with respect to any beneficiary country upon the determination by the USTR that the country has satisfied the customs requirements for such treatment. –See Chronology.)

H.R. 984 (Crane)

Title I (United States-Caribbean Trade Partnership Act). Introduced March 3,1 999; referred to the Committees on Ways and Means, International Relations, Banking and Finance Services, the Judiciary, and Armed Services. Ways and Means Committee held a hearing on March 3, 1999; reported favorably by Ways and Means Committee March 13, 2000 (H.Rept. 106-519, part 1).

H.R. 1834 (John Lewis)

United States-Caribbean Basin Trade Enhancement Act. Introduced May 18, 1999; referred to the Committee on Ways and Means.

S.371 (Graham)

Title I (United States-Caribbean Basin Trade Enhancement Act). Introduced February 4, 1999; referred to the Committee on Finance.

S. 1389 (Roth)

United States-Caribbean Basin Trade Enhancement Act, an original Finance Committee bill, reported without written report July 16, 1999; written report (S. Rpt. 106-160) filed September 16, 1999. Language incorporated as Title II (Trade Benefits for Caribbean Basin) in the Senate version of H.R. 434.

CHRONOLOGY

11.09/00 -Effective date for application of CBI/NAFTA parity benefits to Guyana upon USTR's determination of country's satisfactory compliance with statutory customs requirements (65 F.R. 69988; Nov. 20, 2000).

10.02/00 -In Presidential proclamation 7351 (65 F.R. 59329; October 10, 2000), President Clinton authorized the implementation of the CBTPA by designating 24 countries as beneficiaries of the program, but delaying its effect with respect to each of its individual beneficiary countries until a determination is made by the USTR that the country has satisfied the customs requirements for such treatment.

-Effective date for application of CBI/NAFTA parity benefits to Belize, Costa Rica, Dominican Republic, El Salvador, Guatemala, Haiti, Honduras, Jamaica, Nicaragua, and Panama upon USTR's determination of countries' compliance with customs requirements 65 F.R. 60236; Oct. 10, 2000).

05/18/00 -President Clinton signed H.R. 434 into law (Trade and Development Act of 2000), providing in Title II (United States-Caribbean Basin Trade Partnership Act-CBTPA) for Caribbean Basin countries preferential trade treatment in parity with that of the NAFTA.

05/11/00 -Conference language of H.R. 4343 passed by the Senate (77-19).

05/04/00 -Conference report on H.R. 434 (Trade and Development Act of 2000) (H.Rpt. 106-606), containing Title II-Trade Benefits for Caribbean Basin, filed after protracted informal consultations, reconciling the versions of parity provisions of H.R. 984 as reported by the House and H.R. 434 as amended by the Senate.

-House passed conference version of H.R. 434 (309-110).

03/13/00 -H.R. 984 reported favorably by Ways and Means Committee (H. Rept. 106-519, Pt. 1).

11/03/99 -H.R. 434, including Title II (United States-Caribbean basin Trade Enhancement Act) as added by the Senate, passed by a vote of 76 ayes to 19 nays.

10/27/99	-Language of S. 1389 as reported included as Title II in substitute Senate amendment SP 2325, proposed to an expanded H.R. 434, renamed the "Trade and Development Act of 1999."
09/16/99	-S. 1389 (United States-Caribbean Basin Trade Enhancement Act), reported favorably with written report (S. Rept 106-160).
07/16/99	-S. 1389 (United States-Caribbean Basin Trade Enhancement Act), an original Finance Committee bill, reported without written report.
06/10/99	-H.R. 984 ordered to be reported amended by the Ways and Means Committee.
05/18/99	-H.R. 1834 (United States-Caribbean Basin Trade Enhancement Act) introduced and referred to the Committee on Ways and Means.
03/23/99	-House Ways and Means Trade Subcommittee held a hearing on H.R. 984.
03/04/99	-H.R. 984, containing the "United States-Caribbean Trade Partnership Act" as Title I, introduced and referred to Committees on Ways and Means, International Relations, Banking and Finance Services, the Judiciary, and Armed Forces.
02/04/99	-S. 371, containing the "United States-Caribbean Trade Enhancement Act" as Title I, introduced and referred to the Committee on Finance.
07/31/98	-S. 2400, containing the "United States-Caribbean Basin Trace Enhancement Act" as Subtitle C of Title I, reported favorably by the Finance Committee as an original measure (S. Rept. 105-208).
11/04/97	-H.R. 2644 ("United States-Caribbean Trade Partnership Act") failed of passage in the House on a roll-call vote (182-234).
10/31/97	-H.R. 2644 reported favorably (H.Rept. 105-365).
10/09/97	-S. 1278 ("United States-Caribbean Trade Enhancement Act") reported favorably as an original measure (S. Rept. 105-105).
07/31/97	-Conference report on H.R. 2014 agreed to unanimously by the Senate and with a 389-43 vote by the House.
07/30/97	-H.R. 2014 reported by conference (H.Rept. 105-220) without CBI/NAFTA parity provisions.

06/27/97 -H.R. 2014 passed the Senate amended (language of S. 949, not containing any CBI/NAFTA provisions, substituted for House-passed language) in lieu of S. 949.

06/27/97 -H.R. 2014 passed the House.

06/27/97 -H.R. 2096 ("United Sates-Caribbean Basin Trade Enhancement Act") introduced.

06/24/97 -H.R. 2014 (budget reconciliation bill) reported as an original measure from the House Committee on the Budget (H.Rept. 105-148), containing as Subtitle H of Title IX the "United States-Caribbean Trade Partnership Act," inserted by the Ways and Means Committee during its consideration of the budget reconciliation legislation.

Note: No legislative steps were taken in 1996.

Congressional Hearings, Reports, and Documents

U.S. Congress. Conference Committee. Trade and Development Act of 2000. Conference report (to accompany H.R. 434). Washington, U.S. Govt. Print, Off., May 4, 2000. 146 p. (At head of title: 106th Congress, 2d Session. H. Rept. 106-606).

U.S. Congress House. Committee on Ways and Means. Caribbean and Central America Relief and Economic Stabilization Act. Report together with additional and dissenting views (to accompany H.R. 984). Washington, U.S. Govt. Print. Off., March 13, 2000. 52 p. (H.Rept 106-519, Part 1).

United States-Caribbean Trade Partnership Act; report to accompany H.R. 2644 including cost estimate of the Congressional Budget Office. H.Rept. Washington, U.S. Govt. Print. Off., Oct. 31, 1997. 30 p. (H. Rept. 105-365).

U.S. Congress. Senate. Committee on Finance. Trade and Tariff Act of 1998; report (to accompany 2400 [sic]. Washington, U.S. Govt. Print Off., July 31, 1988. 82 p. (S. Rept. 105-280).

United States-Caribbean Basin Trade Enhancement Act; report (to accompany S. 1389). Washington, U.S. Govt. Print. Off., September 16, 1999. 29 p. (S. Rept. 106-160).

For Additional Reading

Beranal, Ricahrd L. "A Jamaican Case for Trade Parity with NAFTA." *Congressional Record,* v. 142, no. 46, March 29, 1996: E505-506.

Hutchinson, Gladstone A., and Ute Schumacher. "NAFTA's Threat to Central American and Caribbean Basin Exports: A Revealed Comparative Advantage Approach." *Journal of Interamerican Studies and World Affairs*, v. 36, spring 1994: 127-148.

Kornis, Magda. "Is NAFTA Affecting U.S. Imports from the Caribbean Basin?" *International Economic Review,* September/October 1997 (USITC Publications 3065): 3-8.

Lewis, David E. "The North American Free Trade Agreement: Its Impact on Caribbean Basin Economies." *Caribbean Affairs,* v. 4, October-December 1991: 56-67.

"NAFTA Parity." In: U.S. International Trade Commission. *Caribbean Basin Economic Recovery Act: impact on the United States (twelfth report 1996.* (Investigation No. 332-227). (USITC Publication 3058). Washington, September 1997: 24-34.

Scott, Robert E. *Rebuilding the Caribbean: a better foundation for sustainable growth.* (Briefing Paper). Washington, Economic Policy Institute, March 1999. 18 p.

U.S. General Accounting Office. *Caribbean Basin: worker rights and progress made but enforcement issues remain.* Washington, July 20, 1998. B-280379. GAO/NSIAD-98-205. 49 p.

U.S. Apparel Imports from Caribbean Basin Countries and Mexico [Memorandum to the Hon. Ernest F. Hollings], Washington, December 3, 1997. B-278724. GAO/NSIAD-98-59R. 11 p.

CRS Report

CRS Report RS20174, *CBI/NAFTA Parity Proposals: A Comparison*, by Vladimir N. Predgelj.

TRADE AND THE AMERICAS

Raymond J. Ahearn

SUMMARY

The Summit of the Americas, held in Miami during December 1994, led to ongoing Congressional interest bearing on three interrelated trade policy issues. The first involves an invitation extended to Chile to join the North America Free Trade Area (NAFTA). The second focuses on preferential tariff treatment for countries of the Caribbean and Central America. The third concerns movement towards a Free Trade Area of the Americas (FTAA). In addition, a fourth issues has arisen concerning a request by the Andean countries to extend Andean Trade Preferences Act (ATPA) beyond its scheduled December 2001 expiration date.

In a separate action following the Miami Summit, the United States, Canada, and Mexico invited Chile to enter into negotiations to accede to NAFTA. Envisioned as a first step towards creation of an FTAA, preliminary negotiations started in July 1995. Chile, however, shortly thereafter suspended the negotiations pending renewal of U.S. "fast-track" negotiating authority. Four years later, Chile proposed on August 10, 1999, to re-start discussions on a bilateral free trade agreement (not NAFTA accession). In July 2000, nearly a year later, the two partners agreed on a work program aimed at addressing issues that would be covered in a free trade negotiation.

A second issue concerns the treatment of the Caribbean and Central American Countries that may have been hurt in trade and investment terms as a result of the Implementation of NAFTA. These countries maintain that they have been losing trade and Investment opportunities to Mexico as a result of the preferential access Mexico has to the U.S. market under NAFTA.

On May 18, 2000, President Clinton signed into law (P.L. 106-200) legislation that contained provisions (Title II, also known as the "U.S.-Caribbean Basin Trade Partnership Act") providing benefits for CBI beneficiary countries that are similar to the tariff benefits afforded Mexico. The new law, in particular, offers expanded access and preferential tariff treatment to certain textile and apparel products assembled from U.S. fabric, under specified conditions. The key provisions agreed to by conferees reflect compromises between a relatively expansive House bill (H.R. 984) and a more restrictive Senate bill (S. 1389).

The third issue involves movement towards hemispheric free trade. Nearly four years after the 1994 Summit of the Americas, hemispheric leaders formally launched the FTAA negotiations in 1998. Subsequently, the negotiations have been slowed by domestic economic and political problems in the hemisphere and the continued absence of U.S. fast trade authority. At a meeting held in Toronto November 3-4, 1999, trade ministers directed negotiators to compile drafts from all negotiating groups for consideration at the next ministerial meeting in April 2001 in Argentina. High-level political support, however, remains less than overwhelming.

A fourth issue that has arisen involves a request from Bolivia, Colombia, Ecuador, and Peru to extend the ATPA beyond its 20001 expiration date, to reduce the list of products excluded from tariff benefits, and to add Venezuela as a beneficiary country. The 1991 ATPA granted Andean countries tariff preferences for 10 years in an effort to help the countries fight narcotics trafficking.

MOST RECENT DEVELOPMENTS

On October 5, 2000, the Chairman of the Senate Finance Subcommittee on International Trade urged the Clinton Administration to jump-start what he called stalled negotiations to create a Free Trade Area of the Americas (FTAA).

On July 13, 2000, the United States and Chile agreed on a work plan to discuss issues that would be considered in a free trade negotiation. The U.S. –Chile Commission on Trade and Investment will meet in early October to review the status of those discussions.

On May 18, 2000, President Clinton signed into law (P.L. 106-200) legislation that contained provisions (Title II, known as the "U.S.-Caribbean Basin Trade Partnership Act") providing benefits for Caribbean countries. The key provisions expand access and preferential treatment to certain textile and apparel products assembled from U.S. fabric subject to specific conditions. The bill also provides preferences for apparel made with regional fabric under specified conditions.

BACKGROUND AND ANALYSIS

SUMMIT OF THE AMERICAS: TRADE RESULTS

At the Summit of the Americas held December 9-11, 1994 in Miami, 34 hemispheric democracies agreed to create a "Free Trade Area of the Americas (FTAA)." Under the Declaration of Principles, the countries committed to "begin immediately" construction of free trade area and to complete negotiations no later than the year 2005.

The Declaration stated that concrete progress toward the FTAA will occur before the close of the century. Based on the view that substantial progress towards economic integration in the hemisphere has already been made, the declaration called for building on" existing sub-regional and bilateral arrangements in order to broaden and deepen hemispheric economic integration and to bring the agreements together." At the same time, the declaration recognized the need to "remain cognizant" of the "wide differences in the levels of development and size of economies" in the Hemisphere in moving toward tighter economic integration.

The FTAA would have 34 members (Cuba is not included) with 850 million people. The population would be more than twice the 370 million of the now 15 nation European Union. The FTAA would also have a gross domestic product of more than $9 trillion, with the $7 trillion U.S. economy accounting for more than 75% of the total.

In the 6 years following the 1994 Miami Summit, Western Hemisphere trade ministers met five times under the FTAA process. The first meeting was held in Denver in June 1995; the second in Cartagena, Colombia in March 1996; the third in Belo Horizonte, Brazil in May 1997; the fourth in San Jose, Costa Rica in March 1998; and the fifth in Toronto, Canada in November 1999. The next ministerial meeting is scheduled to take place in Argentina in April 2001.

At the San Jose meeting, the 34 ministers responsible for trade in the Hemisphere unanimously recommended that he Leaders formally launch the negotiation of the FTAA at the Second Summit of the Americas in Santiago. As provided by the San Jose Declaration, ministers agreed that negotiating groups are to achieve considerable progress by the year 2000, with a conclusion set for December 31, 2004. The San Jose Declaration also provided recommendations on the initial structure, objectives, venues, and principles of the negotiations.

Canada was designated as the Char of the overall negotiating process for the initial 18 months (May 1, 1998-Oct 31, 1999) and the United States and Brazil were named co-chairs during the final two years of the negotiations (November 1, 2002-December 31, 2004). As head of both the Ministerial and Trade Negotiations Committee (TNC), the Chair will provide overall direction and management to the negotiations.

The Ministers elected to establish nine negotiating groups, which cover all the tariff and non-tariff barrier issues areas identified by the Leaders at the Miami Summit of the Americas. These groups are market access, agriculture, services, government procurement, investment, intellectual property, subsidies, competition policy, and dispute settlement. In addition the Ministers created two committees and a consultative group. A Committee on Electronic Commerce, comprised of both government and private sector experts, was established to make recommendations on how to increase and broaden the benefits to be derived from the electronic marketplace. A Committee on Civil Society was established to receive input at the hemispheric level from labor and environmental groups, and academic, consumer, and other non-governmental groups. Add a Consultative Group on Smaller Economies was established to bring to the attention of the TNC the interests and concerns of the smaller economies.

The United States (Miami) will provide the venue for the negotiating groups and the administrative secretariat supporting those meeting during the first three years. The last four years of the negotiations will be held in Panama and Mexico.

The San Jose Declaration contains General Principles for the Negotiations, as well as General and Specific Objectives. In addition to transparency during the negotiations, the Ministers agreed that the FTAA should improve upon WTO rules and disciplines wherever possible and appropriate. This provision was an attempt to ensure that any final agreement will break down the most serious trade barriers in the region and provide a single set of rules for hemispheric trade. It was agreed that bilateral and sub-regional agreements such as NAFTA and Mercosur can coexist with the FTAA only to the extent that the rights and obligations under those agreements are not covered or go beyond those of the FTAA. IT was also agreed that the negotiations will be a "single undertaking," in the sense that signatories to the final FTAA Agreement will have to accept all parts of it (i.e. cannot pick and choose among the obligations.)

At the Second Summit of the Americas, held in Chile in April 1998, President Clinton and 21 other presidents and 12 prime ministers of the Western Hemisphere agreed to begin the trade negotiations, and to make "concrete progress" toward the free trade goal by 2000. Nine working groups were established and meetings have been taking place since September 1998.

The most recent ministerial meeting, held in Toronto in November 1999, approved an FTAA declaration that instructs negotiators to assemble the texts provided by the negotiating groups for consideration at the next ministerial meeting. Scheduled for April 2001 in Argentina. In addition to ordering the preparation of a limited draft agreement over the nest 18 months, the ministers agreed to implement eight business facilitation measures beginning this year. The agreed measures focus mainly on streamlining and modernizing customs procedures in an effort to expedite trade in goods and services.

VISION OF FREE TRADE IN THE AMERICAS

The vision of free trade in the Americas was put forth initially by President Bush in June 1990. Proposed as the cornerstone of the Enterprise for the Americas Initiative (EAI), President Bush envisaged the creation of a "free trade system that links all of the Americas: North, Central, and South...a free trade zone stretching from the port of Anchorage to the Tierra del Fuego" (the southern tip of Chile). The free trade vision was enthusiastically received in Latin America.

Bush Administration officials at the time emphasized that the goal of hemispheric free trade was long-term, and could take a decade or more to come to fruition. Moreover, the hemispheric free trade vision entailed a variable pattern of economic integration, perhaps involving a number of free trade agreements with individual countries or with the region's economic groupings. Given that he timing, terms, and actual dimensions of the proposal were uncertain, its main significance was an offer of a special relationship with the countries of the Western Hemisphere.

Since assuming office, President Clinton has strongly supported the hemispheric free trade concept. Both he and President Bush have viewed movement towards hemispheric economic integration as supportive of U.S. economic and political interests.

Initially, Clinton Administration efforts to clarify the process by which it would work toward creation of a hemispheric free trade area awaited the outcome of the congressional vote on NAFTA, a trade agreement that was touted as a first step in moving towards the vision of hemispheric free trade. Since NAFTA was approved in late 1993, the Administration restated its intention of negotiating a free trade agreement with Chile next, but declined from naming other specific countries as candidates for future free trade agreements.

The Summit of the Americas in Miami helped create a political consensus in the Administration to take further steps in moving towards hemispheric integration. In remarks delivered at the Summit, President Clinton hailed the proposal to build a free trade area from Alaska to Argentina as producing more jobs in the United States and improving the quality of life for residents of the Western Hemisphere.

Since Miami, the vision of hemispheric free trade has been promoted both by the formal negotiations held as part of the FTAA process, and by the expansion of sub-regional groups and the proliferation of bilateral free trade agreements. Under the former approach, the trade ministers of the hemisphere laid the groundwork for the formal launching of the negotiations, which was agreed to at the Second Summit of the Americas in Santiago. Under the latter approach, Mercosur (the Southern Cone Common Market) has expanded and countries such as Chile and Mexico have negotiated bilateral free trade agreements. Lacking fast-track negotiating authority, the Clinton Administration has not been active under this process.

U.S. Interests and Concerns

Supporters view hemispheric integration as bolstering U.S. economic and political interests in a variety of ways. Movement toward freer markets is viewed as supportive of U.S. prosperity, while the strengthening of democratic regimes is viewed as supportive of U.S. values and security. Closer economic ties are also seem improving cooperation on a range of bilateral issues, including environmental concerns and anti-drug efforts.

In most general terms, a reciprocal reduction of trade barriers by two or more countries usually contributes to improved efficiency and higher living standards for both. As tariffs n Latin America are roughly four times higher than U.S. tariffs, supporters argue that the lowering of tariffs and other trade barriers should facilitate significant increases in U.S. exports.

Supporters point out that the Western Hemisphere has become the largest regional destination for U.S. exports of goods over the past three years. In 1998, the region accounted about 40% of total U.S. merchandise exports and nearly two-thirds of the increase in U.S. export growth worldwide.

Supporters also believe that a higher degree of economic integration should contribute to the consolidation of economic and political reforms that have taken place throughout the hemisphere. They maintain that the reforms have not only contributed to an improved economic performance in Latin America overall, but they have also made Latin America a more attractive setting for U.S. foreign investment. Similarly, they maintain that the stronger Latin America becomes economically, the more likely democratic institutions will continue to proliferate and deepen.

Opponents of an FTAA are concerned that hemispheric free trade would lead to the export of jobs that otherwise would be in the United States. Some critics believe that an FTAA will induce an outflow of American capital to take advantage of much lower wages and weak safety and environmental standards. Many opponents of the FTAA have argued that free trade with poorer countries will put pressure on the United States to lessen its workforce protections and environmental requirements.

Other critics are concerned that an FTAA will inevitably involve the United States in the instabilities, class tensions, and economic turmoil of many southern hemisphere societies. Some cite Mexico's financial crisis in 1995 as an example of potential costs. According to this view, costs include a deterioration in the U. S. trade balance, an increase in immigration pressures, and the need to extend a large amount of credit.

From a very different perspective, some opponents also argue that hemispheric free trade could undermine the achievement of a stronger and more open multilateral trading system. According to this perspective, regional free trade agreements that may weaken the multilateral trading system of not serve the interests of the United States because it has major commercial interests in all regions of the world-Asia, Europe, and North America, and Latin America.

LATIN AMERICAN INTERESTS AND CONCERNS

Over the last few years, Latin American nations have made considerable progress implementing far-reaching trade reforms and opening their economies to outside competition. The prospects of hemispheric economic integration have spurred new sub-regional integration schemes and breathed life into sub-regional groups that had lost their stamina. Most importantly, the political commitment at the Miami Summit to create an FTAA by the year 2005 was a product largely of pressure from many of the countries in the region.

If the 1980s were Latin America's lost decade, the 1990s may be the catch-up years. Since 1991, the economies of the region have averaged roughly 3.5% growth, up from 1.1% in the 1980s. Inflation has been reduced dramatically, averaging around 10% in recent years compared to 550% in 1990. And fiscal deficits are now approximately 2% of gross domestic product, compared to 9% in 1983.

One of the central aspects of the economic transformation of the region has been impressive market-oriented reforms and unilateral trade liberalization. This trend has been, in recent years, complemented by a surge of sub-regional integration efforts and growing hemispheric interdependence.

Since 1990, four sub-regional groups have made considerable progress breaking down intra-regional trade barriers. MERCOSUR, the Common Market of South, consists of Argentina, Brazil, Paraguay, and Uruguay and is the second largest preferential trading group in the Western Hemisphere. The Andean Community, consisting of Bolivia, Colombia, Ecuador, and Venezuela (Peru recently dropped out in 1997), currently is the third largest preferential trading group in the Western Hemisphere. Acting unilaterally as well as under the auspices of the Community (formerly the Andean Pact), individual members have liberalized their own trade and investment regimes in recent years. The Caribbean Community and Common Market (CARICOM), consisting of 13 English-speaking Caribbean nations, has agreed to implement a common external tariff over a period of six years, although members will be allowed to maintain their own non-tariff barriers. The Central American Common Market, (CACM), originally established in 1961, gained new stimulus after a 1990 summit of Central American Presidents. Within CACM, the Central American Group of four-El Salvador, Guatemala, Honduras, and Nicaragua-has taken measures to liberalize and harmonize their trade regimes. Other combinations and the deepening of sub-regional trade agreements are key factors in the economic turn-around. The Group of Three (G3)-consisting of Colombia, Mexico, and Venezuela-signed a free trade pact on June 13, 1994.

The likelihood of eventual hemispheric free trade could provide a further boost to the economies of the region. Hemisphere-wide free trade, according to a 1994 Institute for International Economics study, could boost the region's economic growth by an estimated 1.5% a year, which by 2002 would translate into an additional output of almost

$300 billion a year. Needed inward investment flows would rise by an estimated $10 billion annually.

Most Latin American leaders generally support the establishment of a hemispheric free trade area, believing that an FTAA will help bring about greater prosperity, competition, and entrepreneurial activity. A number of critics, however, caution that the United States will benefit the most from the arrangement.

Similarly, many Latin American understand that negotiating a free trade agreement with the United States opens themselves to increased trade competition and potential U.S. involvement in such issues as environmental standards, workers' rights, and intellectual property rights protection. Some worry that as tariffs fall, the United States would increasingly resort to other procedural ways (such as the imposition of anti-dumping or countervailing duties) to protect its producers and workers. Consequently some nations might not be willing to move as quickly as others toward the goal of free trade. And others, such as Brazil, may attach greater importance and priority to the consolidation and strengthening of sub-regional trade groups before moving towards a hemispheric free trade area.

Beyond that, opposition to hemispheric free trade could grow if the region's unemployment and staggering poverty does not begin to decline. Despite the improvement in economic growth in the 1990s. unemployment has risen from around 5%-6% at the end of the 1980s to 8% in 1998. And the number of people living in poverty is about the same as in 1990. As a result, many workers and groups in these countries believe that the shift towards open markets and free trade has done little to improve their living standards, and that hemispheric free trade may only make things worse.

POLICY ISSUES AND CONGRESSIONAL ACTIONS

Chile: Negotiating A Free Trade Agreement

Canada's Prime Minister Jean Chretien was widely quoted at the conclusion of the first Summit of the Americas on the invitation to Chile to join NAFTA: "For one year we have been the three amigos. Starting today, we will be the four amigos."

Accession negotiations were formally initiated on June 7, 1995 in Toronto, but they remained preliminary due to the fact that the Clinton Administration lacked fast-track negotiating authority. Chile elected not to negotiate on any "sensitive" issues unless fast track authority is renewed to cover the negotiations. Such authority allows the Administration to negotiate a trade agreement with assurances that the legislation implementing the agreement will be treated under special, expedited floor procedures. Differences between most House Democrats, on the one hand, and most Republicans, on the other hand, on the inclusion of labor and environmental objectives in future free trade agreements was a major obstacle to the renewal of fast-track in 12995, 1996, 1997, and again in 1998. The most recent attempt to pass a fast track bill occurred on September 25 1998, when the House defeated H.R. 2621 by a vote of 180 to 243. In 1999, no comprehensive fast-track bills were reintroduced.

Both the Senate Finance and the House Ways and Means Committee fast track bills, as well as the President's proposal of September 16, 1997, provided that a free trade agreement negotiated with Chile would be accorded fast-track legislative treatment. While NAFTA accession is the most likely form that any free trade agreement would take, a bilateral free trade agreement could also be accommodated under fast-track.

The significance of the inability of the Clinton Administration to carry through on its pledge to negotiate Chilean accession to NAFTA or to negotiate a bilateral free trade agreement is mostly political, not economic. In economic terms, NAFTA accession or a free trade agreement would unlikely have any demonstrable effect on the overall U.S. economy because trade flows (approximately _ of 1 percent). Chile ranks as the 28th most important market for U.S. exports worldwide, accounting for $3.0 billion in 1998. U.S. imports from Chile totaled $2.1 billion in 1998, representing the 35th largest supplier. As a country of only 13 million people, with an economy the size of Dallas, and located some 4,000 miles from the United States, Chile is unlikely to become a major trading partner of the United States.

In political terms, the Clinton Administration's inability to carry through on its promise to achieve a free trade agreement with Chile has perhaps undermined to its negotiating leverage in the context of the FTAA. The promise of Chilean accession to NAFTA, for some interest groups, was that NAFTA obligations and rules could be adopted to serve as the foundation for hemispheric integration. After Chile acceded, it was believed that other countries would be eager to join NAFTA when they were ready as well. Lacking fast-track, the Administration, however, arguably was forced to make a number of compromises concerning the objectives and structure of the FTAA negotiations as enunciated in the San Jose Declaration.

Despite the obvious set-backs and delays, the idea of free trade negotiations with Chile took an unexpected turn on August 10, 1999. On this day, Chile's Foreign Minister Juan Gabriel Valdes announced that Chile was prepared to start preliminary discussions on a bilateral FTA with the United States without fast-track negotiating authority in place. The United States termed the proposal "constructive" and "positive" at the October 5-6, 1999 meeting of the U.S.-Chile Joint Commission on Trade in Investment in Santiago, Chile. But no official decision was made on whether or how to proceed until July 2000. At that time the two partners agreed to form working groups that would identify coincidences and convergences in positions on issues such as investment, services, government procurement, electronic commerce, business visas, technical norms and standards, environment, labor and civil society. In early October 2000 the U.S.-Chile Commission on Trade and Investment met in Washington, D.C. to review progress made in those meetings.

How to Deal with Caribbean Basin Countries

Ever since NAFTA was proposed in the early 1990s, Caribbean Basin leaders have expressed concern that Mexico's more preferential trading status would erode its own preferential access to the U.S. market as provided by the 1984 Caribbean Basin Economic Recovery Act (CBERA). At the Summit of the Americas, President Clinton and key legislators supported legislation to address the concerns of the CBERA countries. Legislation to prevent an erosion of the CBERA countries' preferential access to the U.S. market has been introduced in every Congress since 1993, but it was not until this year that legislation was enacted.

The CBERA, which is commonly referred to as the Caribbean Basin Initiative or CBI, was enacted in 1983 in an effort to bolster the economic development and political stability of this strategically important region. A key objective was to help these countries diversify their exports away from traditional agricultural and raw material based exports such as petroleum, sugar cane, coffee, cocoa, bananas, and aluminum ores.

The centerpiece of this U.S. government program is a unilateral, non-reciprocal, grant of duty-free or reduced duty access for certain Caribbean exports to the U.S. market. Most textiles and apparel, certain footwear, canned tuna, petroleum and petroleum derivatives, and certain watches are not eligible for any preferential treatment. The CBERA was amended by Caribbean Basin Economic Recovery Act of 1990, so-called CBI II. This act made the trade benefits permanent and included measures to promote tourism and establish a scholarship assistance program for the region.

Currently, 24 Caribbean, and Central and South American countries enjoy these trade preferences. (Four countries-Anguilla, Cayman Islands, Suriname, and Turks and Caicos Islands-are eligible to become a BERA beneficiary country, but have not requested to be designated). Benefits under CBI are conditioned on various mandatory and discretionary conditions, including intellectual property rights protection, investment protection, improved market access for U.S. exports, and workers rights. In its 15-year history, CBERA has been popular with Caribbean exporters, and in recent years about one-fifth of overall U.S. imports from CBERA countries have entered the U.S. under CBERA preferential provisions.

In 1997, U.S. imports from CBERA countries amounted to $16.6 billion (or 1.9% of total U.S. imports), and total U.S. exports to CBERA countries totaled $17.8 billion (or 2.8% of total exports). The U.S. trade surplus with these countries totaled $1.2 billion in 1997, the eleventh consecutive year that the U.S. ran a trade surplus with the region.

In 1996, apparel was the most prominent U.S. import from the CBERA countries, constituting 42% of all U.S. imports. Traditional exports-petroleum, coffee, tea, fish, and sugar-comprised 21% of total imports, and vegetables and fruits 7%.

Although not eligible for CBERA trade preferences, apparel is also the fastest growing category of U.S. imports from CBERA countries. According to the U.S. International Trade Commission (US.I.T.C.), apparel imports grew from 5.5% of overall imports from the region in 1984 to 41% in 1996. From 1987-1996, apparel imports increased at a rate of 21%, the fastest increase among all foreign suppliers. About 80% of apparel imports from CBERA countries benefited from reduced duties under a production-sharing provision of U.S. trade law (the 9802 provision of the Harmonized Tariff Schedule) which provides partial duty exemption for products assembled abroad of U.S. fabricated components. Shirts, trousers, underwear, and coats and jackets are the principal garments assembled under the production-sharing operations.

CBERA countries compete with one another and Mexico for assembly work from U.S. apparel firms. Since NAFTA went into effect in 1994, apparel assembled in Mexico from "fabric wholly formed and cut in the United States" enters free of duty and quota, but similar CBERA garments are subject to a duty based on the value added offshore. This duty was estimated by the U.S.I.T.C. staff to be equivalent to a 6% ad valorem tariff in 1996. This alteration of the terms of competition arguably has been a factor in causing differential rates of increase in imports to the United States.

According to the U.S.I.T.C., U.S. apparel imports from CBERA countries and Mexico both rose at around 26% from 1991-1993. However, apparel imports from

CBERA countries grew by 15% per year from 1994-1996, while imports from Mexico increased by 44% per year.

Although Mexican apparel shipments to the United States are growing faster than CBERA shipment since NAFTA went into force, the CBEA countries are not losing market share. According the U.S.I.T.C., the CBERA share of leading U.S. imports of apparel increased from 13.1% in 1993 to 16.1% in 1996, while Mexico's share rose from 4.5% to 10.1% during the same period. Suppliers from the rest of the world incurred about a 10% decline in their share of the U.S. market in this post-NAFTA period.

These data have been used by both proponents and opponents of the so-called NAFTA parity or CBI enhancement legislation. Proponents have pointed to a declining rate of increase for CBERA countries' shipments of apparel to the United States, as well as the accelerated growth of Mexican shipments, as evidence that NAFTA has been a force for diverting trade (exports) from, CBERA countries to Mexico. Opponents point to the fact that CBERA countries in the aggregate continue to gain a greater share of the U.S. apparel import market.

"NAFTA parity" or CBI enhancement bills introduced in Congress since 1993 have been premised, in part, on the notion that Mexico's more favorable tariff treatment under NAFTA would lead to a diversion of exports and investment, particularly in the textile and apparel sectors, from the CBERA region. To remedy potential trade and investment diversion, most bills have proposed extending NAFTA equivalent provisions to CBERA countries for products that did not enjoy equivalent preferential treatment under CBERA.

In the 106th Congress, both the House and Senate passed bills that provided a form of parity. The House bill (H.R. 984) provided more expansive benefits than the Senate bill (S. 1389). The differences related most basically to the minimum U.S.-origin content under which textile apparel assembled in a CBI country would qualify for the preference. After protracted informal negotiations between the two houses, the final language of H.R. 434 was agreed to, passed by both houses and signed into laws on May 18, 2000 (P.L. 106-200; Trade and Development Act of 2000).

Movement towards Hemispheric Free Trade

Since the 1994 Summit of the Americas, the goal of hemispheric free trade has been advanced by two different processes. The first process involves the expansion of sub-regional groupings such as MERCOSUR and the proliferation of bilateral free trade agreements. Most all countries of the Western Hemisphere-except the United States-have been active in this process.

The second process involves the formal negotiations among 34 democratic countries of the hemisphere to create an FTAA. As described above, the March 1998 San Jose Declaration formulated a framework for the negotiations and the Leaders formally launched the FTAA negotiations during the second Summit meeting in Santiago in April 1998. And at the fifth hemispheric ministerial held in Canada in November 1999, ministers approved an FTAA declaration that sets goals for negotiators over the next 18 months and directs them to assembled the texts of all negotiating groups for consideration at the next ministerial meeting in Argentina in April 2001.

Assessments differ on whether this combined movement toward hemisphere free trade is "on-track" or "off-track." The former perspective maintains that a solid foundation and structure for FTAA negotiations has been agreed to and that on-going efforts to expand sub-regional groupings are accelerating hemispheric integration. The latter perspective holds that the United States, lacking fast-track authority, has been unable to provide the kind of leadership that is necessary to ensure that the FTAA negotiations proceed according to schedule or in a manner that is supportive of U.S. interests.

Those who see positive developments over the past two years point to the accomplishments of the San Jose Trade Ministerial and the Second Summit of the Americas in getting the FTAA negotiations off to an official start. While some critics doubt much progress can be made in the negotiations until the U.S. President obtains fast-track negotiating authority, others point to agreement on a range of business facilitation measures to date. These include temporary admission of certain goods related to business travelers, express shipments, simplified procedures for low value shipments, compatible data interchange systems, harmonized commodity description and coding system, hemispheric guide on customs procedures, codes of conduct for customs officials, and risk analysis/targeting methodology.

The "on-track" perspective also points to a continuing trend of greater market opening at both the bilateral and sub-regional level as contributing to an expansion of trade flows. In recent years, intra-hemispheric trade has been growing more rapidly than exports to the rest of the world. This trade growth, in turn, has bolstered the economic performance of the countries of the region and enabled Latin American leaders to negotiate with the Untied States more confidently, as well as to embrace the long-term goal of hemispheric free trade.

Those who judge that he process is "off-track" make several points. The first is that the United States, lacking fast-track authority, has not been able to promote its preferred approach (the expansion of NAFTA) to hemispheric integration. Instead it has been relegated to the sidelines as other countries and sub-regional groups have continued to reach preferential agreements. These agreements, in turn, are said to be discriminating against U.S. exports and making it more difficult to eventually negotiate a comprehensive, hemispheric free trade agreement. In the continuing absence of fast-track, this view also holds that the FTAA negotiations have lost momentum. These observers see the Toronto Ministerial declaration as a limited document, calling only for more discussions and compilations of draft texts.

These critics believe that a time-consuming and extended negotiation would provide Brazil, in particular, with significant advantages, not the least of which would be an opportunity to expand MERCOSUR into a larger South American trade bloc. Buttressed by the diplomatic support provided by a larger MERCOSUR, Brazil could be better positioned to negotiate with the United States from a position of strength. This is particularly important because Brazil wishes to extract from the United States concessions limiting Washington's use of unfair trade practices remedies (i.e. antidumping and countervailing duties) and to improve its access to the U.S. market for agricultural goods. In addition, because MERCOSUR currently protects a number of sectors (such as financial services, telecommunications, and automobiles), a longer period of time would provide these sectors with more leeway to adjust to increased import competition. The fact that the hemispheric trading partners remain at odds over the work programs of the nine negotiating groups, as well as the role labor an environmental considerations should play in the negotiations, play into the strategy of delay.

Public support for hemispheric free trade appears to be low both in the United States and in Latin America. Labor and environmental interest groups in the United States oppose free trade agreements that lack strong protections for basic labor and environmental standards. And many Latin American businesses and citizens fear the effects of greater exposure to the competitive pressures of large U.S. companies.

Extending the Andean Trade Preferences Act

The Andean Trade Preferences Act (ATPA) authorizes the President to grant certain unilateral preferential tariff benefits to Bolivia, Colombia, Ecuador, and Peru. The ATPA, which went into effect on December 4, 1991, will expire on December 4, 2001. Often referred to as the trade component of then President Bush's "war on drugs," the ATPA attempted to encourage the economic development of Andean countries and economic alternatives to drug production and trafficking.

The Andean countries have asked the Untied States to extend the program beyond its expiration date, to reduce the list of products excluded from tariff benefits, and to add Venezuela as a beneficiary country. In congressional testimony on February 22, 2000, before the Senate Caucus on International Narcotic Control and the Senate Finance Subcommittee on International Trade, Deputy U.S. Trade Representative Richard Fisher stated the Clinton Administration was prepared to example the request "very closely." Some Senators at the hearing indicated support for an early renewal of the program, saying it would show U.S. commitment to the region and help promote a favorable investment climate.

According to the Clinton Administration, The ATPA has been successful in encouraging a move away from narcotics trade to legitimate business in the region and in increasing U.S. exports. Since APTA was passed in 1991, the four Andean countries have increased their exports to the United States by about 80%. Products benefiting from ATPA, tariff preferences include cut flowers from Colombia, Ecuador and Bolivia; precious metals and jewelry from Colombia, Bolivia, and Peru; and fish and fish products from Ecuador.

CHRONOLOGY

10/05/00- The Chairman of the Senate Finance Subcommittee International Trade, Senator Charles Grassley, urged the Clinton Administration to jump-start what he called negotiations to create a Free Trade Area of the Americas (FTAA).

7/10/00- The United States and Chile have agreed to a work program aimed at identifying issues that would have to be addressed in a free trade negotiation. No decision on beginning a bilateral negotiation is expected to be made until after the U.S. presidential election.

05/18/00- President Clinton signed into law (P.L. 106-200) legislation aimed at expanding U.S. trade with African and Caribbean Basin Initiative countries. The conference bill (H.R. 434) was approved by the House on May 4, 2000 by a vote of 309-110 and by the Senate on May 11, 2000 by a vote of 77-19.

05/04/00- By a vote of 309-110, the House approved the conference report on H.R. 4343, the Trade and Development Act of 2000. Title II expands trade preferences for Caribbean Basin exports of apparel products.

02/18/00- Brazilian Foreign Minister Luiz Felipe Lampreia announced that Brazil is not going to commit to an FTAA until it sees what the final package is and whether the U.S. Congress will approve it.

11/3-4/99- Hemispheric trade ministers agreed at a meeting in Toronto to instruct trade negotiators to assemble the texts of the negotiating groups and to prepare a report for the next ministerial, scheduled to be held in Argentina in April 2001.

11/03/99- The Senate passed a bill (H.R. 434) by a vote of 76-19 that expands trade preferences for Caribbean Basin countries. The bill must be reconciled with a House-passed bill that addressed African trade preferences only.

10/7-8/99- A U.S.-Chile Joint Commission on Trade and Investment met in Santiago to explore possible negotiations on agree trade agreement.

08/10/99- Chile's Foreign Minister Juan Gabriel Valdes announced that Chile was ready to start preliminary work on a bilateral free trade agreement without U.S. fast-track negotiating authority in place.

07/28/99- At a meeting of the Trade Negotiations Committee (TNC) of the FTAA, representatives of 27 countries reached agreement on nine business facilitation measures. The measures will be reviewed at the November 1999 ministerial summit in Canada.

06/22/99- The Senate Finance Committee reported out a CBI bill, S. 1389 (Roth), by voice vote.

06/10/99- The House Ways and Means Committee reported out a CBI bill, H.R. 984 (Crane), by voice vote.

05/18/99- The Ways and Means Trade Subcommittee approved H.R. 984, the U.S.-Caribbean Trade Partnership Act, by voice vote without amendments.

03/04/99- Congressman Philip Crane (R-Il) introduced the "United States-Caribbean Trade Partnership Act. Title I of the bill offers additional incentive for economic development in the region through enhancement of the CBI trade program.

02/04/99- Senator Bob Graham (D-Fla) and nine other Senators introduced the "Caribbean Relief Act of 1999." The bill, S. 371, contains a proposal to enhance the trade benefits offered CBI countries.

01/26/99- Senate Majority Leader Trent Lott stated that he intends to bring a Caribbean trade bill to the floor for a vote early this year.

09/25/98- The House defeated H.R. 2621, a Republican leadership sponsored fast-track bill, by a vote of 180-243.

09/01/98- The first negotiating sessions of working groups on market access and agriculture took place in Miami under the FTAA rubric.

06/11/98- Commerce Secretary William Daley expressed doubts that the 2005 deadline for completion of the FTAA can be met given an enormous negotiating agenda and the large number of diverse economies involved in the process.

04/19/98- 34 Leaders meeting at the second Summit of the Americans in Santiago, Chile agree to formally launch FTAA negotiations.

03/19/98- Trade ministers meeting in San Jose, Costa Rica agree on the principles, objectives, and venues that will guide the FTAA negotiations.

11/04/97- The House defeated by a vote of 234-182 the United States-Caribbean Trade Partnership Act (H.R. 2644).

10/09/97- House Ways and Means Committee approves by voice vote a 14-month Caribbean Basin Trade Partnership bill (H.R. 2264).

10/01/97- Senate Finance Committee approves by voice vote a 3-year Caribbean Trade Enhancement bill (S. 1278).

07/27/97- Conferees on the budget tax legislation deleted the House-passed NAFTA parity provision from the final bill.

06/26/97- The House passed a budget reconciliation bill (HR. 2014) that contained provisions to establish "NAFTA parity" for the Caribbean Basin Initiative beneficiary countries.

07/25/95- Negotiations for Chilean accession to NAFTA officially began in Mexico City.

06/07/05- Trade ministers from the United States, Mexico, Canada, and Chile announce the structure and work schedule for the negotiation of Chile's accession to the North American Free Trade Agreement.

12/9-11/94- Summit of the Americas held in Miami. Political commitment was made to negotiate a "Free Trade Area of the Americas" by the year 2005. In a separate action, the United States, Canada, and Mexico invited Chile to enter into negotiations to join NAFTA.

1/01/94- The North American Free Trade Agreement entered into force.

FOR ADDITIONAL READING

CRS Issue Briefs

CRS Issue Brief IB95050. *Caribbean Basin Interim Trade Program (NAFTA/CBIPARITY),* by Vladimir N. Pregelj.

CRS Reports

CRS Report 97-56. *Chilean Trade and Economic Reform: Implications for NAFTA Accession*, by J.F. Hornbeck.

CRS Report 97-876, *Fast-Track-Authority: Debate Over the President's Proposal*, by George Holliday.

CRS Report 07762- *A Free Trade Area of the Americas: Toward Integrating Regional Trade Policies,* by J.F. Hornbeck.

CRS Report 97-514. *Hemispheric Free Trade: Status, Hurdles, and Opposition,* by Raymond J. Ahearn.

CRS Report 95-940. *MERCOSUR-U.S. Trade Relations: Evolution and Prospects* , by Raymond J. Ahearn.

CRS Report 97-811. *NAFTA, Mexican Trade Policy, and U.S. –Mexico Trade: A Longer Term Perspective,* by J.F. Hornbeck.

CRS Report 98-330. *Summit of the Americas II, April 18-19, 1998: Background, Objectives, and Expectations,* by K. Larry Storrs.

HEMISPHERIC FREE TRADE: STATUS, HURDLES, AND OPPOSITION

Raymond J. Ahearn

ABSTRACT

At the Summit of the Americas held in Miami during December 1994, 34 leaders of the western hemisphere agreed to create a Free Trade Area of the Americas (FTAA) by 2005. At the Second Summit of the Americas, held in April 1998 in Chile, the leaders formally launches negotiations to create a FTAA, in accordance with the March 1998 San Jose Ministerial Declaration. This report evaluates the status, hurdles, and opposition to this objective. Absence of U.S. fast track negotiating authority remains a key obstacle to more rapid movement in this direction. This report will be updated periodically.

SUMMARY

At the 1994 Summit of the Americas in Miami, 34 countries in the Western Hemisphere agreed to complete negotiations to create a "Free Trade Area of the Americas" (FTAA) no later than the year 2005. Since the summit, two approaches have emerged for promoting hemispheric free trade.

The first approach involves the expansion and deepening of sub-regional groupings such as MERCOSUR (the Southern Cone Common Market) and the proliferation of bilateral free trade agreements. Most all countries of the Western Hemisphere—except the United States—have been active in this process.

The second approach entails formal negotiations to construct the FTAA by progressively reducing barriers to trade and investment. Under this approach, the trade ministers from the 34 countries agreed on the structure, organization, and venue for the FTAA negotiations at a meeting held March 17, 1998 in San Jose, Costa Rica, and the negotiations were officially launched by the Heads of State at the Second Summit of the Americas held April 18-19, 1998 in Santiago, Chile.

There are at least two different perspectives on how much overall progress has been made over the past four years in advancing hemispheric free trade. Some observers maintain that the official launching of the negotiations at Santiago, combined with the proliferation of sub-regional groupings and bilateral free trade agreements, are all strong evidence of accelerating hemispheric integration. Other observers hold that the formal FTAA negotiations are likely to lose momentum or drag on interminably, and that hemispheric integration may be evolving in a manner that is hurting U.S. interests.

If one assumes hemispheric free trade is a desirable objectives, several major hurdles stand in the way of moving more rapidly in that direction. The most important obstacle is absence of fast-track procedures for implementing trade agreements. A tacit assurance that Congress will not demand changes in trade bargains struck by the President is considered key to persuading U.S. trade partners to engage in substantive negotiations. In addition, vast differences in size and interests of the negotiating countries, combined with the possibility that a new round of multilateral trade negotiations may be launched in the near future, could undermine the FTAA negotiations.

While the vision of hemispheric free trade was put forth by President Bush eight years ago, the amount of popular support in the United States for this goal remains unclear. A 1996 public opinion poll found that 57% of the American public was opposed to a new free trade agreements with Latin America, while a 1998 poll found 36% opposition. Sources of opposition within the Untied States can be seen n continuing debate on the benefits and costs of hemispheric free trade, as well as on the efficacy of regional free trade agreements per se.

*****

This report provides a current assessment of the movement towards hemispheric free trade in three parts. The first part evaluates the status of efforts to create a free trade area in the Western Hemisphere by 2005. The second part, assuming that hemispheric free trade is a desirable objective, discusses the major hurdles to achieving such a free trade area. The third part examines sources of opposition to the proposal.

Status of Movement toward Hemispheric Free Trade

The objective of establishing a hemispheric free trade area was formally adopted at the December 1994 Summit of the Americas held in Miami. At the Summit, President Clinton and 33 other leaders of the Western Hemisphere agreed to complete negotiations to create a "Free Trade Area of the Americas" (FTAA) no later than the year 2005. In addition, the leaders agreed to make concrete progress toward that objective by the year 2000.[1]

If the FTAA were established in 1998, it would have 343 members (Cuba is not included) with 757 million consumers. The population would be more than twice the

[1] For an analysis of the decision making to convene the summit, see Feinberg, Richard E. *Summary in the Americas,* Institute for International Economics, Washington, D.C., 1997, 261 p.

370 million that comprise the now 15-nation European Union. The FTAA would also have a combined economic output of more than $9 trillion, with the $7 trillion U.S. economy accounting for more than 75% of the total.

While the Summit produced a *Declaration of Principles* and a *Plan of Action* that provided some general guidelines for the negotiations, neither document provided a blueprint or precise plan for achieving the FTAA. Subsequently, hemispheric free trade is being promoted through two different approaches or processes.[2]

The first approach involves the expansion of existing sub-regional agreements such as MERCOSUR (the Southern Cone Common Market) or the Andean Community. This approach entails adding countries to existing agreements with a view towards eventually combining or amalgamating the agreements into a larger accord through direct negotiations. Under this approach, the Clinton Administration initially hoped to expand the North American Free Trade Agreement (NAFTA) southward, beginning with the accession of Chile.[1]

The second approach attempts to harmonize diverse provisions and rules of the various existing regional groupings and potential members with a view towards eventual convergence into an overarching or general agreement. This process of formal FTAA negotiations entails acceptance of tariff and non-tariff obligations by various sub-regional groupings and countries with an eye over time toward blending these provisions into a comprehensive free trade agreement. Under this approach, the trade ministers from the 34 countries agreed on the principles and framework for the negotiations (the San Jose Declaration) in March 1998, and the negotiations were officially launched by the leaders at the Second Summit of the Americas in Santiago, Chile in April 1998.

There are at least two different perspectives on how much overall progress has been made over the past two years in advancing hemispheric free trade. Some observers argue that the process, is "on-track" and others judge that the process is "off-track."

Progress in Expanding Sub-regional Groupings

Since the Summit of the Americas, most countries in the Western Hemisphere, with the exception of the United States, have been actively involved in expanding sub-regional groupings. MERCOSUR, led by Brazil, has been the most active. At the same time, a number of countries have negotiated additional bilateral free trade agreements, with Mexico and Chile leading the way.

Over the past three years, MERCOSUR, which consists of Argentina, Brazil, Paraguay, and Uruguay, has reached free trade agreements with Bolivia and Chile that are designed to serve as steeping stones for full membership into MERCOSUR.

---

[2] Moss, Ambler and Lande, Stephen. "A Critical Year for Hemispheric Free Trade: Can Countries Agree on A Blueprint?" The North-South Center, University of Miami, 1997, p. 9.

[1] President Bush unveiled a vision of free trade in the Americas on June 27, 1990. Proposed as the cornerstone of his Enterprise for the Americas Initiative (EAI), President Bush envisaged the creation of a "free trade system that links all of the Americas: North, Central, and South...a free trade zone stretching from the port of Anchorage to the Tierra del Fuego" (the southern tip of Chile). The extension of the U.S. –Canada free trade agreement to Mexico (what became NAFTA) was to be the first step in creating this hemispheric free trade zone.

Mercosur has also signed an agreement with the Andean Community to negotiate a free trade deal by 2000, and it continues to explore negotiating a trade agreement with the European Union (EU). The main obstacle is beginning negotiations is the insistence by some EU members to exclude the cereals, beef, and sugar sectors from the negotiations. These are all sectors in which Mercosur countries are very competitive.[2]

MERCOSUR hopes to expand its membership to all of South America, thereby creating a South American Free Trade Area (SAFTA). The creation of a SAFTA could position MERCOSUR, and particularly Brazil, to play a much more important role in regional and world affairs.

Mexico, for its part, has been equally active. Hoping to become a commercial hub between North and South America, Mexico has reached trade agreements with Colombia and Venezuela (creating the so-called *Group of 3*) and with Bolivia, Costa Rica, and Chile. In addition, Mexico has initiated talks with MERCOSUR and a number of Central American countries.

Mexico's growing web of free trade agreements have entailed trade and non-trade obligations that are deeper and more rigorous than those undertaken by MERCOSUR and its free trade partners. For the most part, Mexico has negotiated agreements that are relatively equivalent to its NAFTA obligations.[3]

Chile, which envisions itself as a bridge between Asia and South America and Europe and South America, has been similarly active on a bilateral basis. It has concluded agreements with MERCOSUR, Mexico, Colombia, Venezuela, Canada, and Ecuador, and intends to start similar negotiations with Central America.

The United States is the major exception to this trend of expanding free trade agreements in the hemisphere. While the Administration initially expected to pursue hemispheric integration actively under this approach, beginning with an invitation to Chile to negotiate accession to NAFTA at the Summit of the Americas, the absence of fast-track authority has prevented movement in this direction from taking place. Although negotiations with Chile were formally launched in July 1995, Chile subsequently suspended it participation because the Clinton Administration did not have fast track authority-a situation that Chile feared could force it to negotiate twice with the United States (once with the Executive Branch and once with the Congress).[4]

The rapid increase in free trade accords in the hemisphere (an estimated 30 agreements have been concluded since 1990) has been accompanied by a rapid acceleration of exports. Latin American intra-regional trade has grown particularly fast, rising on average by 18% per year from 1990-1997. This compares to an average growth of 9% per year to countries outside the region.[5]

---

[2] See congressional testimony of Regina K. Vargo, Deputy Assistant Secretary of Commerce for the Western Hemisphere, before the Subcommittee on International Economic Policy of the House International Relations Committee on April 29, 1998.

[3] Moss, Ambler and Lande, Stephen. "A Critical Year For Hemispheric Free Trade: Can Countries Agree On a Blueprint?" p.9.

[4] Fast-track authority allows the President to negotiate a trade agreement with assurances that the legislation implementing the agreement will be treated in Congress under special floor procedures, including no amendments.

[5] Inter-American Development Bank. "Integration and Trade in the Americas," Periodic Note, August, 1998, p. 31.

Progress in Harmonizing Norms

In the nearly four years since the first Summit of the Americas in Miami, Western Hemisphere trade ministers have met four times under the FTAA process. The first meeting was held in Denver in June 1995; the second in Cartagena, Colombia in March 1996; the third in Belo Horizonte, Brazil in May 1997, and the fourth in San Jose, Costa Rica in March 1998. While a number of decisions were made at all the meetings, the most significant preparatory work occurred at the San Jose Ministerial.

At the San Jose meeting, the 34 Ministers responsible for trade in the Hemisphere unanimously recommended that the Leaders formally launch the negotiation of the FTAA at the Second Summit of the Americas in Santiago. As provided by the San Jose Declaration, ministers agreed that negotiating groups are to achieve considerable progress by the year 2000, with a conclusion set for December 31, 2004. The San Jose Declaration also provided recommendations on the initial structure, objectives, venues, and principles of the negotiations.[6]

Canada was designated as the Chair of the overall negotiating process for the initial 18 months (May 1, 1998-Oct. 31, 1999) and the United States and Brazil were named co-chairs during the final two years of the negotiations (November 1, 2002-December 31, 2004). As head of both the Ministerial and Trade Negotiations Committee (TNC), the Chair will provide overall direction and management to the negotiations. Consisting of the 34 Vice Ministers for Trade, the first meeting of the TNC will be held no later than June 30, 1998.

The Ministers elected to establish nine initial negotiating groups, which cover all the tariff and non-tariff barriers issue areas identified by the Leaders at the Miami Summit of the Americas. These groups are market access, agriculture, services, government procurement, investment, intellectual property, subsidies, competition policy, and dispute settlement. In addition, the Ministers created two committees and a consultative group. A Committee on Electronic Commerce, comprised of both government and private sector experts, was established to make recommendations on how to increase and broaden all the benefits to be derived form the electronic marketplace. A Committee on Civil Society was established to receive input at the hemispheric level from labor and environmental groups, and academic, consumer and other non-governmental groups. And a Consultative Group on Smaller Economies was established to bring to the attention of the TNC the interests and concerns of the smaller economies.

The United States (Miami) will provide the venue for the negotiating groups and the administrative secretariat supporting those meeting during the first three years. The last four years of the negotiations will be held in Panama and Mexico.

The San Jose Declaration contains General Principles for the Negotiations, as well as General and Specific Objectives. In addition to transparency during the negotiations, the Ministers agreed that the FTAA should improve upon WTO rules and disciplines wherever possible and appropriate. The provision was an attempt to ensure that any final agreement will break down the most serious trade barriers in the region and provide a single set of rules for hemispheric trade. It was agreed that bilateral and sub-regional agreements such as NAFTA and Mercosur can coexist with the FTAA only to the extent

[6] Information on the FTAA can be accessed an official website: http://www.ftaa-acla.org/.

that the rights and obligations under those agreements are not covered or go beyond those of the FTAA. It was also agreed that the negotiations will be a "Single undertaking", in the sense that signatories to the final FTAA Agreement will have to accept all parts of it (i.e. cannot pick and choose among the obligations.)

As expected, President Clinton and 21 other presidents and 12 prime ministers of the Western Hemisphere agreed at the Santiago Summit in April, 1998 to launch the trade negotiations, in accordance with the San Jose Declaration. The first meeting of the nine negotiating committees took place in Miami during September 1998.

Movement toward Free Trade

Assessments differ widely on whether this combined movement toward hemispheric free trade is "on-track" or "off-track". The former, basically positive, perspective maintains that a solid foundation and structure for FTAA negotiations has been agreed to and that on-going efforts to expand sub-regional groupings are accelerating hemispheric integration. The latter, mostly skeptical, perspective holds that the United States, lacking fast-track authority, has been unable to provide the kind of leadership that is necessary to ensure that the FTAA negotiations proceed according to schedule or in a manner that is supportive of U.S. interests.

Those who see positive developments over the past three years point to the accomplishments of the San Jose Trade Ministerial and the Second Summit of the Americas in getting the FTAA negotiations off to an official start. While some critics doubt much progress can be made in the negotiations until the U.S. obtain fast-track negotiating authority, others point out that the absence of fast-track may have made the U.S. negotiating position more compromising and diplomatically effective to date. This view holds that Brazil and other Latin countries may not have agreed at Santiago to begin formal FTAA negotiations if the United States had not been willing to change its original negotiating positions on agriculture and some other issues.

The "on-track" perspective also points to a continuing trend of greater market opening at both the bilateral and sub-regional level as contributing to an expansion of trade flows. In recent years, intra-hemisphere trade has been growing more rapidly than exports to the rest of the world. This trade growth, in turn, has bolstered the economic performance of the countries of the region and enabled Latin American leaders to negotiate with the United States more confidently, as well as to embrace the long-term goal of hemispheric free trade.

Those who judge that the process is "off-track" make several points. The first is that the United States, lacking fast-track authority, has not been able to promote its preferred approach (the expansion of NAFTA) to hemispheric integration. Instead it has been relegated to the sidelines as other countries and sub-regional groups have continued to reach preferential agreements. These agreements, in turn, are said to be discriminating against U.S. exports and making it more difficult to eventually negotiate a comprehensive, hemispheric free trade agreement. In the continuing absence of fast-track, this view also holds that the FTAA negotiations will lose momentum or drag on interminably.

HURDLES

They who identify the creation of the FTAA, as a desirable objective cite two major hurdles to rapid movement in that direction. These are the absence of fast-track authority, and divergent interests of key countries involved in the negotiations.

Fast-track Authority

Many observers doubt that a formal FTAA can be negotiated by 2005 in the absence of an extension of fast track authority from the Congress. Such authority allows the Administration to negotiate a trade agreement with assurances that the legislation implementing the agreement will be treated under special procedures. Strict time limits on consideration and bars on amendments increase the probability of passage.

A tacit assurance that Congress will not demand changes in trade bargains and compromises struck by the President is considered indispensable for persuading U.S. trading partners to engage in substantive negotiations. While foreign countries in the past have agreed to begin trade negotiations without fast-track authority in place, it is considered unlikely that they would offer sensitive concessions in trade talks if they were unsure that U.S. negotiators could live up to their end of the bargain.[9]

Fast track authority was first adopted in 1974, and it has been renewed five times. However, since its expiration in 1994, efforts, first by the Clinton Administration, and second by the House Republican leadership, have been unsuccessful in winning its renewal. President Clinton transmitted to Congress a draft fast-track bill in the fall of 1997.[10]

The proposal and subsequent versions reported out of both the House Ways and Means and Senate Finance Committees proved controversial. Lacking the votes for passage, the President on November 10, 1997 elected to suspend efforts to gain its passage in the 1st session of the 105th Congress. The most recent attempt to pass a fast track bill occurred on September 25, 1998, when the House defeated H.R. 2621 by a vote of 180 to 243.

The inability to obtain a bipartisan majority in favor of fast-track bill has stemmed primarily from divisions on the treatment of labor and environmental standards in future trade agreements. Many Democrats maintain that future trade agreements should contain strong labor and environmental standards, particularly with developing countries that maintain tight control over labor markets and lax standards on environmental protection. Many Republicans believe that these issues should be addressed in different fora and ways. Without a narrowing of the gap concerning the proper relationship between labor and environmental standards and international trade, efforts to pass an extension of the fast-track authority may continue to prove difficult in the future.

---

9 For a full discussion, see Schott, Jeffrey J. ed. *Restarting Fast Track*, Institute for International Economics, Washington, D.C. 1998.

10 For a description of the President's fast-track proposal, see U.S. Library of Congress, *Fast-Track Authority: Debate Over the President's Proposal*, by George Holliday, Report 97-876 E.

The terms of any potential fast-track consensus, of course, could have direct consequences for the FTAA and U.S. relations with Latin America. On the one hand, a fast-track extension that entailed strong labor and environmental provisions in future trade agreements could encounter strong opposition from FTAA negotiating partners. Most Latin American leaders have made clear that they view any labor or environmental provisions that are enforceable by trade sanctions as being potentially protectionist, and have vowed not to negotiate such agreements. Similarly, a fast-track extension that contained authority only for multilateral negotiations could obviously gut the FTAA process. On the other hand, a fast-track extension that was accompanied by measures to help American workers adjust to increased competition could help build domestic political support for the FTAA.

Divergent Country Interests

Even if fast-track negotiating authority is renewed in some form, movement toward hemispheric free trade likely will be constrained by the divergent interests of two key countries in the hemisphere-Mexico and Brazil. In addition, there is growing concern that the possible launch of a new round of multilateral trade negotiations could effectively divert the attention of negotiators and countries away the FTAA process.

Both Mexico and Brazil appear to have an interest in a go-slow approach to the FTAA negotiations. Mexico's interest in prolonging the negotiations is straightforward. Preferential integration with the U.S. economy through NAFTA has been a major boon to its trade and economy. At least in the short-run, it has a clear-cut commercial interest in seeing that the value if its preferential access to the U.S. market is not eroded by the creation of a hemispheric free trade area.[11]

For Brazil, a time-consuming and extended negotiations would provide it with significant advantages, not the least of which would be an opportunity to expand MERCOSUR into a larger South American trade bloc. Buttressed by the diplomatic support provided by a larger MERCOSUR, Brazil could be better positioned to negotiate with the Untied States from a position of strength. This is particularly important because Brazil (together with Argentina) wishes to extract from the United States concessions limiting Washington's use of unfair trade practices remedies (i.e. antidumping and countervailing duties) and to improve its access to the U.S. market for agricultural products. In addition, because MERCOSUR currently protects a number of sectors (such as financial services, telecommunications, and the government procurement), a longer period of time would provide these sectors with more leeway and capacity to adjust to increased import competition.

A final consideration is that gaining unfettered access to the U.S. market may not be as important for Brazil and its principal MERCOSUR partner, Argentina, as it is for many other countries in Central and South America. For both countries, the European Union is a more important trading partner that the United States, which accounts for only

---

[11] For example, Venezuela and Colombia, two frequently mentioned candidates in the past, are now experiencing considerable problems. Venezuela is struggling to return to a path of economic reform and revitalization, and Colombia is deeply troubled by guerilla and drug-related violence and corruption.

29% of Brazil's exports and 9% of Argentina's exports. For this reason, both countries' calculations of the benefit/cost ratio of a special hemispheric relationship may be lower than of other countries that are more dependent on the U.S. market.[12]

The possible launch of a new round of multilateral trade negotiations under the aegis of the World Trade Organization (WTO) could also divert the attention of key countries from the FTAA process. A WTO Ministerial meeting scheduled for 1999 is expected to decide whether and when to initiate a new round.

OPPOSITION

While the vision of hemispheric free trade was put forth by President Bush eight years ago, and subsequently embraced by President Clinton, the amount of popular support in the Untied States for this goal remains unclear. For example, a public opinion poll taken in 1996 found that 57% of the U.S. public is against new free trade agreements with Latin America, while a 1998 poll showed 36% opposition.[13] Sources of opposition within the United States can be seen in controversies relating to the benefits and costs of hemispheric free trade, as well as the efficacy of regional free trade arrangements in supporting U.S. interests.

Benefits and Costs of Hemispheric Free Trade

The debate over the benefits and costs of hemispheric free trade tends to divide along economic and geo-political considerations. Those that emphasize the economic benefits and costs often view hemispheric free trade as an end in itself, while those who emphasize geo-political costs and benefits tend to view hemispheric free trade as a means to achieve other objectives.

Economic Benefits and Costs. The Clinton Administration and most supporters of hemispheric free trade emphasizes the extent to which movement in this direction will help expand U.S. exports, which in turn will create more and better paying jobs. The statistics cited in support of this contention include the following:

- Exports over the last 5 years have accounted for nearly 40% of U.S. economic growth.

- Exports support an estimated 11.3 million U.S. jobs, and over 1.4 million of these jobs were generated by increased exports over the last 4 years.

- Export-related jobs are good jobs, paying 13-16% more than non trade-related jobs.

---

12 Ahearn, Raymond J. *Trade an the Americas*, CRS Issue Brief 95017, [updated regularly] 14 p.

13 Green, Paula. "Study: 57% of U.S. Public Against Free-Trade Pacts with Latin America," *Journal of Commerce, September 8,1996, p.2.* and Schumacher, Edward. "A Meeting of Minds, From Peoria to Petagonia," *Wall Street Journal,* April 16, 1998, p. A19..

- U.S. exports to the Western Hemisphere (including Canada and Mexico) have accounted for two-thirds of U.S. export growth in 1997.

- U.S. exports to Latin America and the Caribbean (the 31 "other" countries which the U.S. does not have a free trade agreement with) have increased by 150% since 1990, making this region one of the fastest growing markets for U.S. exports. As a result, the U.S. now sells more to Brazil than it does to China, and more to Chile than it does to India.

- Because Latin America and the Caribbean have relatively higher trade barriers than the Untied States (tariffs that are four time higher), American companies will have the most to win from a reciprocal reduction of barriers.

- Beyond the potential direct gains from freer trade, proponents see a danger for U.S. exports and investments arising form the movement towards preferential trade agreements in the region without U.S. participation. They cite free trade agreements that Chile has concluded with Canada, Mexico, and Mercosur as contributing to an estimated $500 million in lost U.S. exports. (The effect reportedly is due to the fact that U.S. exporters are subject to a price disadvantage imposed by the 11% Chilean duty that Chile's preferential hemispheric free trade partners do not have to pay.)[14]

Opponents and skeptics can respond that supporters overstate the potential benefits, and underestimate or ignore the potential costs. Regarding the potential benefits, they make the argument that Latin America and the Caribbean (excluding Mexico because it is already a member of NAFTA) represent a relatively small market for U.S. exports. In 1997, for example, the region accounted for only 9% (or $63 billion) of total U.S. exports. Although it may be a fast-growing market, the relatively small trading relationship the United States has with these countries indicates that hemispheric free trade could have only a modest impact on economic activity, including export growth, in the United States. As a result, opponents can argue that movement in this direction is not going to create large numbers of export-related jobs.

Concerning the dangers of inaction, opponents can point out that the trade data, to date, do not support the assertion that the United States is losing market share as a result of being excluded from preferential trade agreements. For example, in the case of Chile, which has negotiated preferential trade agreements in recent years with Mexico, Canada, Bolivia, Venezuela, Colombia, and Ecuador and the four members of Mercosur (Argentina, Brazil, Paraguay, and Uruguay), the U.S., share of Chile's total imports has

[14] See congressional testimony of Regina K. Vargo, Deputy Assistant Secretary of Commerce for the Western Hemisphere, before the Subcommittee on International Economic Policy of the House International Relations Committee on April 29, 1998.

shown little change in recent years. The U.S. market share grew, from 17.8% in 1990 to 23.8% in 1995, averaged 23.1% in 1996 and 23.2% in 1997 (thru the first three quarters).

Oppositions to new free trade agreements in general is closely linked to perceptions of how NAFTA is working. For example, a 1997 Wall Street Journal/NBC News poll showed that 43% of Americans believe that NAFTA has had a negative impact on the United States, while 28% believed it has had a positive impact. In a 1998 poll, a plurality of those polled again believed that NAFTA was having a negative impact of jobs and wages.[15]

Opponents of NAFTA and the FTAA appear to feat that agreements with low wage countries-absent strong labor and environmental provisions that are fully enforceable by the threat of U.S. trade sanctions-can lead to a loss of U.S. jobs, put downward pressures on U.S. wages, and divert investment capital abroad. In particular, many Democrats, labor unions, and environmental groups are reluctant to support new trade agreements on the grounds that the NAFTA is working to lower the standard of living of U.S. workers and encouraging businesses to relocate in Mexico to take advantage of low wages and weak enforcement of environmental laws.[16]

Opponents also point to the huge turnaround in the bilateral trade balance with Mexico, going from a $1.4 billion surplus in 1994 to a $17.5 deficit in 1997, as a sign that the agreement is having a negative impact on employment in the United States.[17] A huge increase U.S. imports from Mexico is estimated by opponents to have resulted in a loss of an estimated 250,000 U.S. jobs.[18]

Proponents of hemispheric free trade-both the Administration and many Republicans-counter that NAFTA is working. They point out that in the three plus years NAFTA has been in effect, the U.S. economy has created 8.5 million new jobs and that there has been no stampede of investment capital from the United States to Mexico. In 1995, for example, when total foreign investment from all sources in Mexico was $7 billion, total foreign investment from all sources in Mexico was $7 billion, total foreign direct investment into the United States was over $60 billion and total gross investment in the U.S. economy was over $1 trillion.[19]

Despite the data confirming strong U.S. employment and investment performance economy –wide since NAFTA went into effect, there may be a growing sense of anxiety

---

[15] Schumacher, Edward. A Meeting of Minds, From Peoria to Patagonia, *Wall Street Journal*, April 16, 1998, p. A19.

[16] For analysis of these arguments, see the following CRS reports: Tiemann, Mary E. *NAFTA and Related Environmental Issues and Initiatives.* Report 97-291 ENR, February 27, 1997, 6 p.; Bolle, Mary Jane. *Worker Rights Provisions and Trade Policy: Should They BE Linked?,* Report 96-661 E, July 30, 1996, 18 p.; and Hornbeck, J.F. *NAFTA, Mexican Trade Policy, and .S.-Mexico Trade: A Longer Perspective,* March 111, 1996, 17 p.

[17] For analysis of the employment effects of NAFTA, see Bolle, Mary Jane. *NAFTA: Estimates of Job Effects and Industry Trade Trends After Two Years,* CRS Report 96-176 E, April 19, 1996, 9 p. For an analysis of NAFTA's impact on the U.S. economy, see Wilson, Arlene. *NAFTA: Economic Effects on the United States,* CRS Report 96-336 E, April 12, 1996, 6p.

[18] Blustein, Paul. "NAFTA Clouds Prospects of New Pact," p. H7.

[19] Testimony by Ambassador Ira Shapiro Deputy U.S. Trade Representative, Before the Subcommittee on International Economic Policy and Trade of the House International Relations Committee, March 5, 1997, p. 3.

among a seemingly larger segment of the American work force concerning trade agreements with lower wage countries. While the anxiety perhaps could be allayed by the existence of viable retraining or adjustment assistance programs, the concerns appear deeply intertwined with the way a more internationalized and global economy threatens job security and places downward pressures on wages and benefits.[20]

A recent analysis assets that these anxieties may also be bound up with a variety of other underlying forces that are transforming the employment relationship in the United States, including deregulation, technological change, de-unionization and the weakening of domestic safety nets. New responses to the social challenges posed by the increased mobility of firms and capital across borders, thus, may be necessary if public support for accelerating economic integration is to be bolstered.[21]

Geo-Political Benefits and Costs. Although there appears to be a broad domestic consensus that U.S. economic interests should receive the highest priority with regard to future trade agreements, the concept of hemispheric free trade confronts a skeptical and perhaps indifferent American public. As concerns about future free trade agreements have become intertwined with generalized anxieties associated with a more open and globalized economy, the question arises whether future regional trade agreements may need larger geo-political justifications to gain the support of the American public.[22]

Historically, U.S. free trade agreements have relied on a combination of interests with considerable variation in the relative importance attached to economic and geo-political objectives. The two most recent agreements-NAFTA and the GATT/Uruguay Round accord-were motivate primarily by economic considerations, but larger political justifications played a role at critical junctures in each debate.

- The 1993 NAFTA debate focused on employment and investment considerations. Nevertheless, a prime U.S. interest was that a more democratic and increasingly prosperous and stable Mexico would provide a sounder foundation for dealing cooperatively on a range of problems that affect U.S. interests, such as narcotics, immigration, and the environment.

- Similarly, the rationale for the 1994 Uruguay Round Agreement was its impact on the overall U.S. economy, specific industries, and workers. But as the GATT vote drew closer (just as the NAFTA debate), attention shifted to broad political arguments concerning the impact that approval might have on the U.S. role and leadership in the world economy.

Some proponents of hemispheric free trade argue that similar geo-political arguments should be given primacy in today's trade debate. While the Clinton Administration

---

[20] For analysis of the relationship between trade and economic welfare, see Elwell, Craig. *Trade and Economic Well-Being,* CRS Report 96-608 E, June 22, 1996, 14 p.

[21] Rodrik, Dani. *Has Globalization Gone Too Far?* Institute for International Economics, Washington, D.C., 1977.

[22] For further discussion, see Ahearn, Raymond J. *Regional Free Trade Partners and U.S. Interests,* CRS Report 95-393 F, March 13, 1995, 27p.

justifies its support for hemispheric free trade (as well as for fast-track extension) primarily on building prosperity at home through export expansion, it also has made the case that stronger trade ties support broader U.S. interests as well. But the Administration, according to some critics, has failed to consistently and forcefully articulate a clear vision of what those interests are in relationship to Latin America.

Accordingly, some supporters argue that hemispheric free trade would strengthen democratic forces and institutions throughout the region and solidify recent moves toward market-oriented regimes. They argue that this is important for helping to create a world that is less hostile to U.S. interest and for contributing to the economic development of the region. A democratic and prosperous region that is bolstered by closer trade ties, in turn, is viewed as a necessary condition for increasing the disposition of these countries to cooperate on a range of issues that are of critical importance to the United States: d rugs, immigration, corruption, and alleviation of poverty.[23]

Opponents of this line of reasoning believe that the United States stands to derive "no benefit" from a close or special association with the other countries of the Americas. This "no benefit" point of view has a long history in viewing the region primarily in negative terms-not as place of economic opportunity.[24] Adherents to this doctrine today can argue that any special relationship will likely involve the Untie States more in the instabilities, class tensions, and economic turmoil of many Latin American countries. And they can point to some problems that continue to bolster these perceptions: These include the persistent inflows of illegal immigrants, drugs, and crime into the United States, as well as continuing widespread poverty, income inequality, and corruption in many of these Latin American countries.[25]

Debate over Regional Free Trade Agreements

A second controversy affecting support for hemispheric free trade revolves around the relative merits of regional trade agreements in promoting U.S. interests. While U.S. policy, in principle, has supported regional free trade arrangements as a means to bolster the multilateral trading system, it has also been clear that these arrangements could lead to some undesirable outcomes. This potential for mixed outcomes has played a role in the evolution of support among academics and policymakers for creating an FTAA via the expansion of sub-regional agreements.

The Clinton Administration initially viewed the expansion of sub-regional groups (to wit, NAFTA) as the most effective approach for promoting U.S. interests. This view was that the United States could expand NAFTA southward as countries or sub-regions became ready to accept the agreement's relatively comprehensive and binding

[23] Perry, William. "Current Trends in U.S. Policy Toward the Western Hemisphere," Testimony before the Subcommittee on the Western Hemisphere, House International Relations Committee. March 12, 1997. p.6.

[24] For a full discussion of the history of "hemispherism" or closer ties between the United States and countries of Latin America, see Feinberg, Richard E. *Summitry in the Americas,* chapter 1.

[25] Schrieberg, David. "Dateline Latin America: The Growing Fury," *Foreign Policy,* Spring 1997, pp. 162-175.

obligations. Absent fast-track authority, the Clinton Administration, however, has been excluded from pursuing hemispheric integration in this way.

Seeking to obtain an extension of fast-track authority, the Clinton Administration argued in 1996 and 1997 that the proliferation of non-NAFTA regional trade agreements in Latin America may be undermining U.S. interests. According to United States Trade Representative Charlene Barshefsky, a number of these agreements wee not consistent with WTO rules. The USTR also argued that the proliferation of preferential agreements, without U.S. participation, was creating a morass of conflicting rules for U.S. business, diverting trade, and undermining U.S. leadership in the region.

Specifically, the Administration maintained that a tangled web of rules governing tariffs, intellectual property rights, and product classification will make it harder for U.S. companies to do business in the region. The Administration also expressed concern that the expansion and operations of MERCOSUR may be diverting substantial trade form more efficient producers outside the region, presumably with an adverse impact on U.S. exports. And the Administration argued that the inactivity of the United States in expanding NAFTA southward has left a large vacuum that is being filled by European countries and Japan in carving out special economic arrangements with the countries of the hemisphere.[26]

USTR Barshefshy more recently has expressed a more benign view on the expansion of sub-regional pacts. To the extent that the agreements open markets, she has argued that they tend to support U.S. interests even in those cases where the United States is not a member.[27]

Whether the proliferation of sub-regional groupings that exclude the United States, on balance, support or hinder U.S. interests and the global trading system is difficult to determine with any certainty. Much depends on whether trade is diverted from lower-cost producers to higher-cost producers-an issue that can be determined only as a case-by-case and product-by-product basis.

From a different quarter, a small but influential group of economists argue that U.S. exclusion from participation in a preferential regional trade grouping is actually a second best outcome. They assert that the eclectic and variable set of trade arrangements that are developing in South and Central America-arrangements devoid of a dominant U.S. role-are positive because they decrease the likelihood of the creation of an inward-looking and entrenched regional trade bloc. Such a bloc, it is feared, is at best a distraction and at worst a hindrance to multilateral liberalization over time. From the perspective of these analysts, multilateral negotiations and a strong global trading system

[26] Maggs, John. "Barshefsky Makes Case in Congress for Expansion of Trade Authority," *Journal of Commerce*, May 1, 1997, p. A2.

[27] Srodes, James. "Charlene Barshefsky on Trade," *World Trade Magazine,* August 1998, pp. 38-41.

are central to the achievement of U.S. interests because of the United Sates holds an equally strong trade and investment position in all three major regions of the world—Asia, Europe, and the Western Hemisphere.[28]

[28] Barfield, Claude. "Regionalism and U.S. Trade Policy." In *The Economics of Preferential Trade Agreements,* The American Enterprise Institute Press, 1996, pp. 136-160.

INDEX

D

E

O

P

Q

R

S

Y